THE SODBREAKERS
An Original Manuscript
By Edith Eudora Ammons Kohl

Presented by her nephew
Clifford T. Ammons

Edith Eudora Ammons Kohl

THE SODBREAKERS
An Original Manuscript
By Edith Eudora Ammons Kohl

Cover design by Margie Ammons
All photographs by Clifford T. Ammons
Editing by Margie Holly Walsh

Paperback ISBN: 978-1514226131
Amazon Kindle eBook ASIN: B00YZP61AY
Published in 2015 by PBJ Enterprises, Inc.
162 Liberty Street, Deer Park, NY 11729 USA
Printed and bound in the United States of America

This book and others written by Edith Eudora Ammons Kohl may be ordered in paperback and eBook versions through Amazon.com.

First Edition

Edith Eudora Ammons Kohl

DEDICATION

This book is dedicated to the memory of
Edith Eudora Ammons Kohl and Ida Marion Ammons Miller

Edith and her sister, Ida Marion, were born and reared in Illinois, near St. Louis. As young women, they were among the very first brave, remarkable men and women who trekked out to settle the untamed, unchartered American West. Our country is forever grateful for their hard work and personal sacrifice.

Edith Eudora Ammons Kohl   Ida Marion Ammons Miller

Ida Marion and Edith Eudora Ammons as young girls
prior to the "Great Trek" going to help settle the West

v

Edith Eudora Ammons Kohl

CONTENTS

Edith Eudora Ammons Kohl

FOREWORD

Edith Eudora Ammons Kohl, is the talented author who wrote "The Sodbreakers," "Land of the Burnt Thigh," "Denver's Historic Mansions," "Denver's First Christmas," and another book soon to be released, "Woman of the Cavalcade." Make no mistake about it … Edith Kohl's writings are truly priceless, historic documents.

Edith Kohl was a young, relatively small lady, barely five feet tall. She was frail and in poor health when she and her little sister, Ida Mary, set out by themselves to join other heroic men, women and children to help settle America's wild, unchartered West. What they expected to be a great, exciting adventure certainly was … but what they encountered was much, much more than they could ever have imagined! They had no way of knowing the many extreme hardships, challenges and dangers awaiting them and the other heroic homesteaders.

That is what Edith Kohl writes about so skillfully for us in "The Sodbreakers."

In addition to her writing achievements, Edith Kohl was quite an extraordinary individual who accomplished several other notable things in her life. She was a "Homesteader" herself; a feature writer for the Denver Post from 1929 until 1954; established a number of U.S. Post Offices; started several newspapers in Montana, South Dakota and Wyoming; was instrumental in negotiating and settling several serious disputes among cattlemen, farmers and American Indians; and more.

In fact, Edith was under contract with MGM for the movie rights to her first book, "Land of the Burnt Thigh" which was originally published by Funk and Wagnalls in 1938. It currently is published by the Minnesota Historical Society and is available on Amazon.com. With Edith's death in 1959, no movie was made.

As you can appreciate, Edith Eudora Ammons Kohl was quite a remarkable lady. She was highly-intelligent, courageous and hard-working, but it was her reputation for fairness and honesty that earned her the respect and admiration of all who encountered her … including high-level government officials and politicians.

Of great literary value, is the fact that Edith Kohl skillfully portrays in words the grueling, perilous settling of America's West … and she does so from first-hand personal knowledge because she was part of it … she lived it!

Her craft of words paints vivid images of what she experienced as she captures the sights, sounds and events as they occurred so well that it allows readers - a lifetime later - to enjoy the grueling realities of how America's West was settled. Readers are given a "peek behind the curtain" as Edith describes the people and exciting, often sad, events involved in settling the West as they actually unfolded. It is almost like hearing her voice telling us this remarkable story.

Now for the very first time since it was written decades ago, Edith's nephew, Cliff Ammons, brings Edith's second book, "The Sodbreakers," to life for readers everywhere to enjoy. The eBook and paperback versions are available on Amazon.com.

Those who had the good fortune to meet Edith could never forget her … and neither will you … once you finish reading her book, "The Sodbreakers." You are in for a treat!

Robert T. Walsh
Publisher
PBJ Enterprises, Inc.

The Sodbreakers

Edith Eudora Ammons Kohl
1879 - 1959

PREFACE
By Edith Eudora Ammons Kohl

In writing this story of the Great Trek, I do not know how I shall tell it. It may not conform to any established rule of word or form any more than the epic itself in which landseekers pushed on to the frontier without plan or precedent, in the greatest mass movement this country ever knew outside of war.

Although I have traveled for the most part with a pencil or stick of type in hand, I know no words adequate to portray the settling of those vast empty spaces overnight. It was the most spectacular (and perhaps predestined) quest for land in world history.

These were the twentieth century trailbreakers of which the influx reached peak in the decade of World War I when millions of acres of land were thrown open to settlement through the great Land Lotteries -- the overflow spreading out over the boundless unsettled areas.

This significant phase of western development, one finds, comes as a surprise to many who have the idea that the settling of the West ended with the prairie schooner and the building of the Union Pacific.

It was a hodge-podge of humanity thrown into a topsy-turvy world in the making without method or experience, without finance or leadership. Band after band of settlers, one No-Man's Land after another, cowboys and Indians, stockmen and homesteader, primitive and progress, all fighting for supremacy. Chaotic, exciting, or desolate and remote and as virgin as in the Beginning.

These armies to the raw frontier were as brave, as ragged and empty-handed as any that ever marched to the colors. This tidal wave onto the land instead of the earlier straggling settlers was like regiments replacing lone soldiers in the winning of a war. And they won the victory against the mighty Primitive.

Without blare of trumpets, without the world knowing they were fighting this great battle for expansion, they built a greater

America little dreaming they soon would be called to fight another great war -- World War I.

It is of this Great Trek of men, women and children and my own part in it that I write.

There is no need to enlarge upon the facts which truly are as colorful and romantic as any fiction. I am using the real names of the characters with many of whom I am still in contact. A very few names have been slightly changed for reasons explained therein.

This story is not meant to be statistical. It is the human drama of these Empire builders interpreted as I trekked and lived it with them. The saga itself already has been indelibly printed on the sage and the sod.

***

The following is taken from a published newspaper article entitled "How-Kola"[1] written by Edith Kohl in 1935. In it, she introduces "The Sodbreakers." (See the full article in the Appendix.)

"Thar's Riches in That Thar Soil"

"Thar's gold in them thar hills," men said long ago. "Thar's feed on them thar ranges," they said a little later. And then, "Thar's riches in that soil," and along came the droves of homesteaders. They all came to practically untrammeled areas as remote as the very first one in this far-reaching frontier West, a vast part of which was once known as the Great American Desert. And the trails that "began nowhere and ended nowhere" led to the building of one of the richest empires in the world by one of the greatest armies that ever marched to conquer.

The truly greatest army, I think, became hungry and ragged and foot-sore and without leadership or direction, they fought, regiment after regiment, the longest and hardest war ever waged for territory. They fought voluntarily and valiantly against the most powerful of all enemies -- the indomitable force of nature. They made their fight unseen, unheard, unheralded by men.

---

[1] "How-Kola" is a greeting of Sioux Indians: "How" (I greet you); "Kola" (friend).

Their families lived in crude makeshifts of shelter -- these "shanties on the claim," crooned about synthetic cowboys, that would disgrace any respectable back lot; and in which no flock of up-to-date chickens would stoop to roost. They suffered from cold where snow blew in through cracks almost as wide as the open spaces. (One of the great mysteries of the homestead world is where the lumber industry ever found all the knotholes it sold the settlers.) They suffered from the searing sun and winds which burnt up their crops and moral courage; and some were parched for water.

Their war munitions in the conquest -- human energy, money if they had any, livestock, were confiscated by the cruel hand of the desert and destiny. The people were wholly unequipped for the job.

"It seems to me," Ida Marion would say, "that it would be a good investment for the nation if our government would help the settlers develop this land." And surely it would have been. It would have come into production and power so many years faster and earlier.

Once I appealed to a large investment broker passing through. "Investment in the development of these new lands is the unparalleled opportunity of big capital," I declared. But he smiled indulgently and called me a Utopian dreamer, a poet. Dreamers, poets, Huh.

But there was no government or financial agencies to grubstake these armies, or equip, or recruit them. All the government did in those days to get the frontier developed was to give the homesteader a plot in the endless vacant space for a song, IF, by the mercy of providence, he could hold out long enough to prove it up without starving to death; and if he could raise money for required improvements of a shack, a few acres plowed and fenced, with a little crop put in, etc. And if he lived on it the allotted time. That was the foremost letter of the law that he live and eat and sleep upon it.

These remote no-man's lands have been enriched with blood from the bleeding hearts and feet of the men, women, and children, who trod them, the toll of progress. But they not only developed a country, they developed men and women. Or rather, while they developed the frontier it developed a people of sterling worth.

And when they laid their sacrifices on the altar of the people for a greater America, a new dominion, the West, there was no blowing of trumpets nor cheering of crowds to hail their feat.

Their victory was signaled by another field of sod turned over, or a lean-to to the shack.

The Last of the Five Thousand

Many there were who fell by the way with only now and then a little wild flower to mark their graves. And there are no tall monuments erected on the border of the frontier to remind the nation they gave their lives to its development -- these heroes who suffered untold privation; who perhaps lay ill and died far away from aid, or perished in blizzards or prairie fires; or just naturally succumbed to the struggle leaving their families to starve, or worse.

Strange, when today we pin laurels on just about anybody, and talk so much about "high standards of living," (when we are already so soft we squash from too much of everything.)

A stripling of a youth sat one night in his bunkhouse on an isolated ranch drawing a picture on a rough scrap of paper. It was the answer to a letter received that day from his uncle in St. Louis who owned the ranch. He finished the drawing and mailed it.

That sketch became world famous. It was Charlie Russell's "The Last of the 5,000," master-piece of the noted cowboy artist.

The picture of a lone starving critter after a blizzard, humped up from the cold, nothing but skin and bones and blocked by snowdrifts with a hungry wolf waiting for the carcass, told the story of what happened to his uncle's large herds of cattle during the terrific blizzard which had swept the plains. It depicts the battle of the cattlemen and sheepmen against the frontier, for supremacy.

A little group of men from St. Louis, who had just filed on land in Wyoming, stood examining a handful of the soil as an old-time cowman came riding over the ridge. A picturesque figure, Tom Bell always made as he rode, and a familiar one over the vast Wyoming ranges. Short, stout, and blocky, he wore white fur chaps and a twenty-gallon hat as white as the chaps, with fancy boots and spurs that glistened in the sun. And he always had a pack of hounds with him. Long, lean, and tall, they trotted alongside the pony, or raced ahead, leaping the barbwire fences of the homesteaders, ignoring these barriers to the open range.

"What do you think of it?" he asked, referring to the soil.

"Well, seems like it's pretty rich."

"It should be," Tom Bell answered calmly. "It has been well-fertilized over these parts."

"Fertilized?" they asked.

"Yes, fertilized by the bones of my cattle and Jackie Mills' sheep that have perished in the blizzards. I found 300 head of my cattle piled up in that fence corner," he said pointing to an old range fence nearby, "when the snow drifts melted one spring. Had been driven by the storm and when they reached the fence they couldn't get any farther."

Herd after herd perished on the plains year after year and there was no government aid, no federal agency to furnish loans for feed or reimburse these pioneers. Yet somehow, they built a sheep and cattle kingdom and became kings of the industry.

Government Ran Lotteries with Land as Stakes
I do not belong to the covered wagon, Pike's Peak-or-Bust era with which the world so mistakenly imagines that the glamour and the romance of the frontier died -- when as a truth they were just an embryo.

None of the immigrants I knew were going to Pike's Peak which was a purposeless destination; and most of them were already busted. I belonged to that last and biggest army which shouted "Thar's riches in this here sod," and tore up the range with their plows.

I had just become well enough set to find the old buffalo waller, three miles away without getting lost, when the sparsely-settled West woke up one morning in the biggest and swiftest stampede of immigration that ever hit any country in the world -- the government lotteries with land as the stakes. One virgin tract after another, millions of acres, with not a track except those made by the wild life inhabiting them, were "throwed open" to settlement through drawings to which thousands upon thousands flocked like grasshoppers in the Kansas grasshopper raid.

"Shucks, it's as simple as fallin' off a log," stage-driver Sam would say to the crowds of excited, confused landseekers. "Just take enough grub to last a couple of days and a bottle or two o' strong whisky and get in line at the land office. The gov'ment will number yuh, put the numbers in a box, shake 'em up and draw 'em out. Lucky numbers win. Like gamblin' on a roulette wheel -- lucky numbers too skeerce for all the suckers that play 'em -- allus rather take my chance on poker."

The players in these drawings had one chance in fifty, sometimes in a hundred, to win. But the land office and the railroads did a "land-office business."

Lucky numbers went wild with the excitement. Surging crowds pushed and jolted and fell down over one another on the border of far-flung, empty space. They had no idea where they were going or what lay before them in the great adventure of this lifetime, for which most of them were wholly unfitted.

The frontier was not ready for this onslaught. Food, shelter and fuel, were a problem. There was no water supply until they went down into the ground after it, and drilled wells which took time and money.

And in some of these boundless areas -- "You'll have to drill clear to H -- after it, and then you won't get water," an old-timer once said.

It was like unloading a world army on desert islands. It caused bedlam, chaos. Natives who had been through the thrill and excitement and adventure of the gold-rush, Indian war days, stood dumbfounded at this spectacular invasion.

The Melting Pot

Lone Star Len rode in from the open range one day. "I'm movin' on," he said. "It's too lonesome with all this millin' around. Too bad to ruin a pretty country like this with pesky homesteadin' herds."

"Ruining it? Making it, you mean." He gave no answer.

"Where are you going?" I inquired.

"I don't know," he replied mournfully. "Some place where it won't be so hemmed in with people."

Lone Star was a strange, lone character, belonging wholly to the silences of the plains. And through the falling dusk he rode on West. But I was to meet him again in one of the many strange coincidences of these frontiers.

Coyote Cal thrived on the upheaval. "Never seed as many skirts in my life. Musta been two trainloads shipped in …" purt near" as human as broncs, when you get to know 'em, too."

Coyote's life had run to broncos.

"You don't get much to eat or wear out here," old white-haired Ma Wagor said next day after the big prairie fire that almost had annihilated us with its red tongue. "But you got a lot o' livin' what with blizzards and prairie fires and young folks fallin' in love and cattle rustlers and Indians -- well, it's almost as exciting as a three-ring circus we had back in Blue Springs once … I told Pa last night that I had always hankered after some excitement before I died.

Pa, nearly eighty didn't hanker after excitement but he figured that eighty-acre homestead would raise corn. The old-timers shook their heads and said, "Too bad. The sun has baked his mind."

But raise corn it did -- and Cain, too, for that dear, brave old couple who became parents to the whole settlement.

Young girls there were, whose tiny shacks sat alone, with the weird cry of the coyotes at night, the only sound. Out of sight and sound and reach of human habitation in case of illness or other emergency, they stuck with an undaunted courage and settled up no small part of the broad frontier.

How they did it is beyond human imagination. But the Great White Father must know -- and remember.

Written Upon the Sagebrush and the Sod

Broad region upon region was settled thus over the West through these spectacular openings; and the momentum of this overnight settlement brought flocks of immigrants into other sections -- an epic of development unparalleled in history.

I traveled with these trail-breakers. Most of the way I trailed a little printing press behind me. Sometimes Ida Marian and I bent the tall grass and pitched our "newspaper shebang" -- as Lone Star Len scornfully called it -- in the middle of a No-Man's land ahead of the settlers. Until – well -- Marian, that brave little torch-bearer was one of those who fell by the way with only a little wild flower now and then to mark the graves and no monuments to mark them as heroes. And then I went on alone.

We were not adventurers. A strange destiny or some other unseen force seemed to lead us into these fields in which we plodded next to the lowly early until our job of aiding the settlers through our little newspaper on each frontier was finished.

I have encountered many people and things along the way -- drama and romance and tragedy and progress, where pathos was oft times filled with humor, and humor became pathetic. And as I come with these stories which have been written indelibly upon the sagebrush and the sod, I say "How-Kola" as a message from those who wrote them there. And now, may you enjoy Sodbreakers!

Edith Eudora Ammons Kohl

INTRODUCTION
By Clifford T. Ammons

My name is Clifford T. Ammons; I am the nephew of Edith Eudora Ammons Kohl, author of "Land of the Burnt Thigh," "The Sodbreakers," "Woman of the Cavalcade," "Denver's Historic Mansions," and "Denver's First Christmas." She was a feature writer for the Denver Post from 1929 until 1954.

Her book, "Land of the Burnt Thigh," was originally published by the Funk and Wagnalls Company in 1938. This book is currently published by the Minnesota Historical Society and is available on Amazon.

Prior to her death in 1959, Edith was writing the sequel and was under contract with a MGM producer for the movie rights to "Land of the Burnt Thigh" and the second book entitled, "The Sodbreakers." No one in my family knew about this second book, "The Sodbreakers," and no movie was ever made.

At the time of her passing, I inherited an old, stinky, ratty-looking suitcase. That suitcase has been in my possession since 1959 and I opened it a couple of times to look at old pictures, some of Edith's poetry, newspaper stories that she had written for The Denver Post, and letters from former U.S. senators and state governors.

My thoughts were, "This old suitcase is taking up space. I'll get rid of it. But wait a minute! What's in this old accordion folder?" To my surprise and delight, I came upon her original typewritten manuscript of "Land of the Burnt Thigh" as well as two additional unknown typewritten manuscripts by Edith that had never been published. Treasures uncovered!

The titles of Edith's two new books are: "The Sodbreakers," and, "Woman of the Cavalcade." "The Sodbreakers" depicts Edith's life settling new ground near Lusk and Van Tassell, Wyoming. "Woman of the Cavalcade" takes her into the Judith Basin of Montana to start her fourth newspaper and to fight the big grain trusts which were robbing the farmers and forcing them into poverty by cheating them out of any profits on their first crops of grain.

She heroically fought for the farmers with the help of several U.S. senators and became involved with an organization called The American Society of Equity, now known as the National Farmers Union.

Edith's books are unique, first-hand, historic documents that take readers back in time with her to hear and see what she personally experienced ... the exciting, difficult challenges she and other heroic men and women encountered in settling America's West.

My Special Memories of "Aunt Edie"

As a young child of five and six years of age, I would accompany my father on his business trips to Denver and stay several days with Aunt Edie - as we affectionately called her - in her one room apartment in an old Victorian home close to downtown Denver.

One time when she was making pancakes for supper, Aunt Edie told me the pancakes were ready to flip when I could count seven bubbles popping up on the surface of the pancake. Several decades later, I still count seven bubbles every time I make pancakes. After we ate, I helped her with the dishes; I got to dry them. When we were finished, Aunt Edie took me - and a dish I dried - to three other ladies on her floor just to show them what a good job I had done. I felt like a celebrity!

At bedtime, Aunt Edie told me stories of children she knew on the homestead of South Dakota. The only name I remember now is Heine Christopherson. He was a little boy who always seemed to be in some kind of mischief. She would also tell me all about the Indians she knew, her horse Dakota, and a cowboy by the name of "Lone Star Len."

Aunt Edie was an expert typist, extremely fast, even though she only used two fingers. She could definitely beat up a typewriter!

I also remember Thanksgiving dinner at my sister Ida's home in 1957. Don, my brother-in-law, picked Aunt Edie up at her apartment in his "California Roadster," as Aunt Edie called it; it was a 1957 Plymouth convertible.

Just as dinner was about to be served, Aunt Edie said, "I'm expecting a call from the Governor; I gave him this number."

It was only a few minutes later when the phone rang.

Don answered, then said, "It's for you Edie ... it's the Governor!"

I will never forget what she said to Governor Steve McNichols.

Aunt Edie said, "The Evanses are not giving **YOU** their mansion! They are giving it to the State of Colorado, and you **DAMN WELL WILL** accept it, whether you want to live in it or not!"

And she hung up the phone!

The "Evans Mansion" is now the Governor's Mansion of Colorado. Aunt Edie was definitely not afraid to speak her mind.

Toward the end of Aunt Edie's third book, "Woman of the Cavalcade," she meets a man who becomes the love of her life, and her husband ... Aaron Wesley Kohl. Unfortunately, I know very little about their life together, but I do know that they had a child who died at birth in April 1921, and Aaron died in April 1928.

Several years before her death, Aunt Edie gave me Aaron's professional drafting equipment and I became a draftsman after high school and worked with architects and engineers for more than twenty years. I am over seventy years old now and still use those tools today designing my dream home.

My grandparents, my father, and uncle are a big part of "The Sodbreakers" and "Woman of the Cavalcade" stories. I never knew anything about this part of my family history until I found these manuscripts. My dad joined the army as soon as our country entered World War 1, and my uncle, Thomas, joined a short time later as soon as he became of age. Thank God they both returned home safely after the war was over.

I feel so blessed to have discovered these truly historic books that lay unopened for well over half a century. The original stories contained within provide personal insight into the remarkable, amazing story of how the West was settled by people like my Aunt Edie and other family members.

I hope you enjoy reading my Aunt Edie's book as much as I did.

Chapter I
OPEN LAND

The train chugged slowly across the sandy plain of western Nebraska. The dozen passengers in the Pullman fretted and dozed, trying to shut out the desolate landscape and the noise of the train as it puffed its way laboriously on the stiff upgrade climb.

To them, this part of the trip was but something that must be endured to reach destination. Traveling salesmen, businessmen from small western towns, women coming home from a visit with kinfolk back East. But in the tourist coach ahead, there was no dozing to escape monotony. Every passenger of the crowded car was scanning the country with an eager eye.

The noise of grinding wheels and belching engine was muffled by their chatter as they exclaimed over a grazing herd, "rolling fat and nothing to eat but dry grass!"

They talked about the grass, and the possibilities of this new West.

It was a strange mixture of people to be bound on a single purpose. I was bringing a colony of landseekers into Wyoming; they were from Peoria and neighboring Illinois towns.

A tall, slim, young man, who was a wage earner, talked to a heavy-set, middle-age man, Charlie Roszell. Charlie, a plumber, made big wages when he had work. But a man could not expect to get steady work at a trade when he got older, Charlie averred. Young men were coming on to fill the trade and labor fields.

The young man, Fred Theilbar, said, "I have a family of small children growing up and now is the time to come west, before the open land is all taken."

Several farmers, one a red-faced, young Swede not long from the Old Country, talked together of soil and crops while a tall, well-poised woman in her early thirties sat gazing out the car window, her eyes fixed intently on the broad plain. She was a trained nurse seeking rest. The free life on a homestead after years in the sick room would rebuild her energy, Anna Watkins figured, and would provide a home when she was too old to work. While she was out on the homestead, she could take a few "cases"

1

to pay for improving the land. In the new towns springing up, a good nurse would be in demand, and a Godsend to the people.

Another, with telltale threads of gray in her dark, heavy hair, sat erect talking in clipped tones to her fellow passengers.

"I owe this trip to a lucky coin. Found it on the street as I left the office last Saturday. With it, I hurried down to the Star office and put an advertisement in the Sunday paper - 'Anyone interested in homesteading please call Catherine Lemmon ...' Only last Saturday - and here I am!"

A modish, young blond across the aisle bestirred herself, "Lucky coin, did you say? Unlucky, I should call it."

There was a flouting smile on her lips as she settled herself again to the book she had been reading. She looked more like an actress than a homesteader. Her husband had gone on ahead to file a claim and she was going to join him, evidently against her own will. She had sat aloof, fussing with her hair and makeup, while the other women merely mopped the dust and cinders from their faces.

The spirited Catherine Lemmon was not to be squelched at the very outset like that.

"Well," she retorted, "if I can get away from punching time clocks and typewriters before I'm thrown in the discard, I'll consider almost anything a lucky break."

And somewhere in the coach, an alarm clock went off. The passengers sat up with a start and turned their heads to locate the persistent **burObrOrr** as the stenographer pulled a grip down from the rack, took out the clock and shut it off.

"There!" She said with a laugh as she threw it back into the bag. "I'm through with you!"

Everyone in the coach laughed with her. With exception of a few, the lives of these folk had been regulated by alarm clocks.

Mingling with the home seekers yet an outstanding figure among them was Ida Van Sant. The Van Sants were old friends with whom Ida Mary and I had made our home while in Peoria taking some special courses. Gathered in the spacious drawing room of the Van Sants, we spent many evenings listening breathlessly to Dr. Van Sant relate his adventures in Klondike and his wife, Ida, told of their pioneering on a Nebraska homestead. Their first son had been born in the homestead cabin

2

while the doctor, a dentist and not a medico, had gone for help. When he reached home with the midwife who was the nearest aid, he found a bouncing baby boy.

The Klondike venture had been unsuccessful, and the Van Sants had given up the homestead. Nobody could make a living on a claim in eastern Nebraska, folk had said at the time. But back in Peoria, the doctor had built a large dental clinic and a neat little fortune. Then one evening, walking with his firm quick tread, head up, he opened the door of the elevator shaft which somehow had been left ajar. The elevator was not there and the strong dynamic John Van Sant went down to death in his own edifice which he had worked long years to build.

In her bereavement, his widow's thoughts often turned to their younger days together and to the new countries where there was gold to be found at the end of the rainbow - or at least opportunity.

And then one day, after Ida Mary and I proved up claims in Dakota, I went back to Peoria. I had been away two years.

Ida Van Sant was jubilant over my return, "Edith, you've come back to live with Mother Van, haven't you? I need you so. You know Birdie has her own home and social affairs."

Birdie was her only daughter.

"No, I have not come to stay," I reluctantly informed her. "I have come to organize a colony of homesteaders and settle them out in Wyoming."

"Homesteaders!" she gasped. "Wyoming. Haven't you had enough of roughing it?"

She was shocked, but as I lay forth the opportunity in this new country, her interest could not be suppressed. She knew a number of persons who would like to get land and I knew others who had written me about homesteads.

The land fever was running high with the people going land crazy. Whether they could go West or not, folks liked to hear about the life out there on the wild and woolly frontier.

The words "Open Land!" carried the thrill of a gold strike. I brought tidings: there was a world of open land out in Wyoming. And a new Homestead law had been passed. It doubled the size of homesteads

3

from a quarter to a half-section. Now one could take up 320 acres; it sounded bigger in acres.

"320 acres? For land's sake! Think of having that much land," men exclaimed.

It was like owning a whole frontier.

What about Dakota where my sister and I homesteaded, many asked. There were no more large areas open in the Dakotas, no reservations being thrown open at this time. The settlers had taken that country. But across the Wyoming border, one could plant colonies. I explained that I was taking settlers into Wyoming in conjunction with The West Land Company of Presho, South Dakota, a well-known locating firm which was expanding its activities to that region.

"Yes," I assured them, "I went out to look the country over. Rich grass, invigorating climate, and pure water, ice-cold, anywhere one drills. New towns springing up, western Congressmen promoting the homestead project and the land not costing a cent. Instead of paying Uncle Sam the regulation fee of $1.25 an acre for the land, you put your money into required improvements."

To a land-hungry people, I was a veritable Columbus bringing back glowing accounts of a new America - a prophet to lead the people to a Land of Promise. A country still colorful and wild with its Indians and cowboys, it conjured visions of adventure for young folk. Its grassy plains created dreams of home and security for the older ones.

Western development was bringing an expansion of commerce and industry, opening new fields for enterprise that interested businessmen. At a reception which Mrs. Van Sant had given last week, a large group had gathered to hear the report of this returned "Columbus." A pompous broker walked around, hands in pocket.

"Looks like a ground floor proposition, folks," he said seriously.

City people talked a lot about "ground floor" propositions.

One morning at the breakfast table Ida Van Sant said, "Edith, I can't conceive of your doing things like this. You were doing fine in your dramatic work. Remember the parties we used to give - and that old actor who wanted you to go with his company?"

That was a far cry from the business I had on hand. She had been a great influence in getting the migrant party together. Now she was trying to dissuade me.

"Well, it is a tremendous undertaking," she went on. "But I like it. I think I'll go along and help you get things started."

I jumped up and threw my arms around her neck.

"Oh, but you can't, Mother Van."

"My grips are packed," she said, laughing, rubbing her strong hands together.

Her two young sons, both dentists, could run the business and look after her affairs.

Noting my hesitation, she added, "You know me," meaning she could rough it with the rest of us.

A sad look came into her face.

"And it will take my mind off my troubles. Now run along," she patted me on the shoulder.

"Louie Prehl of The Star is waiting in the next room for a story about your colony. You know Louie."

Yes, I had known Louie when he had made mention of my recitals and published a few of my poems in The Star.

She sat in the tourist coach that morning, a friendly, large, capable woman, "Just look at eastern Nebraska now - the land where we homesteaded calling for a hundred and fifty dollars an acre ..."

The train lurched and heaved like a bucking bronc as it climbed to mile-high altitude.

The conductor jerked open the door and announced, "We are now crossing the Wyoming line."

Every passenger minus the blond who sat immobile in her seat scrambled to his feet and hurried to the vestibules for a panoramic view of the magic land. Myrtle Cromb, a dark elfin girl grabbed her banjo, strummed a note and began to sing. Myrtle, who had run a little newspaper back in Dakota, was bringing her aged father from Minnesota to file on land.

In the spirit of men putting foot on new soil, the whole colony joined in and there we stood that bright, fall morning on the border of Wyoming, the "Great Plain," our voices ringing far through the clear

5

spaces. The dozing dozen, aroused from their apathy, came scurrying from the Pullman bringing soprano, bass and baritone into the refrain of "My Country Tis of Thee" with la, la, la-la la-la to our words which we quickly had improvised:

"Wyoming 'tis of thee
Sweet land of liberty
Of thee we sing.
Land of new Pilgrim's pride
Where faith and hope abide
From this Great Plain so wide
Le-et fre-e-dom ring."

I slipped back into the coach and sat staring out the window. A land of the free! There was little to be seen but freedom. Nothing in sight except a herd of cattle marching single file to water.

It was a sea of sod.

A vast, undulating plateau, golden as the sunlight with its yellow carpet of grass. Over against the horizon meeting the snow-capped clouds, there was a fluffy, white wave moving on the earth - a band of sheep. And off to the south, like a Goddess of Liberty, stood a great black landmark - old Rawhide Butte. Eternal earth rolling on and on ...

Of all the far-flung space I had seen, this was the farthest flung. Mighty, impregnable, and how cruel such lands could be. The first qualm of fear I had known since the day I had ridden so confidently away from the homestead in Dakota swept over me.

O, dear God! How had I dared?

In this Omnipotence, I, and these people, were but as tumbleweeds before the wind. I closed my eyes, shutting out the bigness but seeing droughts, blizzards, poverty - what would the future hold for them who stayed? Yet who knew what the future held for anyone, anywhere? And always, in America her builders had moved on West. I had more experience than my followers in the settling of new lands and in the homestead laws which governed them ... but it was like the blind leading the blind.

The train (called the "Sage Hen" because it ran for miles through the sagebrush country) was pulling into Lusk, our destination. The old frontier town was squatted there as drab as the range in which it seemed

6

lost. From the station, crossing the railroad, a rutted dirt road ran in one direction as Main Street through a cluster of small huddled buildings with the two-story hotel in the foreground handy for the traveler, and in the other direction, it wound its way over a ridge and on into the vacant prairie to who knew where.

Roscoe McCully, local agent for the West Land Company, was at the station to meet us. He was a personable young man who at once won favor with the landseekers. As they looked after their baggage, Roscoe called me aside.

"I think we had better take these folk over to the boarding house for lunch. It will not be so public as the hotel. Then get them out of town at once."

I looked at him, eyes wide as saucers. Were the stockmen going to run these prospective settlers out even before they filed on land? The news of our coming had spread and the town was astir. Cowboys in chaps and spurs, guns in holsters, leaned carelessly against the side of the small depot. Ranchers, sturdy bronzed men in high-heeled boots and ten-gallon hats, walked briskly up and down the narrow, board sidewalk, heels pounding like hammers on the loose boards, a few going their way ignoring the arrival of the tenderfeet.

Others giving us dark threatening looks.

"If such as them think they're goin' to take this country ..."

The remark was lost as we passed hurriedly on.

Freighting teams stood with their heavily-loaded wagons ready to start on the long haul to remote ranches. Tradesmen stood in the doors of small frame buildings that lined the street while strange characters loafing on the curbs and corners watched us intently.

"Don't look so scared, Miss Ammons," Roscoe said in his quiet, pleasant manner. "You're white as a sheet. But," he explained, "Lusk is an old, cattle-and-sheep town and always there are stockmen or their foremen, cowpunchers and sheepherders, and some of the town fathers themselves ready to discourage new settlers. And worse, are those 'curbstone locators' you see standing on the corners. They are waiting to grab up every new landseeker."

He knew my fear was of trouble for the new settlers.

Mother Van walking behind, talking to various ones of the excited party, had taken but little notice of this strange reception.

She came up to Roscoe, "Something like a wild, Oklahoma town," she remarked interestedly. "I was down there once."

Roscoe took her by the arm and promptly we steered our guests to the "Square Boarding House" set off from the main part of town. It was called "The Square" not because of its treatment of guests but because the old, gray house was a square, squatty structure with square, dormer windows all around it.

Roscoe McCully ushered the hungry crowd straight to the dining room where long tables piled with steaming dishes of food stood ready. He had ordered an early dinner but not so many had been expected. By the time we were settled, however, large platters of fried ham and eggs with stewed corn and piping hot biscuits supplemented the stewed beef and potatoes and other vegetables. Most of the vegetables had come from cans but there was one fresh vegetable new to the easterners. It looked and tasted like turnips but was sweeter - and yellow.

"What was it?" they inquired.

"That's rutabaga," they were told. "A new kind of turnip - grows out here big as - well, as big as your head sometimes. Fine stock feed, too."

Fred Theilbar thought he would plant his farm to rutabagas. Being informed that one acre would produce several hundred bushels, he decided to cut the acreage.

Then came the pie cut in wide thick triangles with big granite pots of coffee carried around to refill the capacious cups. With the second cup, our famished travelers were ready to make over Wyoming - a corner of it, anyhow. Some of them had been too fatigued, others too excited, to notice anything amiss. They were encouraged, too, by the cheery talk of the host and the several boarders who had claims and were working in town part of the time. One of them had a job in the lumber yard, another in a store. The station agent and even McCully lived on a homestead near Lusk.

Immediately after lunch, we hurried the landseekers out of the boarding house into vehicles and got them out of town as though a bomb were ready to be dropped. It was done so calmly the easterners had no suspicion of being guarded or spirited away. We were escaping the land

8

sharks and natives who didn't want the land settled. Drivers were waiting at the gate with automobiles and high-stepping horses hitched to buggies and spring-wagons (the tenderfeet called them democrats.) There had been some trouble in getting transportation and other accommodations for the large crowd of almost a half-hundred people.

The blond who had been met at the train by her husband, waved goodbye as they started out in a rickety buggy behind a rangy, raw-boned horse.

"You'd better hold onto your alarm clocks," she taunted. "Be seeing you in Peoria."

But the boyish young husband called back, "Good luck, folks. Hope you take land."

We started out through the sagebrush flats doubling back toward the state-line with the automobiles pompously taking the lead until we left the beaten road when the cars followed in the rear, waiting for the sharp-shod horses to break a trail over the rough ground. The driver of a light skeleton Ford was afraid his passengers might be bounded out and the owner of a long cumbersome car that chugged like a tractor could not risk getting stalled.

"This country never was made for cars," he complained.

"Never mind," a city man answered, "We'll make roads here someday - paved highways."

Everybody laughed at that, little dreaming that a few years later thru main highways would traverse the region.

It was late afternoon when we came upon our party of surveyors stretching lines across the empty range, marking it off into half-section plots. Here we stopped and the weary travelers, taking on new life, got out and selected their claims - already they called them farms - while Roscoe checked with the surveyors and marked down the numbers of each half-section from his land plot.

A middle-age farmer stood staring, his ruddy face set. "You mean to say all this territory you have marked off is open land?"

"You could drive all day, north and south, and take your choice of almost any piece you crossed," Roscoe replied. "Very little of it ever has been surveyed."

"Lords of all we survey," Catherine quoted glibly.

9

"Well! I'm not going to give a landlord half of my crops any longer," the farmer declared. "I may not raise much here but it'll be mine. What do you say, Jim?"

He turned to a corn-and-hog grower.

"I say Uncle Sam can keep his land. It's too damn dry for me. I think we've struck the Sahara desert. Look at this short grass," Jim Turner grumbled.

Two or three farmers began talking over the rainfall, and I said, "You'll have land enough to fallow," and Roscoe explained the method of cultivating the land and letting it lie for a season soaking moisture into the sub-soil.

Fred Theilbar broke in. "What will we do about schools? This is the first thing my wife will ask about."

"Get the county to build them," I interposed. "By next year, there'll be schools and a trading settlement."

I had helped to build these things in another raw land. After all, they would need a newspaper here to push things, but I had vowed not to start one. My job here ended with bringing the people onto the land.

The women landseekers showed no discouragement. This particular group had no families to consider. They had come to get land and here it was.

Funny about women.

The soil was of lighter, looser texture than that in Dakota. The farmers turned over spades of the sandy loam sifting handfuls through their fingers while the city folk stood by anxiously awaiting their verdict.

"Yes, this is good soil," they agreed.

"This grass," explained Roscoe McCully, "is short because it has been eaten off for years, but the ground has been fertilized by range stock."

Like a sudden flash of lightning, there came to mind an afternoon in my printshop on the Brule reservation. Lone Star Len, that strange character of the open plains, was saying goodbye.

"Where are you going now, Len?" I had asked.

"To an honest-to-God range," he had answered. "Grass short but rich - Wyoming, the Rawhide country."

I now felt a sudden thrill. Rawhide Butte, the old landmark now dimly seen to the south took on new meaning. Only forty miles away, lay the Rawhide region. Wyoming was a great domain Lone Star had said and he knew the frontier.

A group had gathered around me and stood waiting.

"What do you think of it, Miss Ammons?" one asked seriously.

"O," I stammered.

I was thinking: Would I meet Lone Star Len again? What was there about that silent plainsman that made one remember?

"Ha, ha," Bob Kearns, the aggressive salesman said jestingly, "Our Moses gone wool-gathering."

"What better place to gather wool than in Wyoming?" I sallied.

Then turning to the group, I answered earnestly, "What do I think about it? Why - it looks like a ground floor proposition to me."

They laughed, breaking the tension of decision.

"Yah," the Swedish farmer was saying, "but I like to see once something growing beside grass yet."

Ten miles on and still higher than the plateau was a small farming region called "Pleasant Ridge" where a community of early settlers had been raising crops for many years. We drove on to "The Ridge." There also we could find accommodations for the night Roscoe assured us. To those people our coming was a gala occasion. They were delighted to talk to strangers from outside their little world; glad to see new settlers coming into the country. They were a progressive, refined folk with churches, schools and improved farms.

Here we found yellow stacks of grain, green fields of alfalfa, cellars filled with vegetables and wells of pure water with windmills turning in the evening breeze. Now the homeseekers knew what they could do with the land. This was God's country. Pleasant Ridge, in name - and indeed.

We divided into groups according to the accommodations the farmers could provide. All of us were worn out and what a relief it was to the locators and myself to be able to relax without fear of our prospects being "picked from ambush" by the locating snipers.

"I am not afraid of my friends being misled," I told Roscoe, "but a few in this colony are strangers to me. They are naturally skeptical and confused."

11

"We cannot afford to have them discouraged by unreliable propaganda," Roscoe replies. "The land sharks who hang around waiting to pick up landseekers are not bonded, nor responsible to the government as we are. But one dissatisfied person can stir up a whole party."

Set back near the canyons - a hilly, pine-wooded strip which separated The Ridge from a rough stretch of grazing land beyond, was a dilapidated farm home which marked the family as not being the thrifty type of their neighbors. Myrtle Cromb and I, being used to roughing it, took a small group there.

It was wonderful having Myrtle, the little "hammer-and-tong" printer, with me. We had been homesteaders and printers together on the hard frontier. Back in Dakota, she had run the old McClure Press until she proved up, then she had turned her job over to me - my first newspaper. Seeing two small, sprightly girls who had weathered homesteading and the running of a printshop at the same time, not one of these landseekers dared complain about the hardships of a raw country.

"Proving up homesteads is easy money for me - easier than working for a living," Myrtle opined.

Now that she had proven up her own, she would help her father get one.

Gathered around the long supper table with its oilcloth cover and heavy dishes filled with food almost as heavy, I said aside to Myrtle, "What do you really think of the outlook here, Myrtle?"

Getting out onto the land and looking at it in blocks instead of seeing it as an eternity of space had restored my confidence. Keeping one's feet on solid ground is a great restorer of equilibrium and as a rule will carry one as far as hitching his wagon to a star.

"Looks like pickin's to me," she replied. "Are you going to start a paper?"

"We might run one together," I suggested.

"All right. You push the pen and I'll push the press."

Myrtle was like that, wasting no time in parley. She either did things or she didn't. When legal notices must be gotten out in short time, she threw the type into the stick, emptied it into the form, hammered the form into a smooth surface and threw it onto the press. The result was often a smeary job but the publisher and the U.S. Land Office could depend upon her to get them out. Though small of physique, she was virile as a toughened sapling.

"You be editor and publisher, I'll be printer's 'devil'," she proposed now.

The tall, angular woman of the family casually remarked, "Ebe's late. Off helpin' a neighbor thresh."

With the husky, young sons of the family who were lined up at the table on a long bench against the wall, one would think they were a threshing crew.

A few minutes later, Ebe came in, took his place at the far end of the table in his sweat-stained clothes, shirt sleeves rolled up on brawny, hairy arms. A burly figure, who as eldest son, ruled the family clan.

"Course, we ain't like some of our neighbors," he apologized, "slickin' up and sayin' grace at every meal."

The neighbors referred to were the Zumbrunnels who ran a post office and were the center of the civic life in that community, it seemed. I was glad the most persnickety of the tenderfeet had stopped there.

Breaking into the talk about the people and the crops on The Ridge, Ebe said, "I shore feel sorry for folks that's filin' on them bare tablelands around."

There was an uncomfortable silence.

At last the scholarly old man who was Myrtle's father cleared his throat and asked, "Why so?"

"Couldn't make a livin' on a whole township, and the stockman will run you out. No timber - now over here near the canyons you can run stock and get wood to burn ... the canyon country has got them level tablelands beat a mile."

We had run square into a shark. The rough canyon region covered with scrub pine was the place to which Ebe led a poor stray landseeker now and then, locating him for whatever amount he could get. Extra money picked up like that came in handy.

"How much you payin' that Land Company to locate you on a homestead?" he asked of Charlie Roszell, when no one had ventured any further remark.

"One hundred dollars," Charlie replied.

"One hundred dollars! That's highway robbery. I can locate you out here for half that."

Charlie, whom I had known for a long time looked at me, then said, "Well, for me it's worth that money and more to get correct surveying and reliable land-office recordings, say nothing of other valuable service. We can't afford to monkey with Cheap-Johns, Mister."

"You're right, Charlie," from several others.

But Jim Turner who had damned the country that afternoon, began to ask questions. Jim wouldn't have an acre of the land but he was ready to find all the fault possible, for the other seekers.

Roscoe McCully having gone with another group, I spoke up, "I have brought these people here to get the best land and the best locating service to be had. I do not intend to have them misled!"

The traveling salesman who had been preoccupied with his supper looked up at me from a far corner of the table with an amused smile and remarked, "And their Moses was a woman."

With that, he entered garrulously into a discourse on this new Promised Land and no one else could get a word in edgewise. But next morning, I noticed Ebe drawing a few of the seekers out to one side.

After a soft rain during the night, new green grass was popping up and the world about us looked as fresh and clean as through it had been re-created overnight. Everyone was in high spirits. The teams and cars were lined up ready for the journey back, when an old lumber wagon with a farm team hitched to it came out of the corral and went rattling across the rough country toward the canyons. I stood at the rickety farmyard gate as wilted as a morning-glory at noon for perched on the high seat beside Ebe were Myrtle and her father. On a board seat in the rear were two young men who had straggled into the party as we left Peoria and whose names I did not recall.

But the glory of the morning had gone with Myrtle. I should rather have lost the whole colony. She had been my guest and it was from my home that she had met her father and the colony enroute to Wyoming.

Myrtle's independence and quickness of action were her most valuable assets for pioneering. Let it be so. I have always felt she had a good reason, or thought she had, for what she did. The ways of some folk as well as those of our Lord are mysterious.

14

Out on the open spaces, people met on the trail, their ways diverged, and sometimes ran together again in strange ways and places -- sometimes never. I met many unique and interesting characters on the long trek who like a destiny crossed my trail again - and again. Some of them prominent figures in our nation whose influence upon my life and story I herein record.

But I never saw Myrtle again.

The rest of the party were vindictive with, "Well, I'll be danged!" and, "Just let her go!"

As soon as Roscoe arrived with his crowd, we drove over to the edge of the canyons and looked down at the rocky gulleys and up at the steep, timbered hills. In comparison, the broad, grassy plateau looked like a paradise.

The meticulous salesman walked over to where I stood, brushed his tailor-made suit with broad palm and adjusted his tie.

"You're bound to lose prospects," he consoled. "I never sell all mine. Now the law of average ..."

"I know nothing about the law of average and I'm not selling anything."

He took me by the arm.

"Come on now. You know, there's a psychological time to get people to put their John Henry on the dotted line. Let's be getting to the Land Office."

"You're really going to file on a claim?"

"Darn tootin'. It's also the psychological time for me to get my own John Henry on a piece of land."

Roscoe came by with Mother Van and their group to settle with Ebe's folk for our board and lodge.

When I told Mother Van what had happened, she said, "Well, maybe Myrtle's father insisted on her going. And perhaps she was too embarrassed to explain anything. She would not be one to make excuses."

At a railroad siding out on the range we boarded the train for Douglas and the U.S. Land Office eighty miles to the West, sending the drivers back to town with the empty vehicles.

The government filing fee on 320 acres was twenty-three dollars and who wouldn't pay that paltry sum to get his hands on a half-section of land - even if it were on the Sahara as Jim Turner put it. He had concluded to file on a claim with the other colonists.

In the confusion of the crowded Land Office, I glanced up to see Ida Van Sant standing at the Register's desk with Roscoe McCully, a paper in her hand. I walked over to her.

"Mother Van, you are not filing on a homestead?"

She turned and looked at me like a little boy caught in a jam jar.

"Of course I am," she laughed, showing two rows of strong white teeth.

"Why should you," I argued, "with your nice home and friends in Peoria. You'll never stay out here and prove up a claim."

It required living on the land seven months of each year, for three years.

"I'll show you whether I will or not - you know me."

She signed her name and raised her right hand in oath that she was taking the land for a home and not for investment, that she would abide by the requirements of the United States government in the ceding of its public lands to private ownership.

The register looked up as the Swedish farmer made application.

"Naturalization papers?"

"Yah - I bane good citizen, good farmer."

"That doesn't give you the right to file."

The Swede produced the papers.

Our forefathers had seen to it that no foreigner should gain title to an acre of America's Public Lands.

***

I made several trips back East that fall - one to St. Louis, another to Peoria.

On my third trip, Jim Mayes, publisher, lawyer and member of the Wyoming legislature, carried this item in the Lusk Herald:

"Miss Edith Ammons, who headed a party of landseekers from Peoria, Illinois here last week, is still here looking the country over. This is her third trip here and she seems to be more favorably impressed with our town and country with each successive trip. We have been trying to

16

induce her to go in partnership with us in the paper and law business and believe if we were single and more handsome, our persuasive powers would laud her."

My father brought a party of friends from St. Louis, filed on a claim and helped to locate the others. The Ammonses, having been a land people, I was anxious to have his reaction on this region. He was enthusiastic over it and thought it was a poor man's chance to get a foothold. We located the St. Louis folk on the tableland north of the railroad. It became known as the "St. Louis District"; the south table as "Illinois."

Through the influence of those who had taken land, every small party spread to a colony. I have seen landseekers rush back to town and wire friends or relatives to come at once and file on adjoining claims before other seekers spotted them.

Charles West, head of the West Land Company, paced the bare floor of the branch office in Lusk expatiating to Roscoe and me over the success of the colonizing venture. Not often did the dignified Mr. West become so exuberant.

"A woman colonizer. Do you know, Edith, that you are the only woman colonizer in the country - or in the world perhaps?"

Land colonization was then in its infancy.

"Eastern papers and real estate journals have been writing you up."

Two weeks on the ground now and already the rest of the world had receded.

"A woman colonizer!" I sniffed. "Huh. Sounds like a suffragette."

I did not know that Wyoming was the first state to adopt Women's Suffrage.

He laughed. Charlie West had a pleasing personality and some of the droll humor of George Ade, his friend and classmate back in Indiana. He had been a good friend and adviser to Ida Mary and me.

Getting homeseekers to come w5est in that heyday of settlement was not the accomplishment it appeared to be.

As Myrtle had said when I took my first job on a newspaper, "Any fool can learn to set type," so almost any fool, I reflected, could round up settlers with people to be found on every corner of city and hamlet and on

17

every farm district who wanted to take up land. And news on western immigration made headlines for almost any newspaper in the country. Columns had been printed about my heading groups of homeseekers to Wyoming. Open land! Open land! The wonder of it to public and press was, (as it is to me now), that they had followed a chit of a girl.

Bringing in the landseekers may have been a foolproof job, but it was the least of the colonizing problems. The locating business had become an open warfare. And it seemed to me that all the pessimists and stockmen and curbstone locators in the country gathered around waiting for me to bring in a load of seekers.

The cost of colonizing ran high with the locating fees the only remuneration. The West Land Company was under heavy expense of colonizers, of locators, surveyors, and of taking prospects over the country to select their claims. Sometimes Roscoe McCully drove for three days over open territory with prospective settlers that they might have their choice of location.

We could not afford to have our prospects lured away. More than that, I did not want my settlers located undesirably. The groups of friends had expanded to those of strangers. The locating pirates as a rule maintained no offices. They followed the homestead trail like harvest hands the harvest. Cowpunchers and old-timers often conjured wild-west talks to strike fear into the hearts of the strongest.

"Where are the two strangers who came with this crowd?" I asked at the Square House table.

"Those two huskies from Joliet?" the station agent countered. "They took the eastbound with their return tickets. I heard a man telling them how once a sod-buster was so famished he ate his dead horse that had starved to death and then a pack of hungry wolves devoured the sod-buster, and that the penitentiary would be a lot safer."

"They were not escaped convicts from the Joliet prison," I explained. "They were tenant farmers."

And the unsuspecting bank clerk had gone out with that foreflusher, Samson, who stood on the streets trying to catch one or two of a crowd alone and tell of a choice claim that was open.

"Just happened to find out about it - now if you'd like to look at it."

18

The piece of land he was showing the bank clerk was in the Jackie Mills' sheep pasture, the biggest sheepman in that region. What would that tenderfoot do with a claim there?

I pushed aside the slab of pie and refused the second cup of coffee. Back on the reservation I had scared out the claim-jumpers once through expose in my newspaper.

Something had to be done. I refused to be downed by the land sharks.

Edith Eudora Ammons Kohl

Chapter II
THAT LITTLE SKIRT PRINTER

A group of cowboys sat around the chuck wagon of a roundup camp. They had been rounding up a late, fall shipment of steers, driving the cows and young stock to winter pasture. It had been a long, hard day in the saddle.

The boys were famished and at supper there had been an unwonted silence when a long, lean puncher remarked, as if to himself, "Danged if I know what this hyar country is a-comin' to."

"Now what's the matter, Lanky?" one of them inquired. "You're al'lus perdictin' trouble."

"Yeah? Well, when it comes to a noospaper in a Gawd-forsaken cow country --"

"You-all hear what this puncher's a sayin', boys? A noospaper!" He turned to Lanky, "Where you been? You wuz supposed to be out at them corrals a loadin' cattle for Denver."

"Yes, siree," Lanky proceeded, ignoring his companions' remarks. "A printin' shop right in the middle o' the range, 'longside the Van Tassell shippin' pens."

A top hand called Tex took a big gulp of hot, black coffee.

"Aw, he's locoed, al'lus know'd he was locoed."

"No, I'm not locoed," Lanky drawled. "But she is."

Forks and tin cups were suspended in midair.

"She? She!" they exclaimed in unison.

"Yeah, she! A skirt's a runnin' it."

"A skirt!"

Surprise, consternation, disgust all were voiced in those two syllables. Evidently skirt printers were scarce in Wyoming.

"But she won't last long," Lanky consoled his fellow punchers. "Not much bigger'n a jackrabbit. First little Wyomin' breeze comes along she'll be blowed clean down to Cheyenne."

So that puncher had seen her. Their curiosity was aggravated.

"Up at the Van Tassell corrals? Come on Dogie! What would anybody start a newspaper there for? Nothin' for miles around except the Van Tassell and the O Ten Bar ranches," one said.

Lanky took on an important air.

"There ain't now. But you cain't tell -- looks like landgrabbers. One o' the Quarter Circle V (Van Tassell) hands saw a whole bunch o' strangers one day eatin' their dinner up in the rocks over by the corals and the wind raw and cold. All gathered in a pocket to keep warm. Looked like tenderfeet most of 'em-wimmen among 'em."

He stopped to let that piece of news take effect.

"And that very afternoon they wuz seen a nosin' around on the prairie like they wuz huntin' for somethin'..."

Tex, the top hand, broke in. "Don't suppose they could be lookin' for land, do you?

"That's just what the boys suspicioned. Several times there's been people reconnoiterin' around drivin' back and forth and around like they were drunk -- or crazy."

"Well, what about it?" Tex demanded. "Any sign of homesteaders?"

"No hair nor hide of 'em left. But what's that skirt here for unless there's tenderfeet comin'?"

"Well, I'll be flabbergasted," one of the punchers remarked. "What'll Van Tassell say to that? And all the other ranchers in these parts?"

"They cain't do it!"

The foreman's attention had at last been riveted to the conversation.

"That Running Water Divide is the best damned range in the country and no landgrabbers are going to be settled on it!"

The Boston Kid asked, "What kind of a person does this – ah – "skirt" appear to be, Lanky?"

The cowpoke squinted an eye and floundered for words that would accurately describe this enigma.

"Not a bad-lookin' filly, wavy mane -- between a sorrel and a yeller well as I can recollect. Looks like she'd be a pretty high-stepper -- but no heft."

He stopped as a straight, lean-faced young man got up and left the group.

"Now what do you suppose is eatin' him? Ain't said a word all evenin'."

"Nothin' new for Lone Star. He never has much to say. And he ain't like you -- a fallin' for skirts."

A little warning on that score might not be amiss. As they turned in that night, wrapped in their blankets on the ground they admonished Lanky not to go grazin' around any tenderfoot skirts.

"They're the roonation of any cowpuncher."

The Boston Kid who was a wrangler in the outfit had been an impersonator in a road show. It was weeks later that he re-enacted for me the scene around the chuck wagon.

Over a cup of coffee I said, "You mentioned Lone Star. Where is he now?"

"I wouldn't know. He was a kind of roundup boss. Left for a place he called Lost Trail."

"I don't know. It's lost I guess, like every other place out here. Why?" he asked suddenly.

"O, I knew a man by that name in Dakota. And I knew too that the man who had left the table when they were discussing a new printer was he. No doubt he too knew who that skirt printer was."

R.S. Van Tassell was one of the most influential stockmen in Wyoming. He lived in Cheyenne but his home ranch was located up on Running Water Creek. His cattle grazed over miles of open land. It was on this range that my colonies had filed and there, a few rods from the shipping pens, known as the Van Tassell Siding, I started a newspaper which I called THE VAN TASSELL PROGRESS. Putting Van Tassell's name to a settler's publication after filling up his pastures with them was an audacious act. But the irony of it never had occurred to me.

There are two types of persons who forge ahead, accomplishing the seemingly impossible: the very wise man with his great mental power and foresight; and the one who doesn't know he is doing anything out of the ordinary. I was a living example of the well-known axiom, "Fools rush in where angels fear to tread."

The Northwestern Railroad had platted off a town site. The trains had to stop at the corrals to load cattle -- may as well unload passengers, too. So the company switched off another box-car, called it a depot, and I with a few of my immigrants started the town of Van Tassell. By spring when the several hundred settlers returned to live on the land, this new town would be the center of 400 square miles of settled territory. Now, there was not a place in the entire region where a landseeker could find food or shelter.

I bought a fifty-foot tapeline, surveyed off a town-lot for myself and had a printshop built, a mere shack, which I also used as an office and living quarters. This was my third newspaper venture in as many years on as many frontiers. The first one had been as manager of a proof sheet while waiting to get settled on the Brule.

To help meet the emergency, Ida Van Sant put up a store building with a large kitchen in the rear, and lodging rooms above, under the low gable roof. We had the materials shipped from Lusk. Several bachelor settlers who were going to stay the winter to build their own shacks did the work, making Van Tassell their headquarters. We now had a place out on the lone range where we could bring our colonists without the "sharks" at Lusk knowing it.

My toy shop, as a stockman passing through called the shop, sat facing the corrals with its sign THE VAN TASSELL PROGRESS in bold black letters. I had made enough money in colonizing to buy a plant costing several hundred dollars, cash with order. What a shock that must have been to the American Type Foundry Company which had staked me in Dakota.

Several rods from the shop, the store building with its false front stood off at right angles facing the railroad track. Why did we not put those first two lone buildings on the same street I do not know. Streets had been laid out and named though I do not recall a single name. I was not interested in building up towns. Develop the country and towns would pop up like grass after a rain. Mother Van with her flare for boosting business was as proud of that cheap frame building as she had been of the Van Sant Block in Peoria.

The only other building on the town site was a rectangle that looked like a long dry goods box on the end set alone on a bee-line midway between printshop and store -- the outhouse. With no attempt at concealment, it sat perched on the high tableland, its yellow boards glistening in the sun like a beacon on the range.

In a later day of white-tiled rest rooms lining our highways, that one lone rest room on the prairie should have been nothing at which to turn

24

up one's nose. Were it now, it might bear a sign in colored lights. But it is only now that I see that unsightly thing set boldly there for all strangers passing through to see, detracting attention no doubt from The Progress sign. How they must have laughed.

It was a gray day with a piercing tang in the air and spits of snow that I heard a sharp clicking and ringing through the dead silence -- now what could that be? Oh, the railroad phone, I concluded, turning back to my desk. But the **br-rr-rrr** became louder. That insistent ringing might mean an emergency train message and not a soul to take it. The telephone was for the use of the train crews passing through and for stockman notifying the railroad company of shipments ready to go out. There was no station agent. I ran swiftly down the track to the boxcar depot.

It was the station agent at Lusk with a telegram for me, taking the chance that someone would hear the phone and answer. Another party of landseekers was on the way and would arrive the next morning. I gave the operator a message to give to McCully, to be on hand and chuckling over the joke we were playing on the sharks. I ran back to tell Mother Van.

It was an important crowd of professional and business folk who had money for improvements and influence in bringing other settlers. Dr. Watts who had sent the telegram had several friends in the group, so could we locate them near his homestead?

"Mother Van! It's a message from Dr. Watts - a bunch of seekers will be here tomorrow. And they won't have to go on to Lusk. Thanks for our effort."

My elation fell flat as I looked at the older woman. She stood rubbing her hands together as she had a way of doing when greatly perturbed.

"O, Edith," she moaned, "What will we do? Yes, we've got a roof for our guests but no bedding; a kitchen but nothing to cook. And a store with no groceries in it."

The Peoria settler who had leased the store had not gotten in his stock yet and Mother Van now threatened to cancel the lease.

"Wheeler's too slow for a new country," she complained. We were getting along with the few sticks of furniture and supplies hauled out from Lusk; and I bunked in the printshop.

There was no way out that we could see but I had learned that almost anything cold turn up in the Primitive - like the printer in Dakota riding out of the empty space one time when the press would not run; and a little stream trickling between the settlers and a prairie fire; and, the stranger passing through when I was lost that time on the Brule prairie.

Like a magician pulling things out of a hat, the old Primitive produced things to keep one here. Too, necessity developed one's ingenuity.

So I said, "Oh, there'll be a way, Mother Van."

Saying that had become a habit. If there was no way -- well, one just made the best of it.

About four o'clock that afternoon I heard a shrill whistle. A freight train from the West. It would stop down at the tank for water. I called to Mother Van.

"Get on your traveling togs, quick! We're going to Harrison, Nebraska, for supplies."

"To Harrison?" she exclaimed. "What on earth --"

I pointed to the long line of boxcars.

"How are we going to get back?"

"Never mind about getting back," I replied cryptly from the door as I ran to the printshop for my own hat and coat. "We can talk about that when we get there. We can stay overnight if we have to."

She looked at me in stark-eyed wonder as much as to say, "What will that girl do next?" But she did not stop to argue and after all, she was glad of almost any way out of the dilemma.

At Harrison, the first town in the direction the freight was going, we bought a supply of bedding and groceries. We were about fifteen miles from home. The station agent wiring to the division point at Chadron learned there was a west-bound freight due around midnight.

The little homestead-and-cow town of Harrison was dark as a dungeon when the headlight of the freight cast its long yellow line far ahead of it. From the hotel on the corner we made it on time.

Seeing two lone women walking beside the track toward the caboose the brakemen shouted, "Hey, where you going?"

"To Van Tassell," I replied.

"You can't take this train. Not stopping there this trip."

"Well, it could stop there, could it not?" I asked in my most wheedling manner.

He swung his lantern full upon us.

"Oh, it's you!" he addressed me, "and the lady."

By that time, every train crew from Chadron to Lander knew us by sight at least. He called another man and they loaded our heavy boxes of groceries and rolls of bedding (Ida Van Sant was a lavish buyer) which had been delivered at the tracks, and helped us onto the caboose.

The conductor coming through later to stir up the fire in the round-bellied stove looked at us, half asleep on the long benches, lurching back and forth with the bumping of the train; hair tousled, faces drawn and sooty, old coats buttoned tight against the chill of the night. A petite, curly-haired, blue-eyed lass and a dignified, portly lady past middle-age. We must have been a comic and pathetic sight to behold.

I looked at Mother Van as she dozed on the seat opposite. She was really a handsome woman who looked stately in black satin and diamonds and soft brown hair done in a queenly coiffure. The diamond earrings still dangled from pierced ears, making tiny beads of white flame in the dim light of the coal oil lamp in the ceiling.

But she had come from poor, hardy, German stock. And the Van Sants with whom she had spent her mature life were of ambitious and thrifty lineage. The doctor had been a man of business acumen; another was an influential banker; LaPorte, the baritone who had once in his prime sung at Buckingham Palace -- and on whose coattail I had made my debut as an entertainer in Peoria; and there was Cousin Sam, governor of Minnesota. Not so many years ago, Minnesota had been raw country and governor, Samuel R. Van Sant, believed in the West.

He had said to me, then a school girl, "Our greatest leadership in America has come from the soil, from new territory."

There had been two other governors in the Van Sant family -- one of Rhode Island, one of Texas.

No, Ida Van Sant never would be content to sit and rock and she cared nothing for society. But she was showing the strain of roughing it after years of comparative luxury.

Waking with a wrenching lunge of the caboose she said, "Edith, darling. I wish we had gone up to British Columbia, I think it's a better country than this -- big wheat country, big cities, and down in Oklahoma, a big oil boom -- that town of Tulsa is a great place to invest in a growing business or real estate ...”

The next morning with a bright sun and a sparkling air that woke one to the glory of living, I checked my land maps while Mother Van in her Dutch-blue calico set the kettles boiling. Roscoe McCulley was there with locators and surveyors, all of us laughing over Mother Van's and my experiences of last night, all filled with the buoyancy that comes from life in the open. The Sage Hen soon would be steaming round the bend bringing both friends and strangers to whom Mother Van would expound the virtues of old Wyoming, British Columbia and Tulsa forgotten. Ah, but life out here was good with always something to look forward to and Mother Van was singing the first note I had heard her hum since the Doctor had gone.

The train was whistling in. Ida Van Sant soon began to enjoy the free life and the frugal planning of her younger days. No longer did she wring her hands and pace the floor nights over her tragedy. The settlement became a refuge for all who sought food and shelter on their way across the plain. Both friends and strangers, grateful for the hospitality, contributed generously to the expense and lent a free hand to the housework.

A mixture of city folk, cowboys, surveyors and farmers did not perturb Mother Van. Her table back home had ever been a melting pot -- and no servant was allowed to broil the steaks or make the jellies. With Governor Van Sant or other distinguished guest at the table, she would invite any chance caller to “Sit right down and have a bite.”

If it were the lean friends (who usually called at mealtime) she would say, “Come on it, Dolly, (or Mamie or Elmer). This is Cousin Sam, the Governor, you know. Sam, you remember Dolly, the girl who stayed with me when the Doctor was in the Klondike. She has supported her poor old mother for years ...”

One morning I looked out to see Cousin Julia coming up the trail from the station, wearing a rustling black silk dress and heavy gold necklace. Cousin Julia, another Van Sant widow, was a woman of means who lived as she pleased, traveling in the best sets when she chose, ignoring them when she became bored. She was a wiry little woman with a sharp wit that put new life into the settlement.

"Well, Ida," she greeted Mother Van, "I must say -- no, don't tell me anything about the country. I can see for myself all I want to see and you couldn't give me an acre of it. I've come to find out what you're up to."

Cousin Julia lent a ready hand to the cooking and entertaining. For hours, she would sit down by the railroad bridge fishing in the shallow creek for a wary trout that wouldn't make more than one good bite.

"I might catch fish for supper," she said when food ran low.

"No, Ida, I don't want your help. You can't sit still long enough to catch a fish."

While she fished Ida opened up a can of sardines and got the supper ready. (The storekeeper had to get the shelves up before he could order his goods.)

Ida Van Sant could conjure a meal from a cupboard almost as bare as Mother Hubbard's. She was adept at making soups from odds and ends.

"Ida!" from Cousin Julia, "you'd better add more water to that soup -- I see a team coming."

"How many cups?"

"Well," straining her eyes as she shaded them with her bird like hands, "I can't see yet how many are in that rig."

And I would add to myself, "Thanks for a land with plenty of water for soup." I had known the time not long since when water was as manna from heaven. Now we had a well at Van Tassell, and at last, the store and post office had opened up.

The glorious fall was at last giving way to winter. Mother Van and Cousin Julia went home, Mother Van declaring she would be back to live on her claim next spring. Only a handful of the colonists remained, camping on their claims or around Van Tassell.

With leaden fingers, I wrote to Ida Mary, breaking the news.

"Sis, I've started a newspaper. With a railroad and box car depot at my very door. Think of it! My, how I am getting on in the newspaper world. After running newspapers and mail routes miles from established transportation, I find a railroad a real handy thing to have around. I've brought my audiences out and the stage is set, and what a big stage this rangeland is. (How well you know the drama in this homesteading performance.) Yet there is comedy and laughter along with the tears. Besides, this is a great field for development. You will remember that Senator Warren and Congressman Mondell were confident that settlers to Wyoming would make good if they were the right kind. I feel that I have brought the right kind. They possess among other qualifications, gameness. Mother Van has been wonderful. Please do not worry about my overdoing. There is not much the newspaper can do but hole in 'till spring. We have had a lot of fun out here and the work has been thrilling. Somehow, Sis, I can't turn back."

Ida Mary would be perturbed over my starting a newspaper out here.

One day shortly before leaving I had asked, "Sis, what are we going to do when the reservation gets to running smoothly?"

And she had answered promptly, "Just let it run!" then flashed a quick suspicious look at me.

Could it be, after all the hardships of the past months that this sister of hers, so unfitted for the life, was seeing other frontiers?

"Sis, I'm going to start a newspaper on the Rosebud Reservation."

"O, no, you're not, Edith. You're a pretty-looking specimen ..."

Soon thereafter, Ida Mary had just "let the reservation run" and married Imbert Miller, a young rancher, and settled down near the Brule.

Chapter III
LEAVING THE RANGE AND ME BEHIND

For the first time in many weeks, there was leisure to take stock of things. The Department of Interior gave the settler six months' time to establish residence and a newspaper must be published six consecutive months to become an official publication for land notices.

And the land business was the bread and butter of the frontier newspaper. Publication of proof notices was the reason for many of the small sheets scattered over the homestead country. There would be no proofs from these colonists for three years but there would be other legal matters. Also, the earlier settlers adjacent to my territory who had taken land under the fourteen-month law for residence were proving up.

Steps had been taken in Washington to have the six-month Ruling waived for me on the ground that my Wyoming paper was an extension of The Reservation Wand which I was still publishing in Dakota. The Wand had been thus named because it was supposed to wave magically over the new land but it had failed to "waive" in this instance, thus The Progress would not be a legal publication until spring.

The circulation, however, which was mostly in the East among the colonists and others interested in homesteading would keep me going that winter. The paper also carried a few display advertisements from business firms in the West.

To me the income was only a necessary means to the purpose which was to lay the groundwork for development of this region and to prepare settlers for the undertaking. The Progress acquainted them with existent condition and the Land Ruling with which they must comply -- how much land must be cultivated, where supplies could be obtained and at what price, so the settler would know whether to have equipment shipped out or buy it here.

In my mind's eye, I laid out on the virgin floor of earth my pattern which I had made in colonizing the land. Dear me! That colonizing job had been quite a chore after all. There had been no hullabaloo out here as inducement by railroads, development agencies and the press advertising the country and no blare of bands as there had been in the spectacular Lotteries back in the Dakotas.

Wyoming was yet an outpost and these colonists never had seen outposts. They had come from the modern world of commerce and industry and tall corn to find nothing but short dry grass. Grass -- creaking, bending under their feet, popping up again as though in defiance to man. And yet, these colonists had come and seen and settled.

Now, with time to think it over, I wondered how it had been done. But in these undertakings, I must not look back until the job was finished -- lest like Lot's wife I turn to salt.

Starting out on this venture my only fear had been lack of physical strength and it must have been by the Act of God that I had not collapsed in the middle of it.

The long trips back East were wearing. There was the strain of explaining the homestead proposition, making arrangements among the colonists who decided to go back with me and the last-minute confusion of getting them all rounded up. And on the way back to Wyoming, I would find myself completely enervated. It was on one of the trips out when, changing trains one late afternoon at Sterling, Illinois, I remembered having had nothing but a cup of coffee since early morning. The train out of Sterling being late, I had gone uptown for a good hot dinner. When I returned, the waiting room was empty and the train having made up time was speeding on its way West with my landseekers, my bags, and my ticket which had been left in their charge.

After a night of commotion over trains and ticket, with the railroad company wiring back and forth, I arrived in Omaha twenty-four hours late to find my crowd waiting at the gate of Union Station with ropes.

"To lariat our pilot," they jestingly explained to curious travelers who stopped to see what was going on. They were so relieved at seeing me they forgot their annoyance at being held up on the road at extra expense. They had feared I might not be able to finish the trip.

The long hard drives over the prairie by team or shimmying car following these trips sometimes put me to bed for a few days. A few times I had been too ill to accompany the crowds onto the land. Roscoe and his locators knew the land but I knew my people.

In the perverseness of human nature Jim Turner thought the claim Jack Brown filed on must be better than his own else why had Jack taken it: and Jack Brown would rather have a dirt farmer joining him than a highfalutin' eye doctor and must be reminded how lucky he was to have a next-door neighbor who could not only pick a piece of sod from one's eye, but give first aid in almost any emergency.

And the eye doctor wanted a neighbor who could plow for him and look after his wife and little daughter who would be left alone at times while he was attending to his professional duties back in Illinois.

The young Swede hesitantly explained his case with "O Yah, dat stenographer she one fine lady but if you please -- I like a farm woman close by who can wash my clothes and bake my bread yet -- I pay well -- O Yah."

Lone women must be placed near families who could do chores for them and otherwise lend a hand especially in case of sickness. Friends who planned to pool farm equipment and labor must be located in a body.

"Are you going to fence?" became a prime question.

If those who were going to fence their land at once were located adjoining one another they could build line-fences together thus cutting cost and labor in two.

I was carrying out my plan of cooperative action and for harmony between these colonists as it was essential to figure out whose claim should join whose.

Getting the boundary lines and descriptions of each homestead in the boundless space accurate was a responsible job. It was one of the reasons for having experienced locators. Let a man put his house a foot off the line and he could not hold the land.

If one could find a corner-stake that the range stock had not trampled down he was lucky. Finding one, he measured off tracts from that point by counting the resolutions of the wheel with a handkerchief tied to it -- so many turns of a buggy wheel, so many of a car wheel, to the mile. Without thought of familiarizing myself with a surveyor's job, I reached the point where given one corner-stake or stone as a starter, I almost could divide a whole township into sections, or find a location from its numerical description.

After watching a large group select claims, I would hunt corner-stones in my dreams and as I was about to reach one, a drove of cattle would trample it into the grass. But it was fascinating work, this measuring off the untouched spaces into farm units. I have seen big strong men struck with awe as they realized the vast stretches had lain thus since Creation.

That many of the colonists were not experienced farmers did not matter. One must follow different methods on the frontier and it was hard to teach old dogs new tricks. There were a sufficient number of good farmers from which the city folk could learn the basic principles of farming.

Under the 320 Acre Act, one-fourth of the land must be cultivated and other specified improvements made, thus the white-collared settlers who had not given up their interests back East would do their part toward improving the country and would furnish employment to neighbors who needed money to carry on. As a whole, these colonists were better prepared financially to meet requirements than the average homesteader.

The new seven-months-a-year residence provision made it possible for business and professional men like Dr. Watts and Bob Kearns to handle their affairs at home, making trips back and forth, leaving their families on the claim during their absence.

"I figure," said Dr. Watts, "that the improved land will be worth more than the expense of homesteading it. What's nicer than a ranch in Wyoming as a summer home? I can have crops put out each year -- or raise a few head of stock. A new interest, something worthwhile, instead of wearing oneself out hunting up summer resorts and trying to make himself think that when he gets back he has enjoyed his vacation.

"And," he added, "it will make a home when one is ready to retire or in case of a rainy day."

It was not long until many of these Easterners either transferred their business or started one anew in the rapidly growing West.

But plans and patterns faded into the loneliness of the frontier winter in which I was swallowed up. Space eternal, eternal. This was eternity. O, yes, a railroad ribboned the lonely land but when the afternoon express whistled and went rolling on toward civilization it was as though it had taken the last sign of life with it leaving only its lonely echo and me behind.

No cheerful group here as there had been at the Indian trading post in Dakota; no merry parties of young folk skimming across the plain with sleigh-bells and laughter ringing silver in the crystal air. The straggling

34

settler or cowboy out here already had drifted in and on, the storekeeper gone to his claim for the night. And I sat gazing at those two ribbons of steel glistening in the lowering winter sun.

As the sun dropped below the horizon, an array of color would paint the western sky. Flamboyant, as though the great artist had spilled His pot of paints and let them flow one into the other. And as in envy of the gorgeous display, the eastern sky would lift up in a reflected glory with the blood-red shaded to pink, the orange to yellow, and purple to lavender - - the eastern sky more delicate and subdued in its reflection. Just like the West!

I mused, as though the western sun had said as it sank in its majesty, "I am the power and the glory. Men shall follow me."

And the heavens caught up the land making of it a color-draped footstool and one stood awed before this divinity of Nature. No shouting Methodist revivals which I attended in childhood could ever bring one so close to God. The earth lying here as it had lain since the Beginning, waiting. Waiting, poignant, for man to possess it.

Spellbound, as a spirit held in the ether, I watched the colors slowly fade from the canvas and as gray dusk closed in, the evening star came out. I got up, lighted the lamp, and put the kettle on. I drew the heavy, blue-denim curtains close across the windows. I must shut out the nothingness and the night.

I trimmed the lamp to burn its brightest, got out the linen luncheon cloth and a few pieces of china that Ida Mary and Ma Wagor had sent, pushed back the array of papers on the long, home-made, editor's table, making of one end a supper service deluxe, with canned foods heated quickly and steaming tea.

I tacked a few bright pictures cut from old magazines onto the wall. They looked real nice against the natural soft tan of the wallboard which lined my domicile. I pinned a lace collar on my dark wool dress. Then, on to that panacea for all ills -- work.

Holing in, I yet found work to do. Sitting there as obscure and alone as Alice Ben Bolt's grave, The Progress made but little progress that the frontier could see.

So far as current news went, the word newspaper was a misnomer. The general news of the West was gathered from the few exchanges on my copy table. My paper was a four-page publication with two pages of home-print, the other two pages being what we called "patents," furnished by newspaper syndicates, ready printed.

Subscriptions kept coming in from many points and from Washington where officials of the various Public Land Departments must have laughed at the odds and ends used along with boiler plate, and the western poetry I wrote in the winter evenings for fillers.

There were evenings when I sat at the eight-point case under the reflector of the coal-oil lamp hanging on the wall and set my thoughts into type like composing at a typewriter. Clickety-click, clickety-click-click, faster and faster it would go breaking the dead silence until the article was on the galleys and the loneliness forgotten.

I liked the work of emptying galleys into the form and making up the page. That was constructive. I disliked the monotonous inking and rolling, and rolling and inking, to print the paper a page at a time on the old hand-press -- which did not mark the era as antiquated. There was no power but elbow grease for running presses out on the frontier. I hated throwing the type back into the cases letter by letter, undoing what one had just done. I've always hated the 'undoing' of the good things in life. I equally detested the puttering with dirty dishes and other housekeeping messes in the shop when the paper was to be gotten out. In fact, I decided I must have a natural antipathy to everything that was really work. Details and trivial puttering fatigued me to utter exhaustion. And why must I waste time like that with frontiers to be conquered? Next spring, I should probably be able to hire a printer's "devil" or an "angel" -- whichever happened to be available.

Then one day, the largest newspaper in Wyoming -- a Cheyenne Daily -- came out with a write-up about a girl who had started a newspaper in the middle of the range up in Converse County.

I cannot recall the article in full but, in effect, it was very plain that the writer's opinion of both the newspaper and the editor was identical with that of the cowboys, although expressed in different terms than "locoed." The Progress, it inferred, was a sort of freakish whim and its publisher a light, feathery piece of femininity which if blown away would have no special call, I would take it, to stop in Cheyenne.

"And," the writer went on, as though it told the whole story, "her name is Edythe Eudora Ammons."

"That Edythe," the story said in conclusion, "is suggestive of frocks and frills. But that Eudora has got our goat."

The Edythe had been spelled like that, and with it, I had launched my career among Indians and sodbreakers back in Dakota, never giving the name a thought. I do not know whether in my early childhood my mother, or my Aunt Diana Maddux, had changed it to follow a flair for spelling names with a "y" instead of "I," thinking it sounded more poetic for an artistic career. Certainly the name had not been picked for a trailblazer. So I changed the Edythe to Edith.

The night that I read the article in the Cheyenne Tribune, I went to sleep on a pillow wet with tears. To have my newspaper looked upon as trivial and ridiculous was more than I could bear. While many leaders of the homestead movement knew what my work had been, it was evident the writer had not known, so who could blame him?

I had not thought of launching myself with the people and the press through the influence of Wyoming statesmen or the Department of Interior but had it occurred to me I should have spurned the idea. I wanted to carve my own record here. But I now knew I would have to fight all the way to do it.

Edith Eudora Ammons Kohl

Chapter IV
THE WILD SORREL STALLION

I called my printshop the "Aircastle." Not only because of the castles I build there, but because of the air that blew through the cracks and swept around the corners with a sobbing, moaning sound that made my hair stand on end until I grew used to it. After a while, it became company breaking the solitude with its crescendo.

In the long nights of frontier winter, I wrote letters to Ida Mary telling her of the country and of my daily life. And I eagerly awaited the letters from friends and loved ones -- long ones from Ida Mary filled with accounts of herself and news of the Reservation. She and Imbert were doing nicely running the Cedarfork Trading Post in Dakota which was but a few miles from Ammons, and Imbert was helping his father to run their ranch.

It was not lonely, she said, with people coming into the post every day. Old Porcupine Bear had come to ask about "Paleface-Prints-Paper." Ida Mary and I had many friends among the Brules, a Sioux tribe, who were going to celebrate when I came back.

"White squaw she run paper better. Man printer him no good. Sioux no more trade beads and blankets for newspaper."

From back in Milwaukee and later Kansas City where he had taken a job on a newspaper, Alexander Van Leshout, the artist, whose claim was near mine, wrote me in his usual jesting manner. Being cartoonist on the big dailies had lost its appeal for him -- good job, but the open spaces called. His Indian paintings done on the reservation were attracting attention of the critics.

And, "Ladywand (I smiled at the familiar sobriquet meaning ("Lady of the Wand" - my newspaper), I am still listening for your voice in the west wind. Or has your voice been drowned by the bleat of the woollies."

As I read and re-read those letters from the outside, tears splotched the pages and far into the night I would lie staring out the window into a cold, moon-drenched void with nothing to break its continuity except that great cluster of chalky, white rocks which rose like an ancient castle left with only its broken jagged walls towering in the air. They stood there, a few rods to the north, silver in the moonlight, a fortress tower guarding the little settlement -- and me. From that end of the printshop neither the store nor the depot was visible.

In the solitude, I pondered upon the course of life and the small things which sometimes changed its current.

If on that day which I had bolted into her house announcing, "Sis, I'm going on to Wyoming," Ida Mary had said again, as she had always said: "You're a great specimen to break into new country, a frail thing like you. What could you do?"

Or, as Bill, the old stage driver, had reiterated, "You'd better stop and graze 'round a bit or you'll be with the singin' angels."

"Weeping angels, you mean, Bill. Wouldn't it make anybody weep -- being an angel?"

Well, my trail-breaking might have ended there.

But Bill had merely spat his tobacco juice across the prairie and said, "So you're rarin' to step. Funny how tough a little blade of grass can be."

And Ida Mary had only looked at me with that strange expression on her face as though she had known this would come.

And we had wept together over the parting and she had not said, as usual, "What could you do ...?"

It was something not in the pale of words. It was a reaching of a hungry heart, and a wild spirit from the great Holy One of life.

Yet, in the retrospect of that day, I did not know why I did these strange, and what my many friends called outlandish, things. Was I but a tumbleweed in the wind of Destiny? I wondered.

The howling of a pack of wolves and the sharp crackle of walls from the frozen air broke my reverie. I rolled over on my cot, drew the heavy blankets close around me and slept.

Waking to the freshness of morning there was no time nor inclination for brooding. Each morning on the frontier was like a new beginning. The sun streamed in, the crackling fire and the aroma of coffee and bacon filling the shack and wafting into the thin air of the prairie. I was hungry and ready for another day.

Many of the winter days were glorious with a pure crisp air that was putting red into my cheeks and as the season wore on, I settled down to long nights of sleep storing up energy like a hibernating animal.

Two women homesteaders who had stayed the winter came into Van Tassell now and then. Several families from The Ridge came and one day the editor of the Harrison paper and his wife made a friendly visit offering to assist me in any possible way.

After a heavy snow that lay deep over the range, there came a January thaw with a Chinook that melted it in one soft warm breath. The midday sun shone bright and warm and the herds fed peacefully. New grass with its tiny threads of green peeped up under the brownish yellow. The cattle had thrived well on the native grass with no other feed and no shelter.

I went skipping across the track to Running Water, the creek that wound under the railroad bridge and ran for a short distance parallel to the railroad until it twisted away and got lost somewhere on the range or ran itself out. Sometimes I felt like following it to the end. Running Water (Niobrara, the Indians called it), so precious to the stockman, was about as deep as Powder River ("an inch deep and a mile wide"). If there were a skiff of ice left, I would go skating.

I was ready to slip under the wire of the right-of-way fence when I heard a mighty snort and looked up to see a great, sorrel stallion charging toward me, leading a bunch of wild horses and nothing but the barbwire with the old fence posts that would surely give 'way between us. These horses were large with round rump, long mane and tail. I had thought of the wild horse as a smaller breed but I never had been that close to one. I knew instantly, however, this was not a stockman's pasture herd that grazed around like cattle.

Was I seeing a mirage in which things appear larger and closer? No. There was no more time for reckoning, and I stood rooted to the spot as they came like demons of speed, heads and tails up, straight to the fence snorting like ferocious beasts and stood facing me. As the great stallion lifted his hoofs and gave a lunge toward me, I ran up and down the fence, the horses following me on the other side. That fence was going to break against their mighty strength and my only hope was to stick tight to it, leap to the other side, hold fast to a post and dodge the attack -- which was

41

foolish because the posts were too small but I had a chance of rolling back under the fence if I missed their charge through it.

Unable to move a muscle or to scream, I stood staring as the wild herd pushed close, standing opposite me, their heads craned over the sorrel stallion and a big, bay horse pawing the earth. Like a fantasy, I saw them there and in that split second, I heard the swift clatter of horses' hoofs tearing up the ground behind me. More wild horses coming, with no fence between, and the stallion snorting like a ferocious beast. There was no escape. I could not turn my head to look back.

There came a loud whoop and a whizzing of lariats like the cracking of whips as two cowboys brought their ponies to a stop, and the wild horses went thundering across the range. Beautiful proud creatures, graceful in their speed, magnificent in their challenge, they were bluebloods of the range.

The cowboys who had seen the charge as they were riding through became absorbed in speculation about the herd as they watched it disappear down the draw.

"Now where in tarnation did they come from?" one of them pondered.

"Damned if I know," his partner answered. "Do you reckon it could be that drove the Jay Em boys have been tryin' to catch?"

"Yeah, might be -- but ain't that stallion a beaut'?"

Belatedly, they turned their attention to me.

"I reckon you're the printer," the slight, young puncher said superfluously by way of introduction.

In a shaky voice, leaning against a post for support, I admitted my identity.

"Would those horses have attacked me?" I asked. "I thought wild horses kicked up their heels and ran at the sight of a human being,"

"Well, I -- don't know," the older man answered my question. "That stallion is ornery as the devil and wild horses ain't used to meetin' up with wimmen. (Even the horses resented my being here it seemed.) Might be a right good thing we came along."

Dismissing the rescue as though they had sauntered up accidentally, he reached over from the saddle and shook a few posts loosened by the impact of the drove.

"Fence rider will have to fix this ..." he said as the other addressed me.

"If you're all right, Miss, we'll be ridin'."

They followed the fence to the wire gate, the tall slim one lifting it out of its wire loops, holding it as both passed through. Then slipping it back into the wires they rode hell-for-leather in the direction of the fleeing herd -- fifteen, maybe twenty, head, the boys had said. They would never rest until they had tracked down that stallion, a king among his own. It might take months of off-time riding and they may never catch him. But what more thrilling quest?

I "lazed" around a few days and wrote a story on the wild, sorrel stallion to run in several installments in The Progress. Should I have this stallion caught and tamed, spending his last years moping in green pastures? O, no! So my story followed him over great ranges, a leader unsubjected to the end.

"The Wild, Sorrel Stallion." It seemed rhythmic and appealing as I said it over and over to the type falling into the stick. The eastern readers would like it! But the shell of a shop was getting cold and the story of the stallion would have to wait until I did something about fuel.

On the still, though bitter cold days, when the thermometer stood far below zero, the sunrays would penetrate with such force through the thin walls and the windows in the shop-end, that the building in the middle of the day would be warm as toast. But with a penetrating wind, it was like a self-generating icebox.

The storekeeper who attended to ordering fuel for the folk about had shoveled up the last scraping from the bin and carried it over to the shop in two buckets the night before.

"Expecting a man down from the canyons with a load of wood in a day or two; this ought to last ..." he said.

He had gone out to his claim and had not come back. No one would come to town on a day like this.

One of those "Wyoming breezes" to which the cowboys had looked to blow me away had hit the range. It swept everything movable before it; tumbleweeds went rolling over one ridge after another with nothing to stop them. Cattle sought shelter on the sides of the slopes against the cold, piercing blasts.

With that wind, the coal siftings had burned out in a flash. So I went foraging. Dry cow chips which went a long way toward supplying fuel in the cattle country generated a quick heat and left no stench. Having cleared the land around me of its last dry chip, I sat shivering, waiting for a freight to come through. If it stopped at the station, the fireman might let me have a bucket of coal. If none came, I would go to bed and cover up until it became warmer or the man came with wood. Let the newspaper come out next week, who cared except the General Land Office in Washington which would have a hard time checking up on that six months' continuity ruling. I could tell them this issue blew away.

As I planned to get the best of the government with its doggone, red tape, there came a blasting noise from toward Node Siding trying to down that of the wind. I slipped into my red-and-black checkered mackinaw and red tam o'shanter from Snyder's in Lusk, leading ready-to-wear this side of Casper, grabbed my bucket and let the wind carry me down to the station.

Instead of slowing down, the old freight put on steam and whizzed through like the wind itself. It was not going to stop. So I climbed the embankment onto the track, set my bucket down, book off my red tam o'shanter and waved it like a red flag at a bull.

When the train came to a stop, I ran up to the engine.

The fireman glowered at me and yelled through the wind, "Hay you! What you doin'? This is a through freight."

When I held up my empty bucket, he broke into a wide grin and threw a nice little pile of coal onto the ground.

Yes, a railroad was a real handy thing to have around.

"Runnin' a newspaper out here is quite a job, ain't it, sister?" he said sympathetically.

"Oh, not so much of a one," I replied jauntily with a beaming smile of thanks for the coal.

I'd not let anybody in this cow country, not even myself, think I was sick of my job and I cannot say that I really was.

With my scuttle partly filled (I did not possess the heft to carry the full bucket in one trip), I fought my way back against the wind. Hissing through the air, whistling through the dry grass, it came with a mighty force dying down for a moment as if for breath then sweeping with an added velocity that brought me to a standstill, pushed me back. Why was it in such a hurry, I wondered, with no place to go -- like people who travel at death speed, getting nowhere.

Inside the door at last, I sat my bucket down with a sense of exultation. I had <u>not</u> been blown "clean to Cheyenne." The fact seemed to have a significance. I had more resistance than was accredited me.

That evening when the sun went down in an array of gorgeous color, the wind went down with it as it had a way of doing. It had blown itself out and left the world beautiful, warm and soft in the caressing hush of twilight. Harbinger of Spring, when the empty peace of the range would be relegated to the realm of Yesterday. Settlers like the wildfowl of the air soon would be returning.

It was growing dark when I heard the rhythmic hoofbeat of a lone horse coming in an easy gallop in accompaniment to a loud carefree voice:

"O, bury me not -- on the lone -- pr-rr-rarie.

How oft' have I listened to those well-known words

The wild wind a-and the sound of birds -'"

Then a tall, loose-jointed cowboy in checkered shirt and leather chaps stood in my door awkwardly twisting a battered sombrero in his two hands.

"Howdy, Miss Printer," he stammered. "Just ridin' to the store for tobacco. Saw you workin' and thought I'd drop in. Maybe -- I could lend a hand turnin' that contraption."

"Come right in," I invited, as I slapped the ink roller across the press. "So kind of you Mr. -"

He grinned an open boyish grin.

"Just Lanky," he supplied, pitching his hat in a corner, "That's what all the boys call me."

"Lanky, did you say? Oh! I buried my face in a newly-printed page to hide a smile. So he was the cowpoke who had discovered the paper and broken the news to his fellow punchers about the skirt printer. He also had been warned by them to stay away because I was likely to be bad medicine.

"Why, yes, Lanky, I could use some help. If you'll just turn this handle ..."

He ground out a paper.

"Well, dang my skin! Is that all there is to printin' a newspaper? Child's play -- no wonder folks call this a toy shop."

"How about a cup of coffee and some cookies," I said after the papers were run through.

I picked up the pot that sat steaming on the stove.

"Well, now, that'd be right nice, ma'am."

Then as we sat slowly sipping the scalding beverage he asked, "What are you a doin' away out here? Shucks, this ain't no place for a newspaper. Nor a girl for that matter."

"There may be a lot of people out here before long," I replied. Seems as though it would be a good place for folks to settle. Van Tassell will then be a town and it won't be so isolated."

"So that's what you're a figurin' on. You've shore got fancy ideas. But," he concluded as he left, "it's right nice seein' this lone light at night when a feller's passin' through."

Lanky would never tell his fellow punchers how he had compromised the dignity of the cow country by helping that skirt printer turn out the newspaper.

Chapter V
LAND OF TOMORROW – THE PROMISED LAND

The plains that had slept so long were at last awake. The biggest movement any country had ever known outside of war was upon us -- the epoch of greatest expansion.

The flow of immigration now surged like a tidal wave along the main channels of western trade and travel, cut new arteries and overflowed in broken remnants to the remotest parts of the frontier.

While the Old Countries had been settled and the soil developed through the ages, it was but a century gone that a man had astounded this New World by saying, "Let us, the United States of America, purchase the territory of Louisiana."

It was Thomas Jefferson, President, who had spoken. That speech was like the bursting of a bomb. The protest was loud and strong.

"What do we want with that vast wilderness?" men in Cabinet and Congress argued. "The United States never would nor should be expanded beyond the Mississippi."

Heaven knew that would be far enough.

A man named Albert Gallatin, Secretary of the Treasury, was firm in his opposition: "Invest in a wild wasteland like that? Such a financial burden would bankrupt this country!"

The Republic was less than twenty years old.

Voices arose, vigorous, from New England's rock-bound coast declaring, "We would be saddling ourselves with an octopus."

But Thomas Jefferson contended, whether or not we make use of it, this nation should own all the territory between the two seas or it will become hemmed in by European countries which for long years have battled over territorial possessions.

"To buy the Louisiana territory is the only way to prevent trouble over that province, a war between France and England, and a war over territory lying within our shores would cost this young country far more than the purchase price of the land," the great sage proclaimed.

Then added gravely, "And we must preserve our peace!"

Statesmen who held the future of this new Republic in their hands carried a great trust and they were agreed that our people must not become

47

involved in the entanglements of foreign nations and land was land, breeder of conflict among nations. America must be assured of freedom and of peace. For that, the early Colonists had suffered and endured and founded a new country and their work must not be in vain.

But -- fifteen million dollars! That was the minimum sum France would accept and where was the money to come from? The hearts of our government leaders sank heavy as the national debt.

"We'll trust to God," said those of greatest faith, and just let the wilderness lie there -- in peace. After all, that vast territory in the heart of the continent had cost less than a nickel an acre and it gave the United States an open passageway from coast to coast.

Some advanced the idea that development may one day expand to the Missouri, who knew?

And a few statesmen said with Jefferson that "these United States may in time become a great empire reaching from the Atlantic to the Pacific."

To the Pacific! With a little handful of states small and weak and just recovering from a war for independence, weighed down with debt and nothing but wild public land as its resource, and savage Indians roaming the plains? The idea was as wild as the desert itself.

In the short span of a lifetime, the "wasteland" of the Louisiana Purchase was to become one of the richest agricultural regions in the world. From it, incalculable wealth had been reaped. The Indians had given up their great "Hunting Grounds" and settled peacefully on tracts allotted them. From its deep caverns, the West had poured gold and silver into the Nation's vault and from it, grassy plains had built a sheep-and-cattle kingdom and settlement had gone far beyond the Mississippi.

Then one day, there arose on the horizon of Public Affairs another group of diplomats. They were from the range country.

They said, "The United States must turn attention to the development of that vast region lying idle -- our last frontier."

The protest was loud and strong.

"What? Was not most of that area marked on the map as the Great American Desert?" said men who never had laid eyes upon it.

And those who had crossed the isolated sea of space or glimpsed it from afar shouted denouncement. "Impossible! The idea is as wild as the wasteland itself."

And was not development already pushed as far West as was feasible? Into Kansas, Nebraska, the Dakotas -- and the most likely spots farther on?

The Republic was but little more than a century old. Swift America!

But the West had developed some strong, courageous characters along with its gold and its cattle. Those sages from sagebrush had the vision and the spirit of those other pioneers who had founded the country and saved it in the Revolution, and again in the Civil War.

The Frontier, they decried, is another New America around which the affairs of the Nation hereafter must be shaped!

There was "pay-dirt" in the western soil. The country was not a plague-infested jungle but a broad land of sunshine and pure air, endowed by nature as a paradise for man.

In that new-day regime in Washington were such men as Smoot, Warren, Mondell, Burke and other statesmen from the frontier who maintained these natural resources should be developed. And in their midst, there appeared a rugged powerful figure with a resonant voice that resounded above the others like a trumpet warning.

"We cannot let an undeveloped domain like that lie idle within our shores. It is an expanse broader than all the territory lying East of the Mississippi. It may lay this country open to invasion by land-hungry nations. Japan for instance, whose population is too dense and whose people already are flocking into America, onto the West Coast, and penetrating into the continent onto our soil. They are a self-seeking, wily people. Settle it up and avert this danger! Our own people need this land," Senator Borah from Idaho had spoken.

The Pacific lay there an open port-of-entry to a thousand mile stretch of sparsely settled territory with only the narrow strip of west coast settlement between.

But how to populate that desert of space? It surely would take an eternity. It was a gigantic task which those dauntless men from out the

West had proposed. America's Public Lands were her greatest asset, their disposal a great responsibility.

First, put a stop to large corporations, including foreign investment companies, getting hold of enormous tracts. Forestall the speculation which would run riot as the West developed. Speculation on land during the Civil War period had all but ruined the country. It had turned the government from disposing of federal domain through outright sale to that of the Homestead method. This plan of developing raw territory was an innovation and, later, our Homestead Laws of the United States had been adopted in fundamental principle by Canada, Algiers, and other dominions.

The homestead laws of America must now be broadened to meet conditions.

"The thing to do," said western Congressmen, "is to increase acreage in the more arid regions and make laws that will promote permanent home-building."

"The people are clamoring for land. America needs the undeveloped resources," industrial leaders staunchly contended.

"One hundred and sixty acres of dry rangeland is not enough," settlers had argued.

Frank W. Mondell of Wyoming, head of the Public Lands Committee in Congress said, "Double the acreage!" and drafted the "Enlarged Homestead Act" which was promptly enacted.

While the Act was in its infancy, Mondell wrote to me, the young girl on the Dakota prairie, who had popped up as a contender for the settlers.

I had sat in the doorway of the claim shack as I read the letter one hot afternoon.

It said, "I am sending you a copy of the Mondell Act which I am sure will stimulate settlement farther west and do a great deal to encourage actual development. For the right kind of settler, it offers every opportunity for homebuilding. Without doubt, the enlarged homestead provision will bring a wave of settlement to Wyoming."

And then had come the part about my going into that field: "Your experience will be valuable to the people settling there ..."

I had become so absorbed in the new decree I had lost the thrill of having been thus addressed by the Father of it. And it is only now, with many a trail between, that I feel the thrill and the honor as I read the letter once more from this statesman whose faith in the West helped to build it.

It was only three months later that I stood on Wyoming soil, bringing in new colonists.

The Land of Opportunity now stretched far beyond the Missouri and the center of population had shifted like the sandbars of that old river. People pushed on west from the midwest region embraced in the Louisiana Purchase, calling those states, "Back East."

The invasion was upon us. With great regiments marching into our undeveloped domains and the borderline strip of Montana, Wyoming, Colorado, New Mexico and western Texas, it became the western front. But these armies of occupation were America's own! And the movement was one of peace instead of war -- of construction instead of destruction, of new life and not of death, as in the armies of war.

They had come to build homes on the frontier.

What was the explanation for this most phenomenal land settlement of all time? These people were not fleeing from oppression nor depression. They came from the richest sections of the most prosperous nation in the world into primeval space. The East, and even the West itself, did not realize the magnitude of it. But few stopped to analyze it. The homestead world was far removed from that of industry and finance on the other side of the Mississippi, and many of the regions being settled in the boundless expanse were worlds apart from one another.

Escape from tenantry by farmers, risk of unemployment by wage-earners, the seeking of future security and independence were reasons advanced by the landseekers for coming west. Too, a landless generation had grown up in the East and the Midwest who must move on for land.

But this onslaught by every class of American citizen could not be reduced to fact and figure. I was not old enough or sufficiently experienced to know much about public affairs and never had heard the word "economics" used in relation to conditions. I knew but little at that time of the early history of our country, or of Thomas Jefferson. But it did not take a sage nor a prophet to know this move to the West could not be stayed. The Great Trek must go on.

The call of the land was as elemental as the land itself. The virgin spaces must have been created for the use of man. NOW was the TIME. I let it go at that. The West, so The Progress said, was the "Land of Tomorrow."

And so it was. But who could worry about Tomorrow or Yesterday. It was Springtime on the range and this was today.

Chapter VI
ON THE SEA OF SOD

I jumped up, threw open the windows letting the sun pour in. I splashed my face and body with cold water from the basin, slipped into a blue cotton dress and ran out into the sparkling air -- wine of the gods.

The range world was a riot of color. Sky as blue -- well, as blue as a sky on the western plain. Earth, a background of green velvet, was laden with the wildflowers like a bride's altar and birds filling the Great Cathedral with music. I whistled back to robins and meadowlarks in their own carol and they answered. I stretched my arms to the Infinite. Life, life. So big and beautiful. Thank you, God, and let me live! I may be entering a trying period but I'd guard my scant and precious strength, honest I would! I was bargaining with God again as I so often had done back on the Reservation.

For over the plain was a lone rider. If he were only Romeo, this would be an Elysium indeed, or Lone Star Len, even. But it was only a wrangler from the Van Tassell ranch rounding up the cowponies. O, well, one day the Great Romance would surely ride in.

Across from the shipping pens stood a line of emigrant cars and tents in which newly arrived settlers were sleeping. I was glad they could awaken to this new burst of life everywhere. Some of them had arrived in a late snowstorm that all but took their last ounce of courage.

I needed a reporter. There was no end of news items now. I ran down to meet the Sage Hen coming in with her human cargo. She always picked up speed after getting rid of the passengers ticketed for Van Tassell. I worked my way through shipments of household goods on the platform. Beds, tables, stoves -- one would think it was a stove factory.

Piles of lumber, rolls of barbwire, and farm machinery were scattered over the prairie. Farm horses and a milk cow were staked out. A small boy was milking the cow.

Freight trains were switching off emigrant cars, unloading shipments onto the ground. Men with teams lined up waiting for their families to arrive on the morning train or loading their wagons from boxcars. Colonists who had less than car lots had chartered emigrant cars together, dividing freight costs which were high in those days. The railroad company was doing a land office business. I was repaying the Chicago and Northwestern the "hundred-fold" for the coal it had cast upon the prairie for me.

Cowboys milling around the corrals, cattle bawling and breaking herd in the melee. A puncher trying to keep a steer from tearing through a stack of farm goods and a chicken coop with a hen and brook of cheeping chicks.

A foreman shouting, "What the Hell!" Let him go through it, teach the tenderfeet to keep their stuff out of the way ..."

His eyes fell on the hen and chicks.

"Chickens!" He laughed ironically. "Turnin' the cow country into a chicken range, huh?"

If a homesteader had answered and said, 'In a few years, a million turkeys will be grazing the frontier like bands of sheep," he could well have been committed to an asylum.

The first passenger off that morning was Mrs. Van Sant, clapping her hands as she caught sight of me.

"Here's little Edith, looking fresh as a daisy." She threw her arms around me.

"Mother Van! You're really here!"

"I told you when I left that I'd be back this spring with bells on, didn't I? And I can't believe this is the drab range we saw last fall -- Why, Edith, it looks like Paradise."

"And here are Jean and Elmer," she said as a small young girl with keen brown eyes and a thin face descended from the train steps followed by a pudgy round-faced young man loaded down with baggage.

"They got married and are going to get a claim near mine -- I may have to buy a relinquishment for them."

Jean, the girl Mother Van had reared and big, easy-going Elmer Myers whom she had all but reared, giving him jobs, getting jobs for him, taking him under her wing, brought up in the heart of a city without responsibility. I doubted if they would last long on a homestead. But while they stayed, they would be at the beck-and-call of the woman whom Jean called "Mama." Mother Van had hurried this marriage, I mused, so she could get them settled close by.

54

"Have you seen anything of my furniture," she inquired. "Had it shipped last week."

(No wonder the prairie was cluttered up with furniture!)

She noted the commotion around the station. "Looks like a Barnum circle unloading," she chuckled.

We found the furniture. Old stuff, but sturdy. Just the kind for homestead service.

"Mother Van," I said, pointing to the collection, "what are you going to do with all this?"

She looked at me with that caught-in-the-jam-jar expression: "Well, there's Jean -- and Nick and Dick will live with me while they are building. Son Leport will be out this fall. (She called him Son LaPorte to distinguish him from her brother-in-law, LaPorte, the singer.) And Cousin Julia hasn't decided whether to spend the summer here or in Europe. Benny -- Dr. Harsch -- wants to come too and look the country over."

Dr. Harsch, a successful young dentist, was the son-in-law. I hoped he would come. The new West offered wide opportunity for thrifty, progressive young men like Ben Harsch.

"And you could not persuade the governor to take a claim? You are a poor promoter," I jested as we walked up to the settlement where she and her folk would stay until her shack was built.

"O, Sam will be out here before I prove up, and you know his son, Grant. Well, Grant thinks the West is the coming country."

(Some years later Grant Van Sant became owner of an 80,000 acre ranch in the Rocky Mountain region.)

Nick was the late Doctor Van Sant's brother and Dick was her own. Brother Nick of New Jersey had not done so well as the other Van Sants. I presume every family must have its poor relation. At fifty, Nick was starting life anew by bringing a bride with him to a homestead. Brother Nick, an Illinois farmer, had a good-sized family to help him improve the land, but little money.

So Mother Van had her hands full that spring. She hired homesteaders with their teams and tools.

"What kind of a building is that going up on the south table?" folk would ask.

"Just the Van Sant claim shack," some would answer with good-natured ire, others with pride.

It was a peaked-gable house set on a ridge of the high plateau, nothing fancy but roomy. With its upstairs bedrooms filled with beds, a kitchen-dining room and a sizable living room, the house was big enough for kith and kin and all the strangers who might come that way and Mother Van kept set a table large as a pool table, long and wide, ready for the many guests who stayed all the way from a meal to a month.

Locators and surveyors with their parties tried to reach "the Lodge,' as they called it, for dinner or for the night. If either Roscoe or I came that way in getting our colonists settled and failed to stop, Mother Van Sant felt slighted. Stopping there with a crowd was like having a party.

Nick and Dick each built on the corner of his land that joined her claim and Elmer got land in that district so the Van Sant group were all in a huddle. Fred Theilbar arrived with his wife and small children. Clara Theilbar was a tall, angular, light-haired woman who took life very seriously. There was a strained look in her eyes. She was wondering what would come of this venture and of her family.

The St. Louis people were coming in. The Hecklebecks with two or three small girls; the Coburns, a childless couple around sixty years of age; Frank Free, a bachelor, and Dick McHale, a man in his fifties whose family stayed in St. Louis; and, Dryor with his wife and daughter, Eleanor. Hecklebeck and Dryer were painters and decorators; Free had been a foreman in a bottling works; Coburn, a meat-cutter; and, Dick McHale, an optometrist.

It was with a sinking heart that I watched them unload their farm equipment from emigrant cars. What could they do out on the raw range? But George Coburn, a little, dried-up man with long, white moustache, was heaving things into his wagon, chipper as you please. He started out ahead, the others following, to the North Table.

One morning, Carrie, my stepmother, arrived with the two boys. Mitchell was going on fifteen, Thomas, Jr., a year younger, just school children in knickers and caps and long stockings. They had looked forward to coming west as the great adventure. Mitchell eagerly asked questions one after another about the country with nothing escaping his notice. Tommy, a reticent boy, looked around him wide-eyed having little to say. He may have been awed and homesick. But they were both anxious to be off to the claim.

My father had stayed in St. Louis a few days to straighten up affairs but the time for establishing residence on the claim was up and unless the family got onto it, he might be contested and lose the land. He had hired the shack built that winter.

Carrie Ammons was not one to stay alone. She had never known the hardships of roughing it and going onto a raw homestead was a trying ordeal for the bravest. The claim lay about five miles from Van Tassell and they had no team. One of the homesteaders took them and their "jag" of household goods out and Catherine Lemmon and I went along to break the loneliness that night and help them get settled.

The one-room shack sat in the middle of the open range with the grass growing close around it and the tar paper rubbed off in spots where the cattle had found shelter against its walls. But the dried cow-chips lay there ready to start a fire in the big old range which the man who had brought us out was setting up while we put up a bed. An extension table, chairs and dishes with other household essentials completed the equipment. There was no fence, well, or shed. The squat shack was the only object on the claim. But the claim stretched a half-mile in width and a mile in length and probably the feeling of possessing that much land made any lack or hardship endurable, and Carrie made no complaint.

Catherine and the boys took small tin buckets and walked over to the Coburns a mile away for water. The Coburns who had plenty of money for improvements had drilled a well and built a comfortable house with two chambers upstairs. They were former Bostonians and Mrs. Coburn had both shocked and amused the neighbors by talking right out in public about her "chambers." At last they learned that the "front chamber" and the "guest chamber" she spoke of were bedrooms but no one could figure out who there would be to ever occupy the "guest chamber" of the lone couple except the hired man.

It was almost dark when they got home with the water and the boys began to plan what they would do when they got a well and a windmill. They bet they could irrigate -- O, patches and patches of "truck,"[2] and they could build onto the shack. Already they were planning.

By the time supper was over and the dishes washed and a pallet made on the floor for the boys (they would put up the other bed tomorrow), we were ready to fall into bed.

And there on the desolate Wyoming plain, the night black as ink and the coyotes crying like lost souls, another Ammons family started its roots in the soil as Ammonses before them had gone into the wilderness of Illinois, hewn logs for their houses and cleared the timber around them, planting themselves deeper than the corn.

In the middle of the night, Tommy woke up sick with a severe sore throat. We made a fire, heated water and waited on him until morning when Mr. Roberts, the neighbor, took us back to town. We put Tommy to bed in my room at the printshop and Catherine began doctoring him from her kit of remedies, namely nux vomica,[3] her cure-all for stomach upset, for headache, for debility or what had they, singing its praises like the spieler[4] of a patent medicine show.

Carefully she dropped it out, six to ten drops in a glass of water.

"Here, Tommy, take a spoonful of this every few hours. He's tired out as much as anything," she told his mother.

The boy soon recovered and the family went back to the claim where, with their old friends as neighbors, they soon felt at home. They had lived next door to the Coburns in St. Louis.

After she had paid the freight and bought a week's supply of groceries, all the money Carrie Ammons had left was a five dollar bill and my father would have but little to add to it. While I knew it was taking practically all they had to get the family out here and settled, I did not know for some time that their financial situation was quite so drastic.

But had I known before they came, I probably should have said, "Come on. There'll be a way."

Was not this the Land of Beginning Again?

In the bedlam of folk getting settled, I cannot recall my father's arrival. I may have been away at the time. He put in day-work for settlers who needed help, and I put Mitchell onto the newspaper as news-gatherer

---

[2] Market-garden produce
[3] Herbal medicine used at the time
[4] A barker, as at a circus side-show

and general helper, paying him the few dollars a week I could afford. Every penny counted in keeping the family going.

I now had my printer's "devil." But the eager and ambitious lad had the making of a good reporter.

Van Tassell was a beehive of activity and The Progress became a settlers' clearing house. U.S. Land maps with miles upon miles platted into sections lined the printshop walls where settlers checked up their locations.

Alongside the land plots hung that of the town site. Anyone wanting to buy a lot looked at the plot, took the tapeline and measured it off, gave me the money -- front lots, seventy-five dollars, those butted up against the range fence, twenty-five -- and went about his business. There was no time for preliminaries those days, and so I found myself agent for the Northwestern's town site company. I must have been paid a commission -- I wonder!

Catherine bought a lot and put up a shack for a restaurant. Her building faced the North while the store faced South and the printshop East. She thought facing those castle walls of white rock would be much more inspiring than the railroad or the corral.

She was a better stenographer than cook and she started out by serving foods in small side dishes and coffee in her dainty, hand-painted cups that cowboys who stopped in said held only one swallow and who could drink out of toy dishes like those? What did that type-puncher think she was running -- one o' them city tea-rooms the Boston Kid told about? They called her place the Chow Palace. A boycott threatened by section hands and other men customers died a bornin', for there was no other public eating place between Lusk, Wyoming and Harrison, Nebraska, and Catherine was working hard to give up-to-the-minute service. They all liked "Kate."

I had no extra money for board at that particular time and she none for advertising so I exchanged space in the paper for meals and as cheap a' space was, there were times when I felt I was cheated in the deal, so far as good cooking went, but Catherine Lemmon's cheery friendship was sustenance beyond value.

Settlers must have some place to stay and to leave their families until shelter could be provided on the homestead. Mother Van who had reserved the living quarters of the store building opened them up for friends, and for women with children. There were nights when settlers were bedded down in rows on the floors of the few buildings.

The type-puncher was making up for those years of time clocks with a vengeance. She was spreading out. From "way down souf," she imported an old Negro couple to help hold down the claim while she started a "flop-house" in a big tent. Funny how folk getting in on the ground floor of things never know where to stop.

No one could find out how or where she got the old Negro pair. They being the only colored folk in the country, it was like having imported a couple of Texas longhorns into that kingdom of whitefaces. But with the first snow squall the coming fall, they had packed their satchel and headed toward the land o' cotton.

The Widow Putnam (she and her son Dan each had a claim) stretched a tent and went to serving square meals for a quarter. She was a good cook and every now and then, I slipped over to the "Chuck Tent" for one of her "squares." She was a motherly soul and often prepared delicacies for me, sending them over to the printshop when I was unusually busy.

"Well, I had to do some figuring for enough cash during this rush to tide me through the winter and when it is over, I'll pick up my tent and set it up to live on the homestead. Next year, I can have a shack built. Get my half-section proved up? Of course, I will, I must make a home for myself."

Dr. Watts came and had his shack built then went back to Peoria for a month or two and his wife and little daughter Janet came. They would spend the remainder of the seven months' period on the claim.

Mrs. Watts who held a high office in a prominent woman's club had been making speeches here and there just before her departure for the homestead. She was a sweet, refined little woman and a gracious hostess. Out here, she neither received nor demanded any special consideration. To the other women and to herself, she was just another homesteader.

She and Janet stayed overnight at the settlement. I had explained the homestead project to a group at the Watts' home in Peoria last fall. She was not looking to the months ahead with pleasure and relief.

"So many things to do for which I never could find the time back home, sewing, reading."

And she and Janet would have a garden. She wanted Janet at her impressionable age to learn something of the fundamentals of life -- and of nature.

"Children brought up in the city are getting too soft and selfish," Mrs. Watts opined.

Next morning she and Janet went onto the homestead alone. They must depend upon the neighbors with whom the doctor had made arrangements for transportation and other help. Mrs. Watts' sister and family, the McCabes, who had a claim near the Wattses, soon would be coming. And their only child was a little girl, so Janet would have company.

The McCabes came from another city and, I believe, state. It was surprising how many families after years of separation were reunited out on the frontier, working and planning together in the building of a new country where family ties were appreciated.

Mrs. McCabe was a pharmacist and she started a drugstore in Van Tassell -- a badly needed service, Catherine's nux-vomica notwithstanding. (She is still running it as I write this story.)

One early morning, I looked out to see the sun glaring on something that looked like great mounds of gold. A lumberyard had started overnight out on the open prairie between the printshop and the depot. I went down to look it over. Homestead lumber, full of knotholes as usual. Poor homesteader, who of all people needed good solid lumber to keep out the cold and the wind! Some stranger had come into Van Tassell with carloads of cheap rough building material shipped from a western mill to catch the trade of those who had not brought their lumber with them.

With the hard manual labor, men began to feel the need of meat. Those unused to physical work were becoming thin and weak. There were no fresh vegetables to be had and the diet consisted mainly of starchy foods such as rice, bread and potatoes supplemented by dried fruits. The only meat they had was bacon.

Charlie Roszell with several other settlers came to The Progress one day.

"We've got to have fresh meat brought in here," Charlie said, "There should be someone to open a butcher shop."

"It beats the devil," another protested, "that in a country where herds push up to your door, and into the house if the door is open, men should be starved for meat."

Frank Free expressed the irony of the situation, "They trample over everything and knock down our partly-built shacks and fences, and eat our grass."

Bob Kearns, the salesman who had been working hard on his claim for a month, drew in the empty fold of his tailored suit. "Hangs like a sack on a scarecrow. I get so hungry for meat, I could eat it raw and with the hide on."

The outdoor life and long hours of work made folk ravenous.

A dirt farmer by the name of Miller spoke firmly, "This is a serious matter. We must have meat. Men can't break this sod without it!"

There was no way to keep meat fresh at that time of year. It took a day's time to go to town after it. The supply had to be brought in. The settlers had very little stock and had killed every head they could spare.

The ranchers butchered a beef or a mutton as they needed it for the larger outfits every day. No wonder the early settlers killed a range critter now and then. We would try a notice in the paper.

"Moses, we want meat!" The salesman said as the group left the office.

"And ye shall have meat," I answered soberly.

I put a call in the Progress:

"IN A LAND OF SHEEP AND CATTLE - The people are famished for meat. Settlers of the Van Tassell region are calling for a party to furnish fresh meat. Good opening for a butcher shop. Nearest meat market twenty miles. 500 people to be served. Apply to The Van Tassell Progress."

The call brought no Buffalo Bill agreeing to go out and kill buffalo to supply the meat demand. But a few days later, a big flat-footed Dutch farmer from The Ridge shambled into the office and asked for the tapeline.

He laid down his seventy-five dollars for a front lot two doors from the printshop and said: "Now I start a bootsher shop. I got extra cows and hogs and my neighbors on The Ridge got grain-fed stock they can sell.

I come vonce, maybe twice, a week with pork and beef dressed the night before."

He paid for an ad in the paper and at daylight on a Saturday morning Philip Freese and his wife drove into the settlement with a wagonload of cows and hogs covered over with flour sacks, the feet sticking up through the covering.

Meat for the colonists! Beefsteak and pork chops, soup bones and pigs feet. I did not know how sanitary it was but after eating prairie dog with the Indians as I had, I was not bothered about a trifle like sanitation, and the Freeses were clean people.

From the jam and excitement around the market place that morning, one might think it was Water Street in Chicago at sunup. I paid Mitchell his week's wage and he ran through the crowd with it to the butcher shop. He came out with sausage, a soup bone, and a roast for Sunday and caught a ride home with the first team going that direction. What a happy surprise for his family that would be!

The meat must have been good and tender for the butcher shop continued to do a rushing business. But I remember Philip Freese not so much by his meat as by his feet.

He never could get a pair of shoes big enough nearer than Omaha or Denver and his wife would say defensively as Philip traveled to country towns trying to find shoes that fit, "Villip's feet are not so beeg – they're shoost so broad."

Chapter VII
THE GREAT TREK

Like the Canaanites entering Egypt, the army of sodbreakers had marched onto the range. Homestead shacks and crude houses now dotted the plateau, most of them built of the cheapest lumber hauled out from Lusk or Harrison, or from the new lumberyard at Van Tassell. Some of the colonists had shipped out lumber for building in their emigrant cars.

And everywhere plows were cutting into the hard sod. Breaking plows, especially made with long narrow blades, ripped through the tough grassroots and laid over the sod in forms like long, slick ribbons. The sagebrush in the Van Tassell region was not thick like it was farther West, but men and beast strained and sweat as the plows tore through great tufts of buffalo grass and bunch grass. The buffalo grass upon which great herds of buffalo once had fattened was very nutritious for feed and for the soil as it had decayed through the years.

I watched men plodding up and down making long furrows, laying over the rows of sod like hard, slick ribbons, their hands on the handles and the lines around their shoulders. I saw a new expression in the faces of those pilgrims. Their faces, though hard and brown and sweat-streaked, were not so drawn with lines of despair and fear.

"Hello, Mr. Dryer," I said as I rode by his place one morning. "How does it break?"

He sat down on his plow, panting from the labor.

"Tough," he said, "But if I can get these clods rolled down with a roller and then harrowed and cross-harrowed, I think it'll grow oats like everything. Try small fields this year -- next year maybe we can break more ground."

He was one of the St. Lewis colonists.

"Well, I'm just checking up for The Progress -- and, Mr. Dryer, there's a new crop Wyoming is trying out -- hear it yields good. It's something like oats. Rich feed, they say. Yields well, in this high-and-dry climate."

"That so? What is it?"

65

"They call it rye. I am gathering information on it. The Progress will tell you colonists all about it and how to raise it. Well, goodbye, good luck."

I waved at him as I rode on.

A neighboring settler, a farmer, was planting Fred Theilbar's rutabaga patch. Yes, this land must produce! And by the gods, it would.

A prairie schooner hove into sight, a white mast in the sunrise. The big sturdy wagon with its hoop-ribbed, canvas-covered top moved slowly but surely across the plateau.

Men left their plows and women their washtubs to watch it and sent their children to tell the neighbors, "A schooner is coming over the ridge! A prairie schooner!"

A man and a woman sat on the high seat and children's faces peered out of the back end where the canvas was drawn into a porthole. It created more excitement than a showboat steaming up a river.

Folk followed to look at the wagon and to find out where the family was going. They had come up from Oklahoma and had been on the road many weeks looking for a location. They had planned to stop in Colorado but with people coming in that state so fast, they had kept going. Any free land left in these parts? No? Well, they had heard of an open region a hundred miles on to the north. If that were all taken up, there was Montana. They had sold their small farm in Oklahoma, had a few hundred dollars left and 'till next fall to find a place.

The prairie schooner was a symbol of the Old West and the tenderfeet felt more like pioneers now that one had come through. City folk took snapshots and sent them back home with letters telling about it while automobiles as immigrant vans created no particular interest. Not infrequently, an automobile passed through, its high flimsy top wavering under the heavy load that rocked above it, the body of the car shimmying over the rough ground, packed to the hilt, cargo and wooden wheels rattling like castanets.

Suddenly, the car stopped and the driver crawled under it and there it sat on the prairie while he took its insides out and put them back in, "By God, this country never was made for automobiles."

"No, stranger, not all together," the passer-by replied, "but some day it will have surfaced highways."

"The Hell it will!"

But the old prairie schooner and the loaded flivvers[5] were cutting the ruts through that region for Coast-to-Coast Highway Number 20, and Highway 85 from Mexico to Canada.

Many new seekers were following the colonists into eastern Wyoming, into Van Tassell. But these late-comers must go farther out for land. Some went on across the plateau to the south, meeting homesteaders coming from the Union Pacific while others loaded their household goods and their families into wagons and hunted open land in the rugged, hilly country of Old Woman, Lightning, and Lance Creeks to the north until they were stopped by a backfire of settlers coming from the direction of the Black Hills and the Burlington line to the east.

For many years, the railroad companies had been building trunk lines into the West and as immigration spread they built new branches and extended old lines in anticipation of further development.

Always the wagon wheels had cut ahead of the iron trails with the sodbreakers paving the way. But never in their wildest prediction of empire building had the railroads foreseen the network of dirt trails that now cut through the no-man's lands. Trails twisting, winding, or stretching thread-like for long miles through the grass and leading nowhere but to tar-paper shacks. They led out from the railroads like spokes to a wheel, and every day new trails were broken and the dim narrow ones widened by the horde.

Day by day, I watched people cross the range to be swallowed up in the spaces. Selecting land on the virgin plain, visualizing its opportunity, had been an anticipation. Moving on to it was a stark reality.

American immigrants to American soil! It was a soul-stirring sight to see them standing on the border of our frontiers, thousands of them, with their faces turned West not daring to look back.

They came not as immigrants from foreign countries. They came not to get jobs from, but to create jobs for, Americans. They came not to benefit from industry and enterprise built up by another people and another country -- but to build. They came not to crowd the trade and labor fields.

---

[5] Flivver - early 20th century term meaning a small, cheap car with a rough ride. A jalopy

They were leaving places open for others while they wrested their own living from the virgin soil.

Immigrants landing on American shores find civilization and its modern conveniences ready for them. The homesteaders had to carve these things out of the primitive. One heard a great deal of talk among the landseekers about Americans being crowded out by foreigners. The foreigners were coming to the country in ever increasing numbers.

"They are taking our jobs away from us now. How will it be when our children grow up, to get jobs?" men and women would say with a deep sigh and a shake of the head.

"We must get land, make homes for our children!"

It was a cry that carried over the western plain. Here there would be room to grow, and to build, for America's own.

And so, they looked ahead with faith in their souls and hope in their hearts, to this new land and their very attitude was a prayer,

"Land of New Pilgrims' pride

Where faith and hope abide,

From this Great Plain so wide

Le-et fre-ee-dom ring."

Women crossing the border. They have left behind then the things into which years of work and love have been woven. A rosebush tenderly nurtured, trees grown from slim sprouts; an old cupboard which was part of life's routine; the washing machine and the upholstered chairs -- "so heavy and freight so high." They have left behind the house that was a home and deeper things -- friends, loved ones, community interests, and their dreams. Dreams they had for sending Gracie to college or making a bank president out of Jimmy. Before those women lay a span of life stripped of comforts. Inconveniences, frugality, hardships, and perhaps poverty would be their lot, and more than all of these, a patience like the drops of water that wears away the stone.

Children crossing the border, wide-eyed, bewildered before this mystery of life, this new vacant world, following where their father has led, clinging to their parents -- silent and afraid, or crying for their pets and their toys. Homesick children, their childhood dreams broken and they, too, must face stark reality and learn to endure, and to dream anew.

"What is Little Betty crying for," I asked.

"Her old doll and the doll cradle," the mother replied.

"Don't cry Betty," she pleads. "I'll make you another doll -- a big rag one -- and Daddy will make you another cradle."

She turned to me, "We brought only the necessities and the big doll was broken, but Betty wants the old doll, the old cradle."

And older children in notable numbers, boys and girls who soon would be old enough to help their parents, and to carry on the empire building. There were thousands of boys who were to reach maturity just in time to be taken to the slaughter pens of the World War, then in the making. And -- "let the empire building go to the devil!"

Men marching onto the frontier, like soldiers, facing the unknown! They have left behind all they have wrought and which for man is not a thing apart from his very being. To him, beginning anew is like being re-created. He knows not of the tools with which he must build again.

Men conquering virgin domains must experiment. Experimenting without capital, or without money on which to live while they are doing it, is a heart-rending proposition. They know not the soil nor the climate nor how to combat the wild forces of nature.

And man by instinct is a creature of fixed habit. He devotes a lifetime to the routine of a single trade, business or profession -- to hard mental or physical slavery. He is content with the same old house, the same old furniture, the same old slippers at night. He likes to sit down in the same chair in the same spot and why move the furniture around until a man must feel like a stranger in his own home? He wants to scramble through the same topsy-turvy drawer of ties and socks, or the desk with its accumulated letters and papers. Even the time-worn menus suit him better than all the new-fangled concoctions of food. He must meet, and keep pace with, an ever-changing world outside and thus he clings to things stationary in his home life.

To tear himself up by the roots and begin anew with no precedent to follow, weighed down by fear and responsibility for his loved ones -- well, that took mettle and I marveled at the courage of man. Women must suffer and struggle equally with their husbands. But man, by law of nature, is a protector and a provider. If his family suffered, he felt himself helpless, a failure. And when a man's spirit is broken --.

They must not fail!

69

In the past three years, a quarter million people had filed on homesteads. In equal numbers, others were proving up on land which meant they had stuck to it. 25,000 had filed on claims under the Mondell Act, with many others taking land under other laws.

Already the Mondell, or Enlarged Homestead Act, had 8,000,000 acres of public domain into farm Units; and over the frontier were many other thousands of homesteaders who had been coming through the years, ahead of the hordes. There were some 2,000.000 people directly dependent upon the virgin soil for their existence among them many lone women, and widows with children.

Though the government was staunchly supporting the homestead project, prompting and protecting the settlers' interest, Uncle Sam was not donating ready money nor making them cash allotments as he did to his subjects, the Indians. Any such plan would have filled the West with parasites.

The empire builders had no New Deal Administration with Wallaces of Agriculture to feed them, and no Tugwells of Resettlement to take them off the land. They had to make the soil produce or starve. Produce food for that multitude, and as incredulous as it may seem, very few homesteaders ever starved to death. There could be no back-trailing for the land cavalcade. With the driving of corner stakes in the wilderness, they had staked their all.

Land for their children. For their children's children. And there would be no more frontiers! No matter at what deprivation of cost, they must establish this heritage for America's posterity.

A number of settlers around Van Tassell had gotten jobs on the railroad as station hands at a dollar and a half a day, putting in new ties and rails with pick and shovel. But there was no quibbling over the wages.

Toward evening they put their tools at the section house down by the bridge and started home to their claims, my father and Frank Free and Noah behind Noah's plug horse hitched to a rickety buggy, Elmer Myers and Fred Theilbar afoot.

As I watched them fade into the sunset, a lone horseman suddenly appeared on the crest of a knoll. He was sitting on his horse as though they were one, making a clear-cut carving that stood out black against the vari-colored glow of the sky, as the early dusk fell over the peaceful plain.

Then, like a statue come to life, the rider moved slowly on as if he, too, had become enrapt with the peace. He rode with an easy grace. There was something familiar about the rhythm of motion. I sat erect with strained eyes. Then, as he came closer I knew. It was Lone Star Len on Black Indian! He was not turning off at the cross trail. He was coming straight ahead, his shoulders squared, the lines of his serious face alight as he saw me sitting in the open door.

My thoughts flew back to that first, accidental, meeting in Dakota the day he had felled a big eagle and my pony Lakota had leaped and run at the sound of his gun.

With a movement as quick as that of an eagle itself the stranger had run his horse in front of Lakota and grabbed the rein.

"Sorry, Miss, I didn't see you down in that draw."

Then he had turned to pick up the eagle. He measured the wing-spread with his hands as a yardstick.

"More than ten feet."

I was piqued. It wasn't every day a plainsman could meet a young city girl on the trail and his very indifference intrigued me. Not only that, he was the very personification of what girls from the East expected a plainsman to be. He was a typical outdoor product, lean and lithe, his face hardened by wind and sun.

He had been aloof but polite, but in time as I had known him better his reserve had broken to a point of expressing some of his ideas to me.

Lone Star Len resented the homesteaders not because they interfered with the stockmen's business but because civilization robbed the frontier of its grandeur and peace.

"Can't folks ever let things be like God made 'em?"

He was a strange, lone character whose inner self no one could fathom. Lonely, yet seeking far places. So one day he had ridden away as suddenly as he had appeared on my horizon. He had drifted on West to the Wyoming range which he said was "Bigger'n all Creation." I had not dreamed then of ever seeing it but now our trails were to cross again.

At the door he swung lightly to the ground, removed his hat and said, "Howdy, Miss Printer," as casually as if we had met but yesterday but the corners of his mouth were lifted by the semblance of a smile.

"Lone Star!" I exclaimed rising to greet him.

71

"I've wondered what became of you. You knew I was here."

We sat down together in the open doorway and I was surprised that he seemed unconscious of the physical nearness. Lone Star was shy of women. His lean hand with the long tapered fingers lay near my own and I felt the strong muscles of his arm when once he brushed mine.

"Yes, I heard about a woman startin' a newspaper -- knew it was you. And they got you pretty well branded over this range, bringin' a drove o' homesteaders like you did. Was goin' through the Rawhide Country and just thought I'd ride over, not much out of the way."

The Imp of Eve in me smiled smugly -- only thirty or forty miles out of the way. I adroitly turned the subject.

"What was the matter with this range to which you fled for peace?"

The old familiar far-away look came into his gray-blue eyes.

"Too many people." He sighed. "Millin' around worse'n a bunch o' Texas doggies ... Was with the Cheyenne River spread a while and then went on to the Jackson Hole country."

I laughed aloud. "You should have been safe there -- one of the wildest spots in America."

"A few settlers driftin' in there, too," he said disconsolately.

He turned and looked into the printshop, then at me.

"So you brought that newspaper shebang with you?"

"Another one, Lone Star. A new one."

He was silent for a long time and at last he said, "I didn't come when I heard about you bein' here last fall. I told you back in Dakota that if you ever came to Wyoming to leave that newspaper behind and not urge the homesteaders onto the range. This is no place for you."

There was a new earnestness in his voice.

"I remember you telling me. But I thought it was your own personal aversion to settlers."

I knew he considered the matter as serious or he never would have spoken in that objective way. It was not like Lone Star to be personal.

Suddenly he asked, "Can't you find anything better to do?"

"Not just now," I replied, "but someday I want a big newspaper -- a medium that will be farther reaching."

I waved my hand in a circle to all space and said, amused, "You won't do as much damage that way as you've been doin."

"Won't be herdin' at such close range. Sure got this territory cluttered up -- shacks and plowed ground, and ba'b wire strung everywhere. It was one of the prettiest stretches o' country in the West."

"Well, Lone Star," I consoled him, "the stockmen say the settlers will soon starve out. So it may go back to range."

He shook his head.

"You can't starve out landgrabbers. Once they get a start they spread worse than mesquite or cactus and there's no grubbin' 'em out. Well, I must be ridin'."

But he sat there silent for a time and when my eyes met his, he picked up his hat and walked over to his horse. As he stood gently stroking Black Indian's curved neck, I covertly studied him in the starlit dusk. There was a mingled tenderness and strength in the clean-cut, wind-hardened face and in his body lithe as that of a wild animal.

He swung easily into the saddle and rode into the soft summer night and I sat looking after him, not knowing where he was going or when he would return. What was it about him that left me always with that strange loneliness and longing? It must be because he was so much a part of the lonely plain -- or was it the man himself? And had I sensed an undercurrent of emotion in him as he sat so calmly beside me? I could not be sure.

Edith Eudora Ammons Kohl

Chapter VIII
GRAIN OF POVERTY

It was the day of permanent home-builders who cultivated the soil, and who became a distinct people in American history -- sodbreakers. It was they who converted the West to Agriculture.

Homestead shacks now dotted the Wyoming plateau. They were crude abodes built of the cheapest materials. While a few of the colonists had put up better buildings and others would build houses and barns next fall, the majority would live in these make-shift homes until inch by inch they could get a foothold.

For many miles around Van Tassell a shack stood like a corner stake on every half-section, marking the land taken.

The claim-shack is no small part of the West's history. At that time a half-million of them stood on the western plain -- mere specks on the ocean of space.

I wrote: "They stand there, those tiny, flimsy shacks, like fortifications against the Primitive, against all forces which the homesteaders must fight. Pitiably they stand -- those thin, tar-paper walls -- which are the settlers' only protection against the cruel forces of the frontier. What are they worth? Reduced to figures those lowly huts, at the average cost of a hundred dollars, represent an investment of fifty million dollars. But aside from the cracked knot-holed boards, they represent the incalculable wealth of the West's resources now being developed."

Stockmen guffawed. They had seen shacks go up, rot and fall on the range. It was the plows they feared, the plows and the barbwire fences cutting off the range.

And now with shelters provided, the colonists started to plow. It was too late to put in much crop but they must plant what patches they could get ready in time. Every acre of food for their families or feed for their stock would count. During the long winter, The Progress had gathered information from reliable sources, advised them on how to prepare the soil here and how and what crops to plant.

Breaking plows, specially made with long narrow blades, cut through the matted grass roots and laid the sod over in furrows like slick, black ribbons, man and horse straining, sweating, as the shares tore the great tufts of buffalo grass and ripped into the virgin earth which had lain packed since Adam.

Everywhere over the stretches, men plodded behind the plow bending their strength to keep blade in the ground. And yet with the lines around their shoulders and their hands on the handles, the strained harried look of the new Pilgrim seemed to pass.

"Hello Mr. Dryer. How goes the breaking?" I called as I rode by the Dryer claim one late afternoon.

He pushed his plow through to the end of the furrow and sat down on it panting, wiping the sweat from his brow with a big red bandanna. He was one of the St. Lewis folk.

"Tough," he said, "and slow, my golly! This tough sod pushes the plow clear out of the ground."

He held up a black mass of tangled roots almost as large as a man's head, the long tendrils stiff and wiry.

"Settlers can't get so much ground broken this year -- but we can try out small crops and next year ... well some fields will run eighty to a hundred acres I expect."

"You know Mr. Miller over toward Node ranch?" I asked. "He came from Canada and he says the farmers there dug out this prairie wool and raised the finest wheat in the world off the land."

"Well, well! What land, huh? The natives here tell me that this, pointing to a cluster of grass blades -- is gramma grass, richer than clover. Fattens stock like grain they say."

The sagebrush in this area was not so thick as it was farther West. But in addition to the gramma and the prairie wool, the buffalo grass grew thick. It was this nutritious grass on which the great herds of buffalo once had fattened.

Mr. Dryer was going to sow oats if he could get the clodded field rolled and harrowed in time. It had been proven by earlier settlers that Wyoming could produce oats prolifically.

"There's another crop being tried out in Wyoming," I said. "One that is adaptable to this soil and climate. Contains more protein than any grain except wheat."

"That so?" My listener queried eagerly, "What is it?

"Rye," I told him. "Requires less moisture than any other grain, they say. It is sometimes called the grain of poverty. It has furnished bread for the peasants in some of the dry mountainous regions in Europe and Asia, I believe."

And added, "You know what rye bread is," and laughed because neither of us had connected this grain with the common rye bread.

"The grain of poverty," Dryer repeated it thoughtfully. "Guess all the grain we raise out here could be called the grain of poverty. But if rye grows like that we shouldn't starve."

"I am gathering information and will check up on fields of it grown here this year. The Progress will publish the findings for the colonists. In the meantime, you can get general information from the government.

"Well, good bye; good luck."

I waved at him as I rode on and he turned his rested horses and put his plow into the ground.

Fred Theilbar was planting his rutabaga patch behind a neighbor's team and harrow. Fred was exchanging labor for farm equipment -- cooperation in simplest form.

Grain of poverty! I reflected solemnly on the way home. Yes, this land had to produce. And by the gods it would produce. Unless they raised food this very year, some of the settlers would be facing poverty.

But with fences and fields making a checker-board of the range, I realized for the first time the seriousness of the situation. Whereas on the empty Indian lands in Dakota there had been only the Primitive to fight (and a few claim-jumpers), here we would have both the elemental forces and a powerful, organized industry that must give 'way if the settlers stayed. The range men were no longer taking my newspaper as a joke, and in spite of their attempts at ridicule they were stirred up by this invasion.

Settlers fenced their fields but as the grain came up thick and green, they complained that the range stock was eating their crops.

"There's no fence can turn a range herd from a waving field of grain," they declared. "There should be a law against letting stock devour the country."

That had been the cry of homesteaders for years. Many a battle for laws had been waged and lost in the stock country.

Notwithstanding, The Progress came out with headlines: "We Need Herd Laws. Settlers Are In Legal Possession of the Land."

A few days later a stranger walked in to my office. With a distinct manner of the native westerner he asked without preliminary what I was trying to do here.

Startled, I answered informatively, "Why -- I'm running a newspaper."

"Well, you're in the wrong place for the kind of paper you are running," he said curtly.

I looked up at the tall energetic figure, the set jaw, and recognized the man whom I shall call Neil Jordan, a stockman who once had been pointed out to me as a dominant, fearless character who would not brook[6] interference.

"What kind of a paper would you advise me to run?" I asked innocently.

"This is not a farming country," he went on, "and we don't want our range cut off."

"Oh," I replied in a tone that feigned surprise. "I thought the land belonged to the United States government. Or am I mistaken?"

His anger was aroused.

"Possession, you know, is nine-tenths of the law and the stockmen were here long before the landgrabbers ever thought of doing anything with the land. We have run our stock here for fifty years ..."

I laid down my stick of type and faced him -- and the issue -- squarely.

"That's about long enough, isn't it, to have the use of a domain without paying a cent for it, fifty years?"

Ignoring the question he said, "Yesterday we found one of our waterholes fenced off." He took a copy of The Progress from his pocket and pointed to an article.

"Advising the settlers to fence off their land as soon as possible in order to save their hay, asking the city swells who have no use for hay to build line-fences with their neighbors."

---

[6] To allow

"Herd laws!" he said derisively. "Why don't you attend to your own business -- a little upset ..."

I thought, how ridiculous he feels -- a man of his caliber used to combating hard men and a rough world, having to argue with a snip of a girl. He had met an obstacle which he hardly knew how to handle.

"Running this paper is my business, Mr. Jordan," I said as calmly as I could.

The unexpected aplomb irked him. And how should I know his name? He had not introduced himself except as one of the stockmen.

"Who's paying you anyhow?" He fairly fired the question. "There's some Big Interests back of you. Land speculators waiting to buy the homesteaders out for a song as soon as they get the land patented (deeded)."

I was going to cry -- but I must not cry, now! The Ammons temper saved me.

"Like some of the big stock interests are doing?" I retorted. "Financing poor people to prove up land, paying them a paltry sum for it, knowing it is a criminal offense? Or cheaper yet, having cowhands or sheepherders take up land for their bosses, holding waterholes and valleys through fake filings - "

"Don't you accuse me ..." his voice became taut, tense.

"No -- you are not of that class, by reputation, but some of the ruthless, unscrupulous ranchers and land corporations are doing it, are they not? Who? You know better than I -- or even the federal land officials. But, according to reports these perpetrosities[7] are becoming more common every day."

But Neil Jordan was thinking only of the desperate situation. I caught a harassed, depressed look in the man's face. The issue was, what were the stockmen going to do? He voiced the question in that off-guard moment.

"What are we going to do with our range stock and no range?"

"I don't know," I said earnestly. "I'm sorry if the development of the country jeopardizes your interests. It's just the law of progress, I guess."

---

[7] Atrocities

"The law of YOUR progress, maybe," he rejoined caustically, and walked out.

At the door he turned.

"But remember, Miss Ammons, there are not going to be any herd laws!"

His tone augured trouble. So the stockmen thought some financial power was back of this colonization project. Let them think it!

Trembling like a quaking aspen I leaned my head on the rough boards of the copy table and wept aloud. If Ida Mary were only here for a prop.

In her impassive way she would upbraid me for crying as she had back at the Ammons trading post, "You can't expect to do this kind of work and spill tears like a collapsed balloon every time you're pricked. You have no business ... "

That was it -- I had no business in this kind of work. I hated precociousness and shrewdness in women. What should I do now? Hang onto the steer's tail, or slip out some dark night?

And it is no small wonder that I, a fragmentary piece of young womanhood, should have been overwhelmed. For the battle between stockmen and settlers was one of the greatest human and industrial issues this nation ever had, covering as much ground with problems equally as vital, as that of slavery, or more so. I did not realize the preponderance of it at the time. I had that to learn.

From the early days down to the present, there has always been friction and warfare between the stockmen who grazed their herds over government land, and the homesteaders who took up the land and fenced off the range. Sometimes the strife became open mass war; sometimes silent and underhanded between individuals and outfits in which the settler was driven off his land or shot down in cold blood.

Wyoming, often called "The Field of Blood," had been a battle ground of frontier warfare, with the name of being the strongest and wildest territory on the frontier. There had been wars between the Indians and early pioneers, between outlaw gangs and natives, range men and homesteaders. This probably was because of its strategic location as a central passageway from North to South, from East to West, and the early building of the Union Pacific across the state, and because it was rich in minerals and other natural resources, and one of the greatest livestock regions in the world. It is little wonder that men had fought for possession of its wealth and for supremacy.

It was in Johnson, the county cornering our own, that the war against the settlers had become so violent the United States troops had been called out to settle it. That was the bloodiest range war in history. The big outfits ranged far in those days and homesteaders in adjoining territory also had suffered persecution.

The day after Neil Jordan's visit, a quiet middle-aged woman came to see me.

"I don't want to meddle, honey," she said, "but your paper is advocating herd laws and in other ways opposing the stockmen's interests. You do not know me but I've come to tell you my story."

It was in this country that she and her husband, then bride and groom, had taken up a homestead in a creek valley. They had acquired a small herd of cattle, ranging them in the valley. Some of the larger outfits began grazing stock there and when her husband tried to cut his own cattle from the other herds he was accused of rustling. And one by one his small drove began to disappear. One of the outfits tried to push them out of the valley. Things went from bad to worse until --.

"One morning," she said, "my husband started down to the barn to feed the horses. I heard a shot and saw him fall. As I ran to him another shot whizzed through the air barely missing me. I ran back to the house and saw two men ride like the wind over the hill and disappear in a draw. I had no way of identifying either of them or their horses -- and what mattered who they were?"

In faltering, broken sentences she went on: "I had dragged my dead husband into the shack and stayed there alone with him for three days, fearing fire would be set to the house to destroy the evidence -- but what did such outlaws care about evidence? Anyway the blizzard which had come up that morning had covered their tracks. After the blizzard was over I found that the horses either had been turned loose or led away the night before the killing. So I struggled through the snow five miles to the nearest neighbor for help."

She had stayed and proven up the homestead and had married again. Afraid to create any ill-feeling of the range factions toward her

81

present family, she did not want her dead husband's name or her story made known and she did not tell me her name.

Aged far beyond her forty-odd years she treated me as though I were a reckless wayward child.

"Advocating farming and herd laws is like throwing a lighted match in dry grass. I'm afraid you'll get burned with your own fire," she warned me.

Old hidebound natives had told settlers that "the soil here around was enriched considerably by the blood-spillin'."

But, I reasoned, the day when six-shooters were the law, was past. But there were many other ways to defeat the settler's, and the free-range people were making their last stand.

The Whites had run the Indians off the plains, subdued and segregated them. Yet the Indians had thought the land was theirs. They had thought they were justified in defending themselves from the "Evil Spirits" which invaded their hunting grounds and killed the buffalo which was their main food supply. White Eagle, Iron Shell and other of the great Indian Chiefs mournfully had told me of their futile efforts to save the land for their people. And though the White Man had called the Indians sly and tricky, they had merely used the only means they knew for defense.

There had been cattle-and-sheep wars, too.

Cattlemen said sheep ruined the range. Ate it off too close. In the opinion of the cow world there was nothing more despicable than sheep -- unless it were the 'dry-farmers' as stockmen called the settlers. Sheep men declared they had as much right to graze government land as the cattlemen. Neither having any legal rights there was no way to settle the disputes except to fight them out.

But cattlemen and sheep men were now allied against the land cavalcade and only a few days ago, out further west, two men had been killed and another wounded when a little group of settlers filed on a strip of land that had been 'covered up' by sheep men.

The greatest cattle kings in the world were in our West. Kings of a cattle kingdom. They had kept spreading as their herds grew and state lines did not stop them. Many Wyoming outfits expanded into Colorado, into Montana. And one of the largest spreads on the frontier was that of the Hunters.

As a small child, I would listen entranced to Jack Hunter's tales of the Wild West where one day he, a commission merchant in the Chicago Stockyards, was going "to make millions" -- but he had only a million or so. Cousin Jack always thought big.

The Hunter outfit was one of the largest in the West and the Hunter boys (Tom, Will and Harry) were rated among the best cattlemen. Hunters owned seven ranches aggregating fifty thousand acres with ten thousand head of cattle, and one of the largest meadows in one tract in the United States. From the meadow they harvested ten thousand tons of wild hay each year. Cousin Jack, still seeing big, had bought a large ranch in Texas. One had to have vision to do things out here.

But there was talk about his having over-reached, and that he was now having to retrench. Well the stock interests that were fighting to hold their high places as lords of all they surveyed could retrench! However, many in these parts were fighting only for self-preservation as the Indians before them had done.

After Neil Jordan's visit, and that of the strange woman, I was filled with a portentous restlessness and I did not care if I ever got out another issue of the paper, though I must not stir up any feeling among the settlers. I would go see Bill Magoon.

Bill Magoon was a cross between a stockman and a dry farmer. A prominent sheepman, he also ran cattle and raised grain and alfalfa to better feed his stock, paying no attention to the jibes of fellow range men. Magoon often had visited with our landseekers.

If he happened to meet a group in some public place he introduced himself, "I'm Bill Magoon, a stockman fallen from grace -- farming couple a hundred acres or so. Yes, you can find opportunities out here, folks, if you got plenty of backbone."

The Magoon ranch lay to the north of Lusk. I rode horseback through miles of rolling ranch country. The prairie was littered with young. Planted on the green landscape were fields of Wyoming's lamb crop -- little fluffy balls basking in the late spring sun, or scampering over the plain like kittens at play. Lambs thick as soap-weed with their feeble baa-a-aa, an endless treble.

Calves by the thousands lying where they were dropped, still drying from birth or standing on wobbly legs that looked like stilts under their dark red bodies, and their little white faces turned up toward the sun or sucking, nudging, at strutted udders. Cows lying peacefully licking their new-born or grazing nearby with a watchful eye. They threw up their heads and bawled as I passed through a scattered herd. They would not harm me unless I harmed their young. A land of whitefaces.

I drew rein at the crest of a ridge and gazed across the panorama splotched with herds and flocks as far as the eye could see. It was a picture to behold. But shucks! We couldn't build an empire with but sheep and cattle as population.

Bill Magoon, I learned at the ranch, was in Lusk enroute to Denver. I found him in Lusk -- a tall, rangy man with a long, lean face brown to swarthiness. He was dressed in a dark, well-tailored suit set off by a broad, light-colored Stetson which also looked like a cross between the regular cowboy sombrero and a fedora. He walked with a firm, measured stride and talked in a low, slow voice.

Strange, I thought, how he could change from shabby overalls and stogy boots to tailored suit, with boiled shirt and diamond ring and turn from herders and punchers to meet polished men and women without ever changing his gait or his tone. Not many can do that.

We walked down Lusk's dusty Main Street to the Northwestern hotel near the depot, the populace staring after us. Bill Magoon surely was falling from grace hob-nobbing with that range-busting printer!

In the shabby parlor of the hotel he politely pulled a chair forward for me and seated himself opposite.

"Where's the Duchess?" he inquired, meaning Mother Van.

I had not seen her lately -- everyone so busy, I explained.

"Great woman, the Duchess," he remarked. "If I weren't married to a princess of a woman (Mrs. Magoon was a gorgeous lady) ..."

He broke off and looked at me.

"All right, out with it!"

I told him that I had come to get his view of the conflict that lay before us. I wanted his candid opinion.

He leaned back in his chair with all the poise and self-confidence of a big banker, or a publisher at a cocktail party on Fifth Avenue. Leisurely, he puffed a long cigar, holding it in his right hand between puffs, the thumb of his left hand hooked carelessly into the armhole of his vest, the big diamond sparkling.

"It doesn't matter what we think," he said casually, "it's bound to come."

"It" meant agricultural development.

"You say we old plainsmen are trained to see far and big. Well, we've been a helluva long time seeing this coming. Had to be pushed right under our nose. Then we rear and pitch like a scared bronc. Some of the ranchers don't own even the land they live on. Now they are frantically filing homestead rights to the home grounds and pastures. That's plumb unreasonable. Coming here as they did when there was nothing but open space they couldn't savvy its ever being settled."

He grinned a slow broad grin that showed his teeth from molar to molar, white in contrast to his dark skin.

"You know, I've never been sure that God Almighty made all this West specially for a few stockmen. So I figured I'd get some of my land up in shape -- can raise more stock to the acre of range with some grain to feed them."

"That is the way the homesteaders figure, Mr. Magoon," I quickly accorded, "that a section of land will feed as many sheep or cattle for a homesteader as it will for a stockman, and more in small herds well-cared for."

"Some stockmen own a lot of land," he explained. "But their herds are so big they use open range, too. In fact, it was from the free use of land that they made their money to buy up gobs of it. But the stock growers have been trained in a hard school. They've weathered droughts and blizzards and combated cattle thieves sometimes wiped a stockman out, and the big capitalists who tried to hog the range. In the early days, stockmen had to drive their stock hundreds of miles to market, and fight the Indians. They knew how to fight for self-preservation and they're going to do it. You ain't going to find many old Magoons among them. I've fixed myself so I can live and let live."

There was sympathy in his smile and voice as he said, "Kinda playing with fire ain't you, little girl? You've taken on a man's job. A girl like you ought to get married -- now if I wasn't already married ..."

I parried, "That's what Editor Jim Mayes said in the Lusk Herald, you remember, that if he were not married he would offer me a partnership in both life and business. Good alibis, you westerners have."

Bill Magoon gave a hearty laugh.

Jogging home on the borrowed cayuse,[8] my vision expanding over the spaces, the problem seemed to clarify itself. It was not the little Van Tassell Progress and its editor caught between two warring groups. It was the Frontier caught between the indomitable forces of Yesterday and Tomorrow.

Those statesmen from the West had known there would be strife for possession, either by people from within or outside our borders, as long as the frontier remained unoccupied. Thus, they were contending for its development. Yet most of these men were kings in the livestock industry. For instance, Senator Warren. The Warren Livestock Company with 80,000 sheep, great herds of cattle, and vast acres was one of the largest livestock concerns in the world. The Kendricks and the Careys, eminent in both state and national politics, were among the leading cattlemen of the country. Whether or not they owned plenty of range their financial -- and political -- interests were tied up with the controlling livestock regime.

With a new determination I went galloping across the plain. Let the czars of the range retrench -- or get down and dig like the homesteaders who were glad to possess a 320 acre tract. And surely in this far-flung commonwealth of plain and mountain, of valley and foothill, there was room for both. The westerners as a people were broad-minded. I wondered if the day would come when farmer and range men would stand together for the West. Utopian dreams again.

Anyhow, I'd hang onto the steer's tail awhile longer, and like the cowboy who had been dragged almost to death hanging on because he could not let go, I may be pulled through many hard places. Those stockmen who had won against all other obstacles may still win.

That night, I found a letter awaiting me from a stranger who, as the letterhead showed, held an important post in the Public Land Department in Washington.

The missive ran (I copy from the letter on file):

---

[8] A feral or low-quality horse

"Dear Miss Ammons: I am surprised to see the kind of paper you are running out there. It is worthy of a much larger field and puts a good many of the boys in the shade who have vastly more to draw from in the way of public patronage. Keep'er up! And if I can ever be of any assistance it will be a pleasure.

With best wishes for your success ..."

The writer, Robert Kent, was a westerner prominent in political and journalistic fields. As even the best buckers need spurring, so I was spurred to near determination by praise from one in his position.

Edith Eudora Ammons Kohl

Chapter IX
YOU CAN'T TAKE OUR RANGE!

The land sharks who had infested this region had moved on to newer fields and the trouble reduced itself to contesters -- the most unscrupulous of all landgrabbers. They watched every chance to contest claims of legitimate holders. If the U.S. Land Office upheld the contester's allegations that the settler was not living up to the letter of the Homestead Law then he could file on the land with the shack, fences, or other improvements on it. That, too, became a racket. The high cost of appearing with witnesses and making defense at the distant Land Office forced many settlers to let the contest go by default.

I fought this malpractice in scathing articles and several times I appeared at the land office in Douglas pleading the settler's cause, myself.

As a last resort I petitioned the government to establish a Land Commissioner's Office in my district. U. S. Senator Warren at once endorsed the petition and he, with other high officials, recommended my appointment to the Office. The work would go hand in hand with the newspaper and the Office could be established with that of The Progress.

It was not political patronage (I never had heard of the term). The district needed the Office and I could fill it. Back in Dakota I had become an interpreter of the technical land laws which, to many settlers read like a Greek directory. My knowledge had come through printing land documents, and representing the homesteaders in disputes with the Department of Interior. Thus I had experience in the practical application of the Homestead Laws.

Much of the work The Progress was doing was not remunerative. The Office of Commissioner not only would give me opportunity for greater service but added income. I was puffed up like a balloon. Then one day there came a letter from Senator Warren. There was opposition to increasing the number of such offices in Wyoming. U.S. Judge Riner of the State had made a ruling against it.

"But," United States Attorney Burke had written Senator Warren, "It is not a decision that could not be changed if circumstances demanded."

The powers-that-be made appeal against the decision and the political red-tape began to unwind. Senator Francis E. Warren, heading the

89

Congressional Committee on Military Affairs, was one of the most eminent statesmen in America.

People did not say, "Isn't Senator Warren the father-in-law of General Pershing?"

Until the war they said, "Is not General Pershing the son-in-law of Senator Warren?"

Francis E. Warren had a long and enviable record behind him. He had been Wyoming's first Governor, having served as territorial governor before his election to the United States Senate. Frank W. Mondell, father of land laws, was Chairman of the Public Lands Committee then which at that time there was none more important.

Yet working, struggling, in a world far removed, I had absolutely no consciousness of the fact that some of the country's most influential leaders, its laws, courts and constitutions were being brought into action over one little skirt printer. Perhaps we do see only what we are looking for. My eyes were glued to the sod.

The crop outlook was good. We were seeing the Divine miracle of virgin sod coming to life, giving up its wealth. The fields were like magic carpets. Rutabaga and other root crops gave promise of big yield. Already farmers were beginning to talk about Wyoming as a potato country. It was too far north and the nights too cold for corn but patches of it were developing beyond expectation. There were roasting ears sweet and juicy, and gardens producing. The colonists were elated.

But at every turn old-timers tried to squelch their ardor. In Wheeler's store a group of settlers were talking over their crops. One of the settler women had brought in a basket of green onions and radishes and the Roszells, a sack of roasting ears. There was a great demand for garden truck that year among townsfolk and settlers who had not planted gardens. Ranchers bought it when they could do so without the settlers knowing it.

Roszell was bragging about his corn when a sheepman came into the store.

With a sardonic chuckle he put in, "Just wait till the hot winds strike, strangers -- or the hail hits. I've seen it."

He proceeded to draw a tragic picture of drought and starvation.

Anna Watkins, the nurse, walked past with her mail in her most professional manner said, "O, how terrible! How did the stockmen ever manage to stay here all these years?"

"Well, Madam, we didn't try to farm," he haggled. "You can't raise enough in this country to feed a sittin' hen."

Anna Watkins had gone out the door not waiting for him to finish, but Nick Van Sant said evenly, "We hadn't figured on raising setting hens, Mister. We may stick to sheep and cattle."

The sheepman burst out laughing.

"Raise sheep and cattle! On a half-section claim? That's good."

Still maintaining his self-possession, Mr. Van Sant retaliated that as long as there was free range the settlers may as well use it. The sheepman turned on his heels and stalked out, muttering between his teeth. Some of those tenderfeet had more guts than one would suppose.

While the more dignified stockmen did not deign to quibble with settlers the antagonism of the range was obvious. The settlers could not realize it as I did, for I was informed from every quarter.

Stockmen, or their henchmen, would point out to strangers the straggly dwarfed stalks of oats and the dry twisted blades of corn trying desperately to grow along the railroad right-of-way and say, "That's oats, gentlemen. And that's corn. The kind we grow in these parts."

And many of them I think were honest in their belief that nothing but grass would grow. Range men had advanced that theory so long it had, to them, become gospel fact.

Real estate dealers (and settlers too) accused stockmen of scattering seed in the cindered soil to discourage landseekers coming in on the trains. The seed may have leaked from boxcars in shipment and the wonder was that it ever sprouted at all. But the effect of that first impression of the country was disparaging.

One day I went out to see how Mother Van was feeling. I found her talking to Roscoe McCully. She was asking him to find a good relinquishment for Son Leport who was coming out next Fall with a tractor to do breaking for the Van Sants. The young dentist was more interested in machinery -- cars, motor boats, and even tractors -- than he was in dentistry.

91

Roscoe told Mother Van the corn-and-oats story and how real-estate dealers accused stockmen of planting the seed alongside the track. She clapped her hands and laughed.

"Wasn't that a clever trick? The land agents will have to wake up," she chaffed. "Just as well laugh while we can," she said jovially.

Surrounded by friends and relatives Mother Van had settled down to homestead life. She cooked and darned and planned for them all and took up knitting. The Theilbar children and others would need warm heavy stockings next winter.

Cousin Julia, who was coming, had written, "I envy you, out there, and I wish on these sweltering nights I were there to get that cool Wyoming breeze. They say you can't teach an old dog new tricks but if you can sit still long enough to knit, Wyoming has taught you a new one."

Already Mother Van was boosting Van Tassell on the strength of the proposed Land Office, while I reiterated, "Build up this country and the towns will take care of themselves."

New places of business were opening up in Van Tassell to serve the people. The colonists themselves represented trade and professions adequate to make a town.

Dick McHale of the St. Louis Colony started an Optics Parlor. He took in another homesteader as partner, and together they ran a blacksmith shop, while the optical business was growing -- and grow it did -- for Dick McHale, alias Dr. Richard McHale, was a good Optometrist. The long blacksmith shed built onto the small optical shop was like a tail wagging the dog.

Emerging through the door of the blacksmith shop with its flaming bellows, the smithy became the professional man stepping briskly, hands freshly scrubbed, sandy hair and pointed beard neatly combed and wearing a linen coat, the transformation having been made in a corner of the shop.

He greeted a woman customer, "Now, I can fit your glasses while the iron gets hot."

Dick McHale and his brother, Jim, a noted lawyer of East St. Louis, were old friends of the Ammonses.

The community spirit was augmented by the unexpected arrival one day of a missionary from Casper who came to hold services in the new town. But there was not a place large enough for even a small congregation. Then I thought of the hayshed. I did not know how he would take the suggestion.

"What's in the shed?" he asked.

"Bailed hay," I told him. "It is a community shed where folk coming a long way can feed their horses."

That was fine, the missionary said after looking at it. The baled hay could be used for seats.

The Progress made the announcement: Church Service Next Sunday in the Van Tassell Hayshed.

And the announcement ended with, "Why should not the Pilgrims be proud to worship in a hayshed when Christ was born in a manger?"

There were but few of the settlers who had attended church since they came and they gathered from far and near.

With the opening of prayer there came a thundering roar in a cloud of trail-dust, like a band of Indians on the warpath.

The cowpunchers were coming to town in a mad galloping race, singing at the top of their voices, words cut to the sharp staccato of the horses' clicking hoofs: "Shy-Ann. Shy-Ann. Hop on my pony. There's room here -- for two dear -- and after -- the cere-mony ..."

And as the horses slowed down, "On my pony to-oo-old Cheyenne."

As clattering hoofs came to a standstill, a whoopee and a yip-yip pealed through the air. Finding the young town filled with horses and vehicles and business places closed up the cowboys came to the printshop where I was waiting to head them off.

"What's the matter with this town?" one of them demanded to know. "Haint no funeral is there? Everything locked up ..."

I explained that we were having church service and invited them to attend. They gasped in surprise.

"Church. A soul-saver, boys!"

"What's this range a comin' to with skirt-printers and soul-savers?" a short, stocky puncher called Utah remarked.

They argued among themselves as to what they should do while church was in session.

One suggested they might skillfully shoot the bales of hay from under the tenderfeet right while they are prayin' -- just to see what the soul-saver would do."

At last their curiosity got the better of them and they went shuffling along with chaps squeaking, spurs clinking, down to the hayshed. With all their braggadocio the cowboys were a shy, modest class, easily embarrassed in surroundings other than their own. Their environment was far removed from the modern world and its customs.

Standing in the open front of the long shed, or bashfully around the corner, they removed their sombreros and listened attentively while two or three (not all of them had been cowboys always) joined in the chorus of the closing hymn which was led by Reverend Daly's rich voice. There is a Spirit in all mankind which though neither admitted nor recognized comes to life before sacred devotion. The meeting over, the punchers strode quietly back to their horses.

"He's some psalm-singin' son-of-a-gun, ain't he?" Cactus remarked.

The soul-saver joined them, "Hello, boys. Some fine looking hosses you got -- that roan over there is a mean one -- can tell by his eye."

He bore the brand of the famous O Ten Bar (0 10).

"Yeah, he's some outlaw. Enterin' him in the buckin' at the state fair," his rider said proudly.

The missionary knew his West.

On that first Sunday night with no train out until morning, Catherine fixed up her room back of the restaurant for the guest while she slept on a cot out front and that night a family of skunks slipped into town and took up quarters under the floor where the preacher slept. The floor was full of knotholes and wide-cracked, so the soul-saver had to be transferred to the flop tent and next morning in borrowed clothes and good humor, he boarded the train for Casper. It would take more than skunks, he laughed, to daunt a good missionary.

Some accused the cowboys who to their regret, when they learned about the polecats, were not guilty. The story, with a great deal of flavor added, spread for many miles, but reverend Daly seemed not to care

All summer, services were held in the hayshed twice a month. If things went well, the settlers would build a church next year.

One day I found a cheap, finger-smudged envelope in the mail. It bore the postmark of Ammons, S. B. and was addressed in crude childish print: NUSPAPER PRINTER, Wan Tasl, Yoming

It was from little Heine Christopherson, the settlers' mascot back on the reservation. The Christopherson claim had joined my own, and the tow-headed tot had spent most of his time at the trading post watching the movement of settlers and Indians and the wild life, expressing a simple philosophy born of the plains. Heine was wise beyond his seven years.

Without salutation the scribbled note ran: "Mans cant run no nuspaper good. I herd the peoples say so. Why don't you cum back. The dams has got lots of water in. Our corns is big. My Pa is going to faller (fallow) a lot of akers. The piksher man was hear. (Van Leshout the cartoonist.) He drawed me a prity piksher and it was you. I put it in my first reader. We aint got so much prare fire. Might be we wont have to pray no more. If they was railroad traks to your plas I wud come over there some day. Heine."

I read the letter over and over with a lump in my throat. Dear little Heine. He had done more than he knew with his small faith and fearlessness to keep a body of empire builders together. I could see the little fellow looking out from under the tattered straw hat facing life with blue eyes wide open.

When the reservation had run out of water he had said, "Might be it will rain -- I saw a cloud way off."

"No, no, Heine, that was smoke -- the Red Devil (praire fire)."

And when the Red Devil had lapped its tongue against the sky and come sweeping toward the settlement he had come trudging across the plain to the trading post where women had gathered and said calmly, "My Ma says we should all pray."

The need of constant vigilance had been removed. Those few scrawled lines were a page in western history. Good crops. The fallowing plan promoted by The Wand was proving successful. Water stored in dams, reservoirs. Prairie fires checked by plowed fields.

I discontinued the Reservation Wand that summer notifying the editor to get another job, and brought the scrap of a plant (the original plant had burned down in that paper's heyday) to Van Tassell. I never had been able to do two things at once and I must confine my efforts to Wyoming.

We moved things around to make room for the physical remains and Mitchell with great zest set up the type cases which were to be his own and nailed extra galley racks to the bare studding. When I received that federal appointment I would build an addition to the two-room shack, fix up a private room and splurge a little.

Midsummer brought its usual hot winds and burning sun. Or was it unusual -- at least they came a little earlier, so natives said. The stockmen were used to the dry spells and though the grass was dead and brown, well, it was still grass and the range stock had subsisted through such seasons before. But the dry-farmers (and 'dry' had become an apt attachment) were facing a crisis. The plowed fields were holding out much longer than the pastures but farmers must keep a day-and-night watch against the range stock that was seeking better grazing.

Herds with strange brands began to appear either drifting into the farming regions of their own accord, or driven in from other parts. Anyhow, the owners did not turn them back. Fences could not hold great herds from fields of grain and wells of water.

Browbeating bosses and foremen whose word -- or their guns -- had scared many a homesteader out swore that "No goddam dry-farmers are going to push us off the range. We'll tear their fences down."

They said 'dry-farmer' in the same tone in which they spoke of cattle rustlers and sheep-killing dogs -- all enemies to the range men's interests. Fences closing off old trails did not stop them -- they cut the barbwire or pulled out the posts if they chose and went on through.

It was like the constant rumbling of a volcano with one holding breath not knowing when it may erupt. Surely there would be no uprising, for the West had laws now with the power and attention of the government directed to protection of the homesteader. But those vast ranges were a long way from the seats of government and there were still ruthless men on the range -- outfits which also had been a menace to legitimate stockmen. Too many foreign corporations had gotten a strangle hold on our open lands, with hard bosses and underlings to protect their interests.

There were many ways to get rid of intruders. To fill the farming section with droves that would eat the settlers out overnight would be the quickest way.

If the settler-stockman issue came to a western war the settlers could win. They now outnumbered the stockmen many times over. For my region, the newspaper would stick to the policy of settler cooperation. Our very victory might be gained by impervious unconcern toward opposing forces, building up our own interests and strength. And, if it became necessary, we could fight in self-defense on our own ground -- but not many of these homebuilders believed in crossing an ocean -- or a cattle range -- to get into a fight.

Then one day the blow regarding my appointment to office fell. Congressman Mondell broke the news. He sent me a copy of the letter from the Department of Justice, saying it was unconstitutional for a woman to hold the job of Land Commissioner!

At last it was there in black and white.

The letter to Mondell from United States Attorney Burk said, "Dear Mondell: In regard to your action in the interest of Miss Edith Eudora Ammons for appointment to the office of United States Land Commissioner, the question was raised as to whether a woman could hold the office. After a very careful consideration Judge Riner held that she could not, under the Constitution and laws. I think that matter was so carefully considered that we cannot hope for a contrary decision."

High officials had succeeded in overruling a few court decisions, had won in the matter of establishing the District Office, but they could not make over the Constitution just to give a chit of a girl a job. Constitutions were something that could not be meddled with. But if the adamant Judge Riner only had known how I was struggling to help build up the country, he might have found some kind of loophole to give me the job. I've learned since then about political loopholes.

To turn my mind from the disappointment Congressman Mondell had written a personal letter of encouragement: "I am delighted to know of your faith and confidence in Wyoming, particularly the region around Van Tassell. I trust the settlers you have been instrumental in bringing into the country will be successful and I have no doubt but that they will. Assuring you of cooperation in the good work you are doing ..."

There was a penned postscript (I have it before me now): "It hardly seems logical in the state which was the first in the union to adopt Woman's Suffrage, does it?"

Why, I never had dreamed of such a thing in this he-man's country which had made so much ado over a girl editor. And had I known, it would have had no special interest for me. Woman's Suffrage conjured visions of dominant women who tried to wear the pants. The women who had done the most in empire building were those who kept the home-fires burning and let the men run public affairs. It was with and for such people that I worked -- not as their voice but as its echo.

Wyoming had come into the Union as a suffrage state in 1890. Colorado came in as the second, and Utah third. It seemed incredible that the women of the wild and woolly West should be first to have equal franchise. Yet Wyoming was barring women from office -- at least the office of Land Commissioner.

With failure of my appointment, the matter of establishing a land office in my district was dropped. At last, the final decision gave the Departments of Interior, and of Justice (Injustice I thereafter called it), a rest, and with this country drying up and the newspaper financially dry, I took the shock with dry eyes -- it took time to wipe one's tears and there was no time. It was too bad, I grumbled, that one should be denied even the pleasure of moping in self-pity.

The all-absorbing question was ... when would it rain? How much hay and grain and food would the colonists be able to save for the winter, and most vital of all, would they keep up their courage? As the parching heat and intermittent hot winds (no one ever heard of dust storms in the grass country) continued, I was troubled. Not particularly about the condition, which was the history of every new frontier, but these city folk would not see as far as I who had trekked farther and battled worse conditions. Could I make them see this?

I had known homesteaders to win through greater obstacles. I had not been responsible for their coming. I was too close to these people -- my family and friends, and my soul was burdened with the realization that I was responsible for most of them being here. And that was too heavy to rest on shoulders as slight as mine.

Now too was the opportune time for propaganda to take root. One word against the country would have more effect than all one could say or write about its advantages.

It was typical that the few settlers who did the most complaining were those who had accomplished least back in "God's country." And the people who tried to discourage the settlers most were those who could not be driven out with a double-barrel shotgun, both barrels loaded.

Old settlers in adjoining regions seemed not to be panicky over the dry season and the prosperous Ridge farmers who had coped with all the destructive forces of droughts and blizzards, etc. said that one had to learn how to manage, and prepare himself to tide over such things. One of the ways, I deliberated, was to fallow -- hold the moisture in the subsoil. But that took time and these colonists must live next winter! In the main, however, their attitude was that of patient acceptance, with no word of reproach or regret. It was they who filled me with compunction.

One day I saw Clara Theilbar coming. She was carrying a child on one arm, leading another. Her face was brown and care-lined and her eyes held a woe-be-gone expression. I dared not to ask her how things were going with them. Herds were devouring the farmers' hay lands, and stacks. Dryer's oat field was beginning to shrivel. The Ammons truck patch -- cabbage and potatoes -- curled and dried. Stockmen were laughing up their sleeves.

Bill Magoon riding through one day wisely remarked, "Well, it takes more than one dry summer to make a good empire builder. Trouble is, sod don't hold moisture. It bakes."

But I, too, was losing sight of the fact that defeat lay more in fear for the future than in a sod-crop shriveled. I was tired and there was no rest. If only I could lie down and rest. The old physical uneasy I had long suffered was returning. The plains were as hot as Hades and not a breath of air to turn the windmills and stock bawling for water. I couldn't stand that bawling. I wondered if that day would finish up the crops. I rode out to a nearby field to watch the corn stocks shrivel and twist and fall. The stocks were short but it would have made good feed had it matured. I listened to the rustling in grain fields like that of cured straw in a straw mattress. And what about the rye, the grain of poverty? It would be shattered on the ground. It might have survived on cultivated soil, but not on sod.

I watched the Noah's Ark outfit cross the range, the rotund Noah a little thinner, beside him my father sitting straight -- why did he have to sit so straight as though defying fate to bend him. The old horse was a little more bony, the buggy wheels a little looser.

I dreaded to see the settlers coming. I could not bear the creaking, rattling, of dry wagon wheels with their loose spokes bumping over hard, baked earth. They struck a nameless fear into me, bruised my tender conscience. Hot and dizzy I stumbled back to the printshop, drew the checkered curtains tight and locked the door, hiding until the last homesteader had gone and the cool still evening had come.

Evening, the cradle of the range, its gentle breeze a soft lullaby to which the tired and weary lulled to rest and no matter what the morrow may bring, the Wyoming nights brought sweet refreshing sleep. I slept.

Chapter X
WOMEN ARE SURE FUNNY

I do not recall what I thought or did in that first desperate hour behind the locked door but I am sure I did not wish I could die as many did in extremity.

I was more afraid of death than of anything in this world and as a child I had prayed fervently during sick spells, "God, don't make an angel out of me!"

That petition, in different form perhaps, still was foremost in my prayers.

It was a few days later that a cowboy said nonchalantly, "You must be a lookin' to the Lord."

Surprised at the remark from a cowpoke I could only gasp, "Why?"

"Wasn't that what the Psalm-singer said 'tother day – 'Look to the Lord and He'll provide?' Don't see nothin' else much for you to look to."

I pondered that.

Perhaps, unconsciously, all of us were building on faith, so I admonished in an editorial: "Do not become discouraged about conditions. Here is a munificent domain favored by the gods with a health-giving climate, with pure cold water - that elixir of life so lacking in many regions.

"These settlers do not live in constant dread of prairie fire, the Red Devil, which often annihilates the tall-grass country. While there are hot winds and blizzards we have no cyclones to wreak havoc, no high floods to destroy, the soil is rich and the land is ours. By federal law it is ours. All we need is time. The frontier cannot be tamed in a day. And remember! The stockmen did not give up."

Such editorials bore more weight than controversial argument, and the following Sunday Reverend Daly took up the theme of optimism, comparing our conditions to those of the early pioneers in the West, and the colonists who first settled in America. What if they had given up?

And to the tune of "America" and a band of sheep a herder was driving through, the colonists again sang ...

Wyoming 'tis of thee

Sweet land of liberty
Where faith and hope abide
Land of new Pilgrims' pride ...

I had gone out to see Dryer's field of rye, and to my surprise it was resisting the drought. A few other fields of it were holding out better than other grains; it was better adapted to this region.

With the grass-and-water shortage stockmen began to make early shipments. I now saw stockmen, brands, and herds I never had seen before. I had not realized I was surrounded by so many stockmen. I was fascinated, yet overwhelmed, with the capacity of this industry which ruled the range.

I learned the nearby Coffee ranch, the famous O Ten Bar (O-10 Bar), was one of the largest and oldest outfits in the state reaching over into Nebraska. All summer I had watched the portly superintendent of the Quarter Circle V ride by, attending to his own business as befitted the dignity of such stockmen as the influential Van Tassell. I wished he did not live so close by and I hoped he had not read that article in my last week's paper. He was not easily approached but his antagonism to the settlers who closed in much of the range was obvious.

Spreading over the range to the east and south were the Voorhees and the Thorp herds. I had been intrigued with the Thorp brand, which no one seemed to be able to figure out but which had been registered as the "Revolving H," or "Damfino," so-called by all who looked at it and were asked to name it.

George Voorhees and Russell Thorp, Jr., could be seen frequently in the towns or over the range during that dry spell looking after their cattle, getting them from one range pasture to another. Seeing that type of westerner with their unassuming air and commanding figures was almost like watching royalty pass by and to enhance that feeling, among the plain homesteaders at least, was the sight of young Mrs. Thorp riding into town trim and stylish in her English riding habit. Folk said the Thorps were descendants of a dignified old English family.

Of course we had among the settlers, also, people of culture and education, and a few, like Mrs. Van Sant, with money, and Mrs. Watts, with social prominence. It was rather surprising that all this should be lost to the people of a sheep-and-cattle country.

But many of the Westerners, particularly the younger generation, were highly educated and widely traveled and they were not stopping to separate the tenderfoot sheep from the goats. To them a homesteader was but one of the horde, and the Westerners were no satellites. The old timers whose schooling as a rule had been the wild-west did not give a dang about a homesteader's background. They recognized only grit and principle, the qualifications by which they have carved success.

Truly it was the "Land of Beginning Again." I met many on the long trail who had left wide gates (or iron-barred doors) closed behind them and lost themselves in the West. Men with titles and men with prison numbers concealed their identity, built a new life under a new name and the West accepted them on face value.

Old Luke Voorhees (as natives called him) had operated the first stage line between Cheyenne and Deadwood during the gold rush. He had been responsible for passengers and for gold bullion pouring out of the Homestake mine. In that day of warring Indians, desperadoes, and road agents running the line was one of the most hazardous undertakings in all transportation history.

It took two-fisted and two-gun men like Quick Shot Davis and Wild Bill Hickok. It took armored stagecoaches, freight wagons, and 500 head of horses (each with its own fitted harness or saddle) stationed at strategic points of ten or fifteen miles apart along the 300 mile route. It was a miracle if a coach made a trip without the shot of a bullet or an arrow, but the stagecoach went through!

Then Russell Thorp, Sr. had purchased the line and had operated it until the railroad was built through that region.

Now the homesteaders were broadening the old state trail into farm roads, plowing up the country through which it had run. Would men like the Voorhees and Thorps or their posterity let a peaceful people like the homesteaders usurp them? I asked myself as, on the road to Lusk, I passed the Thorp ranch where one of the old stagecoaches stood as reminder. "Full of bullet holes," folk said but far be it from me to cross the Thorp grounds to take a look. The rambling old log house set out on the sagebrush flats seemed to me a bulwark of strength and security -- something that separated one from the flimsy homestead shacks.

Yes, those old pioneer families were tradition. They never had known fear or defeat.

But, even the Who's Who of that part of the range knew me at least by sight though I did not aspire to their recognition socially or otherwise. I was more of an outcast than the homesteaders because I represented them as an issue.

I was washing type one day with the form propped up against the wall outside the shop when George Voorhees rode by. My hands and smock were black as ink. Pretending not to see him I peeked out from under my old straw hat that served as an umbrella against the broiling sun, but ostensibly, he was paying no more attention to me than if I were a fencepost. Those self-assured figures with their diffidence cast more fear into me than all the stockmen on the frontier in the abstract, or the Neil Jordans who threatened me. They appeared to be invincible ... the range itself.

Why could I not have that air of confidence which they carried? I represented almost as many people in the land movement as the stockmen did sheep and cattle, but I felt no solidity except in my own field of endeavor and with my own class.

Everywhere I went I met curious eyes and heard words of comment: "You mean that little girlish-looking person? With the timid look?"

"Huh! Looks like a skim-milk calf," a stockman jeered. "She can't be the one who brought in those colonists. And fighting for herd laws and everything! Well, I do declare."

I felt that I had been weighed and found wanting. The people had expected to see a Calamity Jane or a Carrie Nation.

Then one hot sultry day Neil Jordan came again.

"You can't expect patronage for your kind of paper in this country," he warned me. "You're on the wrong side of the fence. You will never get anywhere working with homesteaders. It's a waste of time."

"Yes," I said appearing unperturbed, "I remember. You told me that before."

"Not ready to quit, huh? Did you know that in another week there won't be a blade of anything left. What are the dry-farmers (such scorn in the word) -- and you -- going to live on?"

"On your cattle, perhaps. Wasn't that what the poor settlers used to do -- kill range critters to keep from starving?"

His look seemed to say, just try it. I interpreted its meaning.

"A penitentiary offense, is it? So is the covering up of open land with fake filings."

It suddenly occurred to me that part of this land graft was through political pull.

The stockman ignored the thrust, which was not aimed at him personally. (How I hated sharp women. Why did I let this man drive me to being pert?)

"You know one of the reasons I am running for public office? To help lick you."

That meant the dry-farmer.

I was startled County Commissioners and other local officers could hold up the building of schools and roads and other improvements. How did I know what powers they may exercise in Wyoming? This man had influence. For what office was he running -- or was that a ruse to scare me?

With forced composure I said, "Thank you for telling me. Forewarned is forearmed, you know."

Forearmed. He smiled at the presumption.

On the wrong side of the fence, he had said. I wished it were so that I might break over, and I believed that was the idea of Jordan's visit. And then he informed me that in this campaign I could make more money by supporting the "right" people.

"Meaning the free range interests?"

"That's what this country is," he replied. "A free range country."

I made no further comment. I knew the homesteaders could give my paper but little financial support. Bravely, doggedly, they were going through a Gethsemane of hardship, uncertainty and adjustment. But I had withdrawn myself from a too close personal contact that I may not weaken again.

I did wish those heat waves would stop coming up from the ground like thin white smoke, spreading into vapor. It made one's eyes shimmer. Like a fan they swept in at the open windows picking up the copy on the type cases, on the desk, wafting it across the shop. The constant rustling of paper was nerve-wrecking.

"Shut the windows, Mitchell, shut them." ... "My it's hot, let's open them up."

The sun penetrated like flame through the thin air and not a sign of shade to break its force. The tar roofing on the low ceilinged shack was as hot as fire, and the ink ran all over the press. But the shack would cool in thirty minutes after the sun went down, and the wind would go down like the turning off of electric current.

"We must do the printing at night," I told Mitchell.

I was at the end of the lariat financially when one morning I saw a horseman coming across the range. A short, stocky man in a bright shirt, white Angora chaps and twenty-gallon hat as white as the chaps. He wore the fanciest boots and spurs and rode the finest saddle to be seen in those parts and he loped along on a little cowpony at an easy gait with a pack of tall lean greyhounds running, baying, ahead. It was a picturesque scene.

I knew him by the trappings and the greyhounds. He was Tom Bell, one of the most typically western characters in the country. His home ranch lay between Van Tassell and Lusk but his cattle ranged over the Old Woman and the Lance Creek country and now and then critters bearing the Carlink brand could be seen grazing over into Dakota or Nebraska. His horses, branded with a Round Top T, ranged in droves. And worse than sheep -- he had a flock of Angora goats. To track down the goats, or cattle rustlers, he kept bloodhounds.

He stopped at my door, walked in and said, "I'm Tom Bell."

"Yes, I know," I answered, wondering what had brought him.

"I am shipping out a few carloads of cattle. Like to come down to the corrals? News item maybe."

Knowing him as I did by reputation I was not greatly surprised at the friendly overture.

"Get on your bonnet."

He watched me as I tied the bows of the pink chambray hat under my chin. I was glad I had put on a fresh white blouse and the pink pleated chambray skirt that morning. He walked the short way down to the corrals, pony and greyhounds following.

"Pretty lean pickings around here right now, isn't it?" he said in affirmative tone.

"You mean for the homesteaders -- or the cattle?"

His round ruddy face became serious. Tom Bell's countenance and manner were as open as the prairie.

"For the cattle, yes. Reason for shippin' part of the stock early. They're not ready for beef. Getting leaner every day though. What I meant was your newspaper -- going to be a helluva fight in elections here this fall, I'm thinkin'. Wondered how you were goin' line up."

"I'm for issues and candidates that favor development," I told him.

"Huh! Well, if you want patronage, better trail with the Republicans. Me? I'm no politician."

We had reached the shipping pens where a group of cowboys were gathered, sitting on the high rail fence, or their ponies, or leaning against the fence lazily, leisurely, waiting to load. They had been riding hard for days, hazing the cattle over a scorching, new desert, land to railroad, driving them slowly, hunting the waterholes to keep the "beef on hoof" from shrinking. Inside the pens the cattle were milling restlessly with continuous bawling.

"Hey, boys," Tom Bell called. "Here's the skirt printer -- Miss Ammons. Maybe some of you know her."

I recognized several of them. At once they came to attention, straightened up, climbed down from the fence or rode into the circle 'round their boss. Tom Bell was not the executive type of man but to every hand in the outfit his word was law.

He took a copy of The Progress from his pocket.

"Now, boys," he announced (some of the "boys" were husky, middle-aged men) "I'm subscribing for The Van Tassell Progress. One of the best dog-gone papers in the country -- the big Washington chiefs say so. And it'll tell you where all the good looking girls are homesteading, where the shindigs are held – there's talk of a town hall for social events.

"I've heard about you-all attending the ice cream socials, and the church services. Boys, this paper has helped to build a town right under our noses. Now, how many of you are subscribing?"

Hands went down into pockets, each puncher bringing out the money or borrowing it from the boss until pay day. Looking on with amusement were two cattle buyers from Denver. That was just like Tom Bell, they averred. What would his fellow stockmen say to this? Tom Bell didn't care. The two men came forward and were introduced.

"Of course," the cattlemen explained, "it's a homestead paper but it will keep you posted on what the gol-danged homesteaders are doing! And they may have stock to sell one day. Can't ever tell."

The buyers not only subscribed, the contracted advertising for the fall months paying for it in advance, as I jotted down the copy.

I stood peering through the rail fence watching the whitefaces being prodded through the narrow chutes into the cars on sidetracks.

"Why did you not use a bell for your brand?" I asked.

Tom Bell gave me a quick look. "Well I'll be gol-darned. Never thought about it. Say, you'd make us stockmen a good publicity agent -- if you weren't on the wrong side of the fence."

I walked back to the printshop carrying my gingham hat into which fifty dollars had been dropped without my passing it; I was indifferent to the midday sun beating down on my bare head blistering my face.

Compared to the gigantic outfits Tom Bell may not have been considered a Cattle King. But he was a king among cattlemen. Fellow range men assailed him for not making more of a fight to hold onto the range.

"Are we going to let the homesteaders come in here right under our noses?" they demanded angrily.

"Let 'em come?" Tom Bell would retort. "Hell, they're here, ain't they! God Almighty no, I don't want the range settled -- but it is. Get rid of them? Well, I'm thinking there'll be plenty of them pulling out in another year or so. (And I'm saying over and over, give us another year.) And if not ..."

He would lease pastures, buy hay or grain from the danged dry-farmers, and cut his herds if he had to, Tom Bell figured, and went his whole-souled, western way, serene. He owned a couple of ranches on which he could make a living and he couldn't be pestered by fighting with fate.

Tom Bell was ready to make the adjustment which in time all plainsmen must make. But he and Magoon were only two and they were not among the czars who ruled the range.

Following upon the heels of the small financial lift from the Tom Bell crew there came word from Senator Warren advising me that the state campaign in progress should enhance the business of my paper to a considerable extent.

"In this connection," he said, "I have conferred with the State Chairman who advises me that he has sent you material and will be able to increase the amount as the campaign progresses."

I received a first, small check from the Republican Party.

In the long late dusk (nine o'clock and still the summer twilight lingered) I heard the cry of a wolf, saw it emerge from the cluster of white rock and slip craftily toward the little row of settlement buildings. I sat outside my door and waited, not moving. The animal was so nearly the color of the yellow grass I could barely see it. It came so close, I was ready to run inside when it saw me, stood for a moment head up, eyes glaring, bushy tail extended, then turned and ran back into the labyrinth of jagged rock.

The wolf had come not quite to my door! I applied it as an omen of the desperate situation of the past few weeks. By sitting steady, the wolf which had stalked me to my very threshold had turned back.

There was a heavy dampness in the air. The gray clouds that moved through the sky like a dark rolling sea, became black and it was still as death.

And that night it rained.

Next morning the new station agent trudged through the downpour to my office with a telegram.

"From Washington, D. C.," he announced with a knowing grin.

A telegram was an event in the homestead country, and having it delivered in a pouring rain made it doubly important.

It was from Robert Kent, the man who had written me that I was "putting many of the boys in the shade" in the newspaper field and urged me to "Keep 'er up!"

The message read: "Passing through Van Tassell Wednesday enroute west. Trust you can meet the train. Looking forward to seeing you."

109

I was exuberant. Robert Kent of the Land Department wanted to meet me! The message like his letter was unofficial, but there were some matters of interest to be talked over. And it was raining!

The soaking rain would bring out the late grain, bring a fresh growth of prairie hay, and hope to the settlers who had begun to think it never rained on the range.

George Hecklebeck had said, "Rain? It can't rain in Wyoming," and Jim Turner from Iowa added, "Well, I've never seen it rain here!"

He had come out in the early summer, his family having come ahead to settle.

Like everything else in the big West the rain fell big and with a flourish and though it fell upon the dry-farmer as well, the stockmen welcomed it with joy. The ground was soft, no more rattling of dry wheels.

The following day Robert Kent wired to know if there was anything he could attend to for me while in Omaha.

"If so, commission me. Hope to see you tomorrow."

It was a considerate gesture knowing as he did how I was cut off from things. I wired my thanks. But – I'd not meet that train! He should not think just because I was a frontier printer that I'd go rolling like a tumbleweed at a word from a Washington official. Then Mitchell reminded me that tomorrow was the day I had urgent business at the Land Office in Douglas and I would be a passenger on the same train with Robert Kent.

I ran to the trunk that served as a window seat, threw off the grass-stuffed pillows and cretonne cover and from the very bottom I pulled out a dress and the paraphernalia that went with it. Simple, but all right for the occasion. I had no more suits and frocks designed by a fashionable modiste as I had when I lived with the Van Sants in Peoria. They had burned up with the Ammons trading post.

I smile in reminiscence at the picture I must have made on my first trip to Wyoming and belated tears of self-pity are stayed only because of the more significant things in which I, that poor girl, was wrapped. C. H. West had wired me to meet him and a group of eastern folk in Lusk. My sister and I left shorn as sheep at shearing time from the big fire had been going around in clothing furnished by settlers and Indians -- faded calico

110

dresses, brightly-beaded moccasins, a fringed doeskin skirt. Starting out to Wyoming, I had stopped at Presho to buy a few clothes.

I was going to Wyoming as a colonizer, a homestead leader. To get there on time I had to take the train at Presho sending my Indian pony Lakota back home and I had landed in Lusk, with Mr. West and his landseekers at the station to meet me and the natives looking on, in a dark-blue, sateen thing called a dress with a heavy stripe running through it a little bluer and more satiny than the other. But it was the best Martin's general store in Presho had to offer and it had cost all of three dollars and a half.

The dress, at least two sizes too big, was belted tightly around my small form making the skirt hang in folds entirely hiding what was conceded to be a graceful figure, the big long sleeves were puffed out at the top like the then old-fashioned mutton-leg (I did not know how long the dress had been in stock) tapering down to the slender wrist and hanging an inch or so over my hand, and the blue "creation" was topped off with a coarse white lace collar. (I never can forget that dress!) I cannot remember the hat.

But I had bought a few presentable, rather modish, garments when the West Land Company sent me east on the colonizing project all expenses advanced. That had been less than a year ago. My! I thought, I have traveled far in that short time; or am I going around in circles?

Getting ready to meet Robert Kent, I had no time to lose. The garments had to be pressed and there was not a flatiron to be found in the village and -- the few women trades-folk did their ironing on the claims. Out front was a scrubby cayuse that had been grazing around all afternoon with the saddle on. I could find no owner so I straddled it, tied my bundle to the saddle and rode out to Mother Van's, four miles, to do the pressing.

Mother Van, elated over the rain that may prove the settlers' salvation, lighted the oil stove and put on the heavy sad-iron. Of course I must meet the man from Washington, she said. Perhaps he was meeting me on business, being connected with the Land Department as he was. Or ... every man I met was, in her match-making eye, a prospect for romance. She had tried so hard in Peoria to develop a romance for me, giving parties and inviting the most eligible young men to steak dinners, but somehow, no great romance had developed.

To me, meeting Robert Kent was release from the drab monotony and the strain. He was a man from my field of activity and of my own class socially. And, secretly, I wanted to find out if the finer edges of my feminine-being were deadened, or if that spark of attraction which lights between man and woman still lived. If it still pulsed, I would have more confidence in myself and my work.

Mother Van folded the pressed dress and underskirt carefully, so they would not get wrinkled.

"Robert Kent will think you're a debutante when he sees you in this," she laughed as she kissed me goodbye.

Back home, I turned the cayuse loose never knowing who the owner was. A Ridge farmer, probably, who had taken the train to a neighboring town and ridden back home that night.

There had been spasmodic showers as though the rain, once started, could not give up. The next morning the range was a golden aura with raindrops, still fresh on the grass, sparkling like diamonds in the sun and there was a new vibrancy in this land turning verdant again.

I put on the blue, polka-dot dress with its two soft flounces. It was almost the color of the deepest blue of the sky. I put on the white slippers and got out the white leghorn hat with its blue, polka-dot band and bow that matched the dress. Standing before the small, cracked mirror that hung on the wall, I set the hat at the most girlish angle. It looked real nice over the softly waving hair. (For the first time in Wyoming I wished for a larger mirror. I had not seen myself from head to foot since my last trip East.) I pulled on the white gloves, grabbed my portfolio and went skipping down to the depot.

Humming a little tune, I danced along to its rhythm. What mattered whether it was the sparkling air or the rain's value to the colonist or whether Robert Kent had something to do with my happy mood. Why spoil things by analysis?

As I went pirouetting down the trail, I turned to see a little, sorrel bronco do a sunfish in front of me.

"Now what in dangnation," the rider exclaimed, bringing his horse back onto the trail.

I stopped and said, "Hello, Lanky. Sorry I scared Skit."

He stared at me, gaping. "Scare any hoss meetin' up with a whirl-a-gig thataway. Didn't know yuh myself all groomed and slicked like a blue-ribbon bronc."

I lifted my flounce with a curtsy, and a "Thank you, kind sir."

It was the last straw. And, as I heard the train whistling in, I left Lanky stoutly charging that "Women are shore funny -- haint no independence to be put into 'em."

In capricious mood, I waited in the deserted boxcar station where from the dirty little window I watched, without being seen, a well-dressed man in light suit and hat swing from the Pullman, look expectantly around, then walk down the platform toward the depot, his eyes focused on The Progress office which he could distinguish by the big black sign.

There was no doubt that the broad shouldered, self-possessed man so meticulously groomed was Robert Kent. Funny, I thought, how men's clothing marked the range to which they belong, like brands on cattle. I noted the perfectly pressed suit, (those creases were never put into the trousers by laying them flat under the mattress and sleeping on them as cowboys and homesteaders did), the highly-polished shoes and the watch-fob[9] glittering in the sun.

I may put some of the boys in the shade, as he had expressed, running newspapers, but Robert Kent put me in the shade when it came to clothes. I was glad I had selected the simple girlish outfit that Mother Van said would make me look like a debutante. I had none to mark me as a sophisticated business woman.

Anyhow, the glum look I saw in the man's face as he came slowly back to the Pullman gave me the inning. He was actually disappointed that I was not there to meet him. Quite young -- in his thirties I concluded -- medium height, well-built, and a boyish expression, not in keeping with his poise, had come into his face.

With the conductor's "All aboard," I stepped out to join him.

And with a quick gesture he came forward and held out his hand, "Why, Miss Ammons!"

---

[9] A watch-fob is a chain or ribbon attached to a pocket-watch worn hanging from a vest or waist-pocket.

He was frankly delighted when he learned I was boarding the train. And as it chugged out of the station, he voiced the glad surprise I had seen in his eyes upon meeting me.

"Do you know," he confessed, "I expected to see a tall dignified woman, severe in dress and austere in manner. I can hardly adjust you to the kind of work you are doing. Now tell me how you came to be running homestead newspapers."

"Is it so incredible?" I asked refusing to take the short time we would have together to explain.

"A conundrum to us in Washington," he declared as he looked out over the well-settled region which he had last seen empty.

Amazed at the progress which had been made in a few months, he said, "Tell me how it was done."

I tried to think what there was of unusual interest about it.

"Well, first of all, we had the right kind of people. And solid settlement."

I told him of my plans and ideas in locating them advantageously, as the groundwork.

"And you already know what my newspaper has done -- its methods and policies."

"Yes, indeed!"

He was silent for a moment then spoke in quick decision.

"That's what homesteaders need -- leadership. As a rule, they go out to fight the primitive singly with no knowledge of the country or the homesteading project. The homesteaders have had no system, no program, no head, and no other industry operates in that haphazard way. Now stock growers are organized. The Wyoming Stock Growers is one of the oldest and strongest associations in the West."

At that I became wild-eyed.

He turned to me abruptly.

"I know of no one else who is promoting the homestead movement under your ideas and plan, do you?"

"You mean as a cooperative system with a newspaper as their medium?"

"Yes. And colonizing. The Van Tassell territory is being cited in The Department as an example of land settlement."

114

Then I presented the other side of the situation -- the drought and the strong stockmen opposition.

"I once knew a cowboy who always said of an undertaking, 'any old cayuse can enter a race. It's coming in under the wire that counts.'"

"We're not under the wire." I reminded him.

His eyes twinkled in amusement, then grew serious.

"The free range controversy is one of the greatest problems the government has in getting this public domain developed. In Washington we realize its significance. It's going to be a political issue in the western states, particularly Wyoming."

'But," he went on, "I'll bank on you" -- he smiled broadly – "even if you are not austere and middle-aged and dominant."

And the conversation drifted from homesteaders into pleasant personal things -- he had not planned our meeting to be official, he said, and why did the old train run so fast that day, I wondered, when other times it poked and chugged and stopped at every water tank and for the cattle to get out of the way? Yet, today, the trainmen hadn't stopped to run a single cow off the track or wait for a bunch of sheep to cross. But I never had known the old Sage Hen to run so smoothly, the sage was white-gold in the sun, its pungent aroma sweeter than roses and the baa-ing of sheep more lyric than harps.

We had lunch together in Douglas and as we parted he said, "Your work and your writing are worthy of a larger field," and then admitted that he had been curious for these many weeks to know what the editor of the Van Tassell Progress was like.

"And now, that your curiosity is appeased?" I bandied, a bit coquettish perhaps.

"I'm satiated with interest," his quick reply, "in your work -- and you."

Then with a sober concern he said, "We are entering a new political period out here -- but, just stick to your guns, Edith. And you'll hear from me again."

Chapter XI
SECTION LINES BEFORE PARTY LINES

"Ballets instead of bullets" was the slogan of the new West.

Hard old natives shook their heads and said, "We had an honest-to-God country when six-shooters were the law. Got rid o' undesirables, pronto. Now it will take bullets to get rid o' the crooks who are going after the ballots."

Over the far flung plains, a new political force was arising -- the Homesteaders, whose interests were varied from that of the old regime. It was a notable epoch in the history of the West and of the United States when this people came into power. It almost was parallel to that of early colonists of New England establishing a new form of government after the Revolutionary War. Their needs were distinct, yet relevant to the country as a whole. Meeting the demand of a young agricultural empire with its millions of people required governmental expansion in many branches, and many new provisions. The western states themselves needed new policies and new laws to keep pace with conditions.

What a conglomeration it all was, I would sit aimlessly jabbing at the buttons on my dress with the point of my pencil -- cattlemen, settlers, politics, sheep. Cattlemen, settler -- no, there was another button -- politics. Always the little game ended on politics and who had time for politics! The campaign had started early before the primaries.

With the rise of a new social order, mushroom politicians began to invade the field. I was besieged by questions as to the policy and politics of my newspaper. Democrat or Republican? "What difference!" I exclaimed. The Progress stood for good government and settler representation. It was not a political newspaper.

In the homestead world, section lines (lines dividing the land) came before party lines. Settlers talked but little of party affiliations. There were no factions among the homesteaders of the West. They were governed by the same federal laws. Their municipal needs were the same, and their primary interest was that of self-preservation which was more basic than partisan politics.

"PARTY LINES?" I shouted in black ink and the biggest type I could find! (My goodness how I was using up ink -- I almost fainted when I saw the ink bill.)

"Let us build more section lines. Cut the West into farm units. For the people! If a half-section is not enough, give them a whole section. We want supporters of this farm movement in public offices."

I was ridiculed by range men and by the people in general. But already a 640-acre law called the "Grazing Act" was in enactment to stimulate settlement into the rougher, left-over areas, and to promote increased production for our people. For the war of 1917.

And it was in the Great Depression of the 1920's and 1930's with collapse of agriculture that the cry of "Save our Farm Units!" was heard over the nation.

"Do not let the West fall into the hands of the speculators. Mechanical corporation farming will ruin the farmers."

And it was not droughts nor dust storms nor barrenness of soil that had wrung that cry from the people. Because they had known droughts, and the dust storms which were but regional, had not yet swept, nor never were to touch many of the vast domains from which that supplication came. It was mainly market manipulation of farm products, and inflation and economic upheaval, far away from the land itself.

They may say the Great Depression with its dire effect upon the West was a far cry from this period of development. But it was not so far, (from one to two decades) and it led straight back to that epoch and to those same homesteaders with their slogan: "Section Lines before Party Lines. Let us build Farm Units."

I had that pronouncement for the coming election with the non-partisan policy set in type. But before the paper went to press, a bunch of range cattle went on a rampage one dark night, crashed against the print shop and knocked the galleys that were nailed to the wall, and the newspaper's policy lay piled in the middle of the floor.

I had been awakened in the middle of the night by a crashing noise. The flimsy walls were swaying, window panes shattering, then down went the galleys of type. I jumped out of bed, dazed. I thought it was an earthquake. Then I heard what sounded like a thousand stamping hoofs. The range cattle were on the prod. And my loud "Hay, Hay, Hay!"

failed to stop them. If they kept on, they would knock the shack down crushing me under it.

So I rushed to the door waving a broomstick in one hand and the ink-roller in the other shouting, hitting, working my way out a foot or two but staying in reach of the door. If the cattle pushed in on me, I'd jump back into the shack. But if the walls went down I'd go forward taking the consequences.

The milling animals stood and looked at me as if they were going to charge, their heads showing up white in the dark, then turned and went running across the prairie frightened almost to the point of a stampede. They were not used to women in white nightgowns.

Even the cattle, I wailed, were trying to push me off the range.

Next morning while the editor, the "angel" and the "devil," threw back pied type, the blacksmith and the butcher squared the printshop back on its two-by-six foundation and braced it by driving posts into the ground at each corner.

"That will hold 'er a spell," Phillip Freese, the butcher said.

Which was satisfactory. I may not need it longer than a "spel," with the political stampede that was closing in on me.

The Progress, being run by a "weak" woman, a few candidates and campaign promoters had trusted to their persuasive powers to get the paper's support. It was the lesser groups and the local issues which would most directly affect the settlers.

According to promise, the Republican State Committee was furnishing The Progress a goodly amount of business. Wyoming was a Republican state, and thus had most of the campaign advertising. Its public officials were almost unanimously Republican, but other political groups, taking note, began to use the paper as a campaign medium.

I published the political matter without editorial comment. And the land notices were increasing.

As the cowboy said when the goat ate his last shirt off the clothesline, "Him who has, gits. And from him who has not, it shall be took away."

That bit of distorted Biblical Truth was being proved for me and I needed more help in the office.

Burleigh Humphrey had come onto the paper early that summer working now and then as an apprentice, becoming known as the paper's "angel." I now put her on full time.

The Widow Humphrey had come out from Presho, South Dakota, and settled on the South Table. She had a family of children ranging from tiny tots and half-grown boys to three grown girls two of whom were employed back in Dakota. Burleigh Blanch was seventeen. Raising a large family on a homestead was no easy task for a widow, but Mrs. Humphrey was a courageous, hard-working woman and Burleigh had assumed a responsibility beyond her years.

She was a blond with a lovely complexion, thin, close-woven features, sober, blue eyes and she was smart as a whip. In white blouse with Peter-pan collar and Windsor bow-tie (always red or blue,) she looked as though she had come out of a bandbox instead of the wash-tub. She rode to the shop every morning. If the mother were away, she put Ivy June on the pony behind her, their lunches tied up in a paper sack.

Icy, her six-year-old sister (born on an icy June morning), was a scrawny, wiry child who seemed to be Burleigh's special care. She kept an eye on Icy while she learned the printing trade. But keeping an eye on Icy who flitted from one place to another, turned out to be a full-time job so the little tyke was let to go her willful way. And Icy June Humphrey could look out for herself. Born on the plain, wasn't she? Children born on the plain were self-reliant.

"Angel" learned rapidly. She and my brother Mitchell were able to handle most of the mechanical work. The girl had become very efficient, and the boy was a keen reporter.

Then one day an automobile stopped at my office. A stockman from the west end of the county and a man who seemed to be a sort of henchman, slated for appointment to some county office, by the name of Horton (which is not his real name) came in and put the issue of support up to me, without quibbling.

"We are lining up this part of the county," Horton explained.

"Many in this district are not yet legal voters," I reminded him.

"You can give the moral support of your newspaper. It carries weight over the east end of the county in sections where many folks are legal voters, take the Ridge for instance."

120

I went on setting type.

"This newspaper is published in behalf of the agricultural interests, you know, and the settler."

The stockman from the West End spoke in a direct manner: "Agricultural interests? Development? That's a lot of theory. Now, we have nothing against you, Miss Ammons. In fact, we hate to see you waste your energy. You are working hard to get a foot-hold and for what?"

They were taking in the meager surroundings: The rough floor with the cracks in it, the home-made copy table, and through the open doorway with its checkered curtains pulled back, they could see the small living room with its folded couch and a few rugs thrown promiscuously on the floor. The closet was made by stretching a curtain cater-cornered across one end of the room. I am told that Mr. Van Tassell's rooms on the ranch are covered with lovely thick furs.

The idea advanced by stockmen that The Progress was backed by eastern financial interests had now exploded. You cannot fool the people long about your financial standings.

The day was cool and windy and I recall vaguely the squeaking of the joint of stovepipe wired above the roof as a chimney -- it must be wired more tightly. A piece of loose roofing flapped up and down -- I'd have to put on a new roof before cold weather. I was doing fairly well now, if I could just stay out of this political jam. How was one to know what cards office-seekers had up their sleeves?

Joe Horton, exasperated at my silence blurted out, "I've got a mule at home that you could teach a whole lot about stubbornness. We haven't time to fool here all day. What are you going to do?"

"Why – why --," I was stammering so, I thought I should never get it out, "I'm going to back-fire! And I've got the matches ready."

Even the blatant, cocksure Horton was frustrated. He did now know what I meant by "having the matches ready." Neither did I.

"In another year or two" the rancher, a sheepman, reminded me, "there won't be a handful of dry-farmers left. Then, where will you be?"

I'd heard that statement so often it was trite.

"In Van Tassell," I retorted, "Running The Progress."

That remark also had become stale.

When they were gone I smiled to myself. If the human powers did try to push me out, Old Man Primitive, as usual, would turn some trick at the last minute to keep me here. I could depend on that.

But I knew now how this gigantic open land-free range controversy between settler and stockman in the West would be fought: Livestock monarchs who would not stoop to picayune, lawless methods, would try to maintain control through the ballots. And the frontier newspaper would be a pivot in the issue.

I saw that I had been letting the settlers down. They were becoming victims of exploitation at the hands of political aspirants seeking settler support. Also, it was the duty of the newspaper to keep them informed and to voice their policies.

The West End was a vast grazing territory and a strong-hold of sheep men. It was thinly populated while the East End was settled almost solid. But the West End had the county seat, and the power to run the county.

Again, in this issue, the settlers' interests ran to lines, this time to county lines. The Progress said: "The East End must be cut into a separate county where the farmers can establish their own local government. The homesteaders in the East End want a county of their own. The present county seat for many settlers may well be on some other planet. Converse County is larger than Rhode Island and Connecticut put together!"

The Colonists would not launch the move until the majority had the right of franchise in the state. This campaign should be a defensive one to block any further legislative control by the West End politicians or the stockman regime.

On Sunday I went out to my father's claim. I found him looking over the truck patch (vegetable garden), and small fields. Paying no attention to the drought twisted cabbage leaves or the corn nubbins that hung pitiably to bare stalks, he proudly pulled up late-sown turnips and rutabagas and pointed to a potato field that somehow survived the hot winds. Food and stock feed.

"Turnips is one of the best cow feeds you can find," he said.

Wild sunflowers with their big saucer heads were taking the fields. He pointed to them.

"They make good feed, like cottonseed," he informed me, "especially for chickens."

Next year, they would raise chickens.

"I'm going out to cut and stack these sunflowers. I've been telling the neighbors about it."

The city folk of the community looked to Tom Ammons for advice on their farming problems.

Sitting in the oblong patch of shade at the side of the shack, I told him how the politicians were hounding The Progress to get my support. He rarely made suggestions or voiced ideas regarding my activities.

"They would like to see all of us run out of here," he said. "And that big-mouth Horton! All he wants is a political job -- he couldn't sell enough fire insurance to make a living so ..."

"As I see it, I said, "if the settlers are to gain representation out here, Converse county must be divided!"

"We are all agreed upon that," he said flatly.

"And if I stand by the homesteaders," I now came to the point, "I may have to make an open fight."

The shade moved on. A streak of hot midday sun cut across my father's face. He shifted out of it.

"I think you will, Edie. But -- we must have a voice in public affairs. It's going to take more than final-proof receipts from the government to make us owners of the land."

I struck my matches to county division and started the backfire which I had so idly threatened when the small-job office-seekers tried to force my support. It surprised the people and brought on a drenching from the west-end cattle-and-sheep kings. Political henchmen began to spread propaganda about tax levies and exorbitant costs of setting up and operating new counties, enumerating with staggering sums "and figures do not lie" they said.

But I was finding they could be juggled around by experts to suit any purpose or group.

"We are not interested in figures," I retaliated. "Except as they apply to the size of the county."

Statistics and red tape records had little part in the conquering of the primitive.

Candidates for all offices were requested by settlers to stand for division and herd laws and those were the very issues they wanted to avoid. County officials were not going to spend money to build up the East End for dry farmers, and they could do a great deal to push them out.

"Things are getting lively out here," Mother Van enthused, rubbing her hands together as though getting ready for a bout. "But I can fight like the Old Nick if I have to," she chuckled. "A number of our colonists can stay here a long time without starving and we are here to help improve this country."

I was invited to make a talk over at Jireh College, some fifty miles, perhaps, to the west. Jireh College had been established by a religious sect from Indiana which had formed a colony of settlers among themselves. Preachers and college professors and many of the students held down claims. Their interests centered in the college, this double duty left but little time to deal with outside issues.

West-end stockmen had tried to persuade Tom Bell to run for office -- county commissioner maybe, or the Legislature; he could handle the settlers.

"Dammit, I'm no politician," Tom Bell argued. "I'm a cowman and I'd have to import more greyhounds to keep track of what is going on."

"We can't let these landgrabbers come into legislative power, can we?" they had flared back at him.

"They are in, man -- same as in."

Neil Jordan for some reason had decided not to run for office or perhaps he had been bluffing.

With a few exceptions, old-established business firms supported the stockmen who supported them through the years.

Businessmen said, "We are for the free range people."

"Their trade is steady and reliable. Homesteaders drift in and out; couldn't pay for a sack of flour when they got out. Some of them traded their claims for a suit of clothes or a grubstake or fare back home. We've seen it time and again."

Yes they had, we agreed. That was the way shrewd stockmen and business men often had come to own many tracts of land.

124

But the stockmen stay, merchants would add, ready to pay merchants goodly profits without quibbling. Come shipping time he asks, "How much do I owe you, Sam?" and writes out a check for a thousand, two thousand maybe -- just a scratch of the pen, like that. And they load their wagons with supplies, starting another year -- yes, sir! If they get short of money, they walk into the bank and say, "Let me have five thousand or ten, Bill, 'till shipping time. Pay you good interest."

A stockman's word was as good as gold bond.

I had not gone through great land lotteries without learning something of what the land booms brought to the West.

The Progress counter blasted: "The new homesteaders have created more business than small western townsmen ever heard of. Why, they have built towns. Look at Van Tassell, Jireh, dozens of others. New enterprises have been established. Old stockmen towns have come to life, many have grown beyond recognition since the land has been settled.

"The towns carry the stockmen for large amounts. But the homesteaders must pay cash. They cannot get a sack of flour or a package of salt without the cold cash. It takes material and money to build empires! The homesteaders are bringing new money into Wyoming -- into all the West. They have brought money from the cities and towns and farms of Illinois, Iowa, Missouri, from almost every state in the Union. And the businessman will get it as long as it lasts.

"Their dollar does not go as far as it would back east -- but you, Mr. Merchant, Mr. Banker, will handle their last dollar. If these homesteaders leave, others will come, bringing more money."

And The Progress lost much of its advertising. The bulk of its other income was thrown back into the campaign. Yet there was no move made to appoint a guardian for me!

Chapter XII
THE ROUNDUP

The Roundup on the range was not only the great pageant of the Frontier, it also was one of the great industrial events of America, when the "beef on the hoof" was garnered in from the boundless stretches.

Cattlemen gathered their cowhands, their horses and their camping equipment together. It was like moving a cavalry that divided into contingents that separated in every direction, combing the broad tables, the deep gullies, the long valley, and the high crags with their hills and pockets where stray bunches or lone critters lose themselves. Winding creek beds, timber bordered, underbrush and steep rocky canyons where it is all but impossible for horse or man to travel.

The many ridges, leading to wide plateaus, and then honeycombing miles upon miles of range to bring all the cattle of one brand together, is like hunting needles in a haystack. It takes a cavalry of trained men and trained horses.

When the range was wide open, the larger spreads rode for weeks with their crews in the saddle from dawn to late dark and at night they centered into camp with its mess wagons, and its cavvy[10] with the wranglers and nighthawks to look after the horses. The cavvy (or remuda) of the roundups may have a hundred horses or more, each cowboy having a string of eight or ten, changing horses every day -- or several times a day depending on the kind of country, the distance covered, and the number of cattle hazed. Always the wranglers must have fresh horses ready. And the nighthawks must herd the cavvy through the nights.

The O Ten Bar started out from Van Tassell with seventy-five to one hundred roundup horses in the cavvy. The Quarter Circle-V (Van Tassell) outfits gathered and milled and launched like a troop getting ready for attack.

The great cattle companies had their ranges and their roundup divisions in various sections. The Hunter (Cousin Jack) roundup which covered the hundred square miles of privately owned land and additional open range kept three hundred horses in the remudas.

---

[10] A group of ranch horses used to herd cattle

From every direction, cowboys ride into camp with their day's screenings and the cook calls, "The roast cow's out, the biscuits are done, the coffee's a boilin', so grab your tin plates and your pint cups! Come and get it!"

Bed rolls of canvas and blankets are spread on the ground under a tent or in the open, boots for pillows.

"O, gosh but I'm tired. Legs stiffer than a branding iron ..." a rider complains.

"Shut up, you tenderfoot. Cain't you let a feller sleep? Gotta break camp here at three in the morning."

"Oh, oh," the moaning answer. "I'm too sore to lie down. Where's that liniment?"

"Liniment! You'd better go back to Chicago, to your old man."

"Yeah," from another puncher. "Don't see why the cattle bosses back east have to push their weak, wayward sons onto us, just to make men of them. Hell! It's all we can do to look after the cattle. Better put him on the night-hawk, boys. He can't ride Roundup – ain't got no bridle path out here."

And the scion of a wealthy family, Beau Brummel of society, eats his humble pie from the hands of the lowly cowpuncher.

The father, who was head of a large cattle corporation, had cut off the playboy's allowance and sent him out to the ranch with orders to the superintendent to "pay him thirty dollars a month and make a man out of him."

Before daylight the camp is broken and the contingents move on scouring more country, bringing the straggling animals together, the number increasing each day -- rivulets of whitefaces that broaden through the miles and converge at last into one wide stream that moves slowly to separating corrals, to branding pens and on to shipping points while others are turned back to open range until the next roundup. And yet in the vast network but few cattle can be lost without the owner missing them. In the days before the railroads broad rivers of cattle moved in their course for hundreds of miles across the range to market.

With the range already drastically cut by homesteaders, the roundups were not so vast as in the early day, when a cattle king's roundup might cover 100,000 head, but the system was the same. That fall great droves of whitefaces traversed the range, smaller outfits driving together thus swelling the herds to an early-day size.

But we were seeing the last of the Great Roundups. The last of the Frontier! Or was it? Could the sodbreakers ever overthrow, or resist, a force so great? The very air was surcharged with a poignancy as of waiting between life and death. The new life of empire building, and the passing of the open range. And the stockmen must have felt the pall hanging heavy over them now, as they rounded up their herds.

It suddenly occurred to me that this was an important phase in American history, and the event one of national interest. I was going to follow the roundup and write an account of it for a syndicate. (The foregoing is part of that story).

For a week, I jaunted here and there over that part of the range and over into Nebraska, skirting the droves that were being driven in, riding through scatterments that were spreading back to range and staying at night with an isolated, settler family, or at a ranch home.

The sparkling fall days bathed the frontier in a golden glory of dazzling sunlight on yellow grass. Fall, when the West is in the zenith of her majesty. As though an unseen curtain had been drawn, great shadows fell upon the plain throwing vast blocks of the landscape into shade. Birds skimmed here and there like small floating vessels on the still, blue sky and once a large, lone bird soaring high, wings outspread like a great airship, swooped easily to lower strata and up again -- an eagle.

Time was when the range cattle would run and scatter at sight of strangers. But now they paid little attention to people passing through. Tired from long driving, some of them lay chewing their cud, refusing to budge off the trail. But when I came to a wild steer, or a bull that began to bellow like – well, like the low, deep rumbling of a bull on the range -- I got out of the way as fast as I could without arousing suspicion that I was running from him and rode down into a draw, out of sight.

Once I looked back to see a massive, old bull coming slowly toward me. I dismounted and slipped under the first fence until he had turned back. As always when traveling over the range, I wore no bright clothing and waved no red flags.

I passed a camp now and then where I was cordially welcomed to "chuck," and I met punchers and cowmen I'd never seen.

One day, I had met Russell Thorp Jr., on a beautiful horse riding at an easy gait. Straight and vital, he expressed the strength of the range folk and his dignity was disconcerting. He lifted his hand, touching a forefinger to the wide brim of his hat -- the gesture of courtesy to take the place of lifting the heavy sombrero -- and passed on. These were busy days for cowmen.

Russell Thorp, whose holdings lay in the heart of that region, which was settled now to the last quarter, already had been hard hit. Some folk said he was bound to go under.

It was mid-afternoon in an outlying district, back in the rough foothills that I came unexpectedly to a branding pen where late calves, and critters missed in the last roundup – "slicks" the punchers called them -- were being branded.

Cowhands drove their cattle in shouting and cursing to keep the solid mass moving while top-hands stood by giving orders. Outside the high, weather-grayed, rail fences, the riders circled their ponies, swirled their lariats as they rode, roping a calf at each throw and dragging it into the branding pen without looking back to see whether it had been lassoed at neck, leg or body, and the cowpony loping on until he felt the rope in the hand of the rider go taut.

A stubborn calf with the lariat around its neck, set its four legs together, braced itself, and refused to more. The pony stopped short.

"Why, you ornery little cuss," the cowboy scolded as he got off and pushed the struggling animal while the horse pulled it into the corral.

He picked it up in his arms, laid it down on its left side for the brander.

"You little devil, you're goin' to make a fine critter someday, got breedin' in you."

Another cowboy brought in a steer with the pony wheeling, stopped like a circus horse at the drop of a hat, in front of the branding fire. In a flash another man had released the rope and held the angry critter down while the brander slapped the white-hot, sizzling iron onto the flesh. Turned loose the animal stood shaking from bright and pain, then went bawling into a corner of the corral.

And so the branding went on with lassoers as expert as any whoever threw a rope in exhibition, and trained horses that knew every move, turning in a split second as though on a pivot. Without a rider, the highly-trained cowponies raced after escaping critters, circled in front of them and turned them back. They had done their stuff day after day, year after year.

The thrilling performances of cowboy and western bronco in the wild-west shows are but repetition of their daily routine. Those daring riders of the range took life in their hands as unconcerned as a city man boards a street car. They were skilled artists as well as courageous men, faithful to their calling.

Cowpunchers never struck for shorter hours or better pay and if a puncher became dissatisfied, he joined up with another outfit and fell in line with its hands.

Inside the corrals, calves were bellowing mournfully. Outside the fence, cows bawled madly for their young, making pandemonium in the smooth order of skilled operations. Leaning against the fence overseeing the performance as though it were dull routine was Neil Jordan! (Although the name and brand has been altered the character is real and typical of many stockmen, and his story exemplary of free-rangers at that time) I did not know whether to run or stay.

In the melee, no one took note of my presence and as the activity slowed up, I dismounted, threw the rein down and walked up to Jordan. He straightened in surprise, giving me an inquisitive look as he turned to give an order. He was thinking, I knew, that I had come either as a sightseer with other city folk -- or to make a compromise on the policy of my paper.

"Drive that heifer over here," he commanded a puncher. Stepping up close to the animal, he examined the brand carefully and spoke more to himself than to me.

"Just as I thought. This heifer belongs to me."

I stood beside him peering intently as he carefully traced the brand with his index finger.

"That '4' has been made over a bar. And see here -- by God! That 'O' has been traced over a 'J.' Been rebranded and has wandered back home."

We had forgotten for the moment that we were enemies, but coming to himself, the rancher moved back, cold, reserved.

But in that unguarded moment, I had seen the troubled look in his face so I said boldly, "I've heard of some rustling going on lately and that stockmen have missed a few mavericks."

"Ye-es, been a bit of trouble lately -- some of the little fellows trying to round up herds of their own maybe; the rustlers used to wipe cattlemen out in the early day."

He stopped short and almost looked a hole through me.

I ignored the insolence.

"Settlers are missing some young stuff and they cannot afford to lose any stock, nor be accused of appropriating range cattle," I explained.

"Thought you said they could live on range cattle next winter if they got hungry."

"It isn't winter yet. And it rained. You gave a week's time for the drought to starve them out. It rained the tenth day. So they may get by without butchering your stock."

My facetiousness did not amuse him. He let it go by.

"Between rustlers and homesteaders – " he shook his head in quandary.

I noted the deep lines in his face. The vigorous middle-aged man who had seemed young, appeared suddenly old, forgetting I was there.

Then he turned on me, his voice hard and level.

"What are you here for? Been thinking over what I told you?"

These plainsmen were men of few words.

"O, about coming over to the right side of the fence? No – O -- I thought perhaps we could tear the fence down."

Naturally he ignored that remark and turned on his high-heeled boots, saying he was busy.

I stood beside my pony a moment, then threw the rein down and followed him.

"Mr. Jordan!"

He checked his gait, then strode on.

"Mr. Jordan, I do not want to see the stockmen lose their herds -- not the individual stockmen, like those of this territory. Neither do the settlers."

I caught up with him, took hold of his arm -- he could shoot me if he wished.

132

"Let's all work together."

"Get out with your soft stuff! This is the cattle business. Who are you to come in here?"

I was no longer afraid.

"The United States Government you mean, not I. This land is not yours, nor ever has been. But you've used it well and built a great industry on it. There's room for us all."

"Room for us all," he said, "with the landgrabbers filing on every acre? Now don't you try to argue with me! Tom Bell and Bill Magoon can be easy marks if they want to but ..."

He resented the two stockmen's acceptance of conditions and the sarcasm in his tone implied that he knew of their amity toward me. He may have known of my conference with Bill Magoon in Lusk that day, and that Tom Bell had his punchers subscribe to my paper.

"They are not easy marks," I interjected. "They merely recognize the situation."

Then I added conclusively, "If the stockmen run the settlers out, others will come."

Others will come. The man's dejected look and manner showed he was facing that eventuality.

Now we were leaning against the fence, he with a bootheel hooked over a rail, I with my little duck riding hat in my hand, pushing my hair back from my forehead.

As a class, the stockmen of the range were of the country's greatest. Men who were men. Strong, courageous and progressive. Too progressive. They would have to curtail, I reiterated, and let the capitalists who had made their fortune off our range get out! Foreign corporations had coerced our own stockmen long enough.

But many individual growers like Neil Jordan would feel the blow and my head was burdened as I said, "Heaven knows, Mr. Jordan, the homesteaders have enough to bear. And they have a legal right to the land. You stockmen have gone through a lot, too. I know that! Hardships, blizzards, cattle thieves -- and the isolation. Loneliness for the women. Sickness, and cut off from help -- that must have been awful."

Unknowingly I had struck a vulnerable spot in this hard man.

"Yes, I know, I've seen plenty of it."

133

He spoke in a low constrained voice as though emotion damned these many years had found an open channel. I heard later that he had lost a child once -- a little girl -- with diphtheria. A blizzard and the roads blocked -- took the doctor three days to make it. Anyhow, these early settlers had suffered many such tragedies. The activity around the branding pens had ceased, the day's work finished.

"Why not lease from the settlers the same land you've been ranging? Let the settlers feed your stock with the hay they put up. For several years to come, they will have idle land. Many of them have no money to stock it. Either lease, or let dry-farmers run cattle on the share."

He stood pondering and I said, "Tom Bell is planning to do that, and I hear that Russell Thorp is leasing from the settlers."

"Let's say that I am a spokesman for the settlers. They do need the money and the stock, for they will raise grain for feed."

Tears trickled down my cheeks as I held out my hand to him.

Reluctantly, he took it and said, "You can't get home tonight, and then there are no houses around here."

"I'm staying at a settler's down the creek about ten miles, I guess I'll make it," I replied.

Neil Jordan was an obstinate man. But a bar had been let down between us. Between the stockmen and the farmers.

Chapter XIII
WITH PLOWS AS ARMANENT

The cattle rustling and other violations had quieted down, and there were other things of importance in which I all but forgot, the harrowing experiences of the past few weeks and even the political battle lost some of its significance.

Settlers must make preparations for the winter if they would survive; even in the thick of the strife, many of them were consumed by that vital problem. And the fall plowing must be done.

Man can live a long time on the isolated frontier without law or government but nowhere can he exist without the products of the soil.

That fall, the West's half-million sodbreakers garnered their meager crops off sod land; larger harvests in the longer cultivated regions. After fall rains, they broke more sod, fallowed the already broken land to absorb the winter and spring moisture into the subsoil.

And you cannot stir up an ardor for war, a thirst for blood, in men whose spirits are imbued in the soil. The soil from which all sustenance, all wealth, comes. Little did they dream that a world war was brewing.

All over the illimitable, inexhaustible frontier, reaching into the Great American Desert, to the Rockies and beyond, this half-million men splotched the virgin landscape with blocks of turned-over soil; while the million women and children gathered precious foods from the earth. The earth that lay unperturbed by the strife among men for its possession, majestically impervious to the selfish greed of weak man for its wealth. The wealth that comes from grain and oil and vast herds and gold and silver.

But these people of the sod lusted not for power nor wealth nor glory. The soil to them meant food and home, contentment and wholesome labor. Its peace flowed into their veins like rain into the soil and those who plowed knew a harmony with the Universe that was greater than the discord around them.

And they raised their eyes unto the high heavens and lowered them again to the lowly earth and found them One, and also One with those who tilled the soil. And from the Heaven and the Earth there came that strength and courage beyond understanding of the pioneers who had conquered the wildernesses with plowshares as armament -- the armament with which they had stretched the United States from Plymouth Rock to the Hudson, to the Mississippi, to the Missouri, to the Rockies, to the Pacific.

The homesteaders had put their roots deep that Fall into western soil.

In the East, in the centers of trade and finance and industry, men talked about expansion and prosperity and larger profits and built more factories, promoted larger corporations, and bought more stocks and bonds and became opulent. They bought their wives expensive furs and diamonds, and dined on rich foods, drank champagne, and tipped the waiter a dollar instead of a dime without asking whence the flush came, not looking beyond their smug world for the cause of this interesting prosperity. And certainly, they would not look beyond the old Missouri for it.

Wall Street, the temple of the money-changers, did not proclaim to the people, "It is the land armies, the construction regiments moving West that is stimulating finance. Transplanting a people puts money into circulation. Building a modern empire as big as the frontier from scratch takes everything."

It took horses and plows and wagons by the thousands. It took harness and saddles and building material and folding wire cots and small shack (monkey) stoves by the carloads. It took a million miles of barbwire, and more farm machinery than the manufacturers ever had dreamed of making. It took iron and lumber and steel and all raw materials. It required materials, labor, and finance to build new towns and cities and new railroads and bridges and dams and highways on the million square miles of western plains. No army of war up to that time ever had taken the amount of equipment, or boosted trade and labor as had the land cavalcades with the tide of immigration that followed.

It took transportation, too, with railroads over-run with business. (And just wait until the sodbreakers began to ship out their products. That was to laugh!)

But the United States Government knew the reason for this solid expansion. Men at the head of the Nation, of The Department of Interior, needed no swivel-chair economists to tell them it was the western land movement. Those sages from the sagebrush had spoken wisely when they said, "Let's develop the vast frontier!"

And the nation grew and strengthened while the homesteaders built their barbwire fences and plowed their furrows.

The future of a greater America rested within the furrows.

Edith Eudora Ammons Kohl

Chapter XIV
THE NINETY AND NINE

In Wyoming that fall, plows ran through sheep pastures, through cattle ranges. On the great plateau of the Running Water, the colonists from farm and city alike plowed their fields in furrows a half-mile, a mile long without a break, so smooth lay the land without rock or tree or stone to stop the plow. Three and four-horse teams went up and down in the warm bright days of autumn. Men plowed the fertile sandy loam and rolled the great lumps of sod down with heavy rollers and pulverized it with harrows.

A few tractors steamed across the range. Dr. Leport Van Sant had filed on a claim and his tractor tore up fields of sod on the claims of all and sundry of the Van Sant folk -- Mother Van, Dick and Nick, Elmer and himself. The engines chugged through the crisp, moonlit nights throwing their bright lights across the cow-trails of the Van Tassell, the Coffee, and the Vorhees ranges. They pulled the plows through the heavy gramma grass, ripping the sod, cutting through the matted roots of the buffalo grass.

Others ran their tractors by day but Leport ran his also at night. He loved the feel of the night in his veins, the throb of the engines, the steeling of plowshare against the stubborn earth. The big open life of the range called to the stalwart young Van Sant scion of a family which had furnished the country with three governors of as many states.

Men resting their teams at every round looked at the tractors and shook their heads.

"God! But that's getting over the ground! Look at that row of plows behind the engine."

"Yeah, but it eats up gasoline. Horses eat the native hay -- and the grain we raise."

"Pulls the liver out of man and beast though, plowing with horses."

But they all plowed on. They must raise food to eat or leave. And they must meet the government demands on having one fourth of the land, eighty acres, under cultivation when they made final proof.

And they must gather in food and fuel. With thanks in their hearts, they watched the Fall lengthen and linger; and with anxiety they saw the days shorten. Getting ready for that first winter on the wind-swept stretches was a gigantic task.

The colonists gathered in their dabs of crop that had survived the drought or matured thereafter. But their food and the feed for their stock would have to be stretched if it held out. Some of them had raised but little. The hardy root crops had yielded fairly well. Rutabagas, turnips, and carrots grew large in that soil and climate and had a delicious flavor.

What potatoes the settlers had raised were smooth and mealy.

"Looks like a potato country," the settlers said to one another, "when we can grow potatoes like this the first year, and it's so dry."

They noted the absence of potato bugs, of cinch bugs.

"Tater bugs?" A native farmer pondered. "Cinch bugs? Never saw one."

He scratched his head in doubt.

"But -- there may be such things. I've never seen a street-car either. But I've seen people who have seen 'em."

And grasshoppers? Wyoming plains never had experienced a grasshopper invasion. Nor were these settlers ever to see one. Nor a dust storm. If they only could get through the winter, through another year, till they could get a foothold!

The women around Van Tassell, trying to beat the early frost, worked desperately to store food for their families. They made pumpkin butter and citron preserves with what sugar they could afford to buy, storing the rest. They peeled off the dead outside leaves of drought-burnt cabbage and cut the small green centers into sauerkraut; made pickles from green tomatoes and small cucumbers that had not matured before frost. Mrs. Coburn and Carrie had raised endive. It had grown large and was rich in flavor and color. This was salted down for salads or for greens. The root vegetables were stored in deep sod-covered caves or trenches.

The Heckerts and a few others bought coffee mills to grind barley for coffee, rye for flour. Before the winter was over, those same mills went many a round over the neighborhood.

Fuel was a vital problem. It was going to take plenty of it to keep from freezing in those thin walled huts on a Wyoming plain with its bitter cold and blizzards. Despite the work the settlers had done to make them comfortable, banking them up with sod, chinking the cracks up with cloth strips or batting them with lathe, and lining the insides with heavy paper, they were still shells through which the cold would penetrate. There were but few plastered houses and the price of coal was high, with freight exorbitant.

Settlers gathered up loads of cow chips from the open range and they began hauling wood from the pine-covered canyons, a thirty, forty -- and for some, a fifty-mile round-trip taking two days to get a jag of wood. Men took their families and camped in the hills and while the men and older boys cut and gathered wood, the women and children picked wild fruit. They found gooseberries, currants and grapes growing in the breaks, and chokecherries abounding in the canyons and along the creek beds.

I watched the teams and wagons go by in almost continuous procession as the food and fuel gathering went on. After the fruit picking was over, the wood hauling continued.

The wood was to be used to make the precious coal hold longer by those who bought coal. Other settlers would try to make the wood do without buying other fuel.

My father came into the office with a sprightly step, his face beaming.

"I've got good news, Edie."

"You look as if you had struck oil over at Casper," I bandied catching his bright mood.

"No," he chuckled. "I've got a team. A good one."

"A team!" my brother Mitchell and I gasped together.

"Come and see for yourselves. Right out here."

In front of the shop two heavy horses -- one brown, the other gray -- stood hitched to a wagon. Seeing the exuberance of father and son over so small a thing, I hardly knew whether to laugh or cry. But things on the range were valued by their need. A team may mean the difference between proving up, and giving up, for a man.

"Got them from Tom Bell," my father explained. "He has more range horses than he can use, or feed. Breaking young horses in all the time. This is one of his older work teams. The harness went with them. Took my note on a year's time. I got the wagon in Lusk cheap. Second-hand, but good as new. That's 'Si,' pointing to the gray, and 'Star.'"

They were branded with the round top "T," the brand of Tom Bell horses.

141

"Even the brand fits," Mitchell enthused. "T' for Tom Ammons. Someday we'll have a brand of our own."

They did. The Ammons brand is registered as A.

No more printshop for Mitchell that day and the two drove away sitting straight and proud on the wagon seat, the boy holding the lines over Star and Si.

Now the Ammonses could plow, haul hay and wood. While the father worked on the section, Mitchell and Tommy joined the wood haulers. They got up at four o'clock in the cold fall mornings and drove fifteen miles up into the canyons. There they gathered wood, trees that had died and fallen through the years. They tied ropes to the large dead logs and pulled them up the steep cliffs, over rocks, and through the timber up to the level where they could load. They gathered the twigs and branches and carried them up.

All day the two lads, both small and light-weight for their age, cut and pulled and heaved to get their wood gathered and loaded before the early dusk settled in the canyons. Then they made the long slow trip over the rough trails home, boys and team tired out. Often they went with the Heckert boys, taking two wagons and teams. That was easier and more fun, all working together like that. Sometimes they camped overnight, taking two days for the trip.

My father and Carrie went along whenever it was possible and they all gathered wood and what wild fruits were left. Once they took a tent to camp a week, but on the second night, they were awakened by the strange deep cry of a mountain lion coming down the canyon. They heard its stealthy step as it stalked nearer to their camp. They stirred up the fire into a blaze, crawled noiselessly into the wagon bed and lay there, not moving as the lion stalked on, along the side of the canyon above them, its roar sounding farther away. They had no gun with them, so next morning they went home.

With a supply of wood for the home, Mitchell took a heavy load all the team could pull, and hauled it thirty miles to a homesteader down on the south table for three dollars. The boys hauled wood every now and then, sometimes through bitter cold and snow for two to three dollars a load to buy themselves heavy shoes, warm clothing, and other necessities. They, with other settlers, took these things as a matter of course, making no complaint. Glad there was wood to be had; thankful for the three dollars.

My family took over the "Square Boarding House" in Lusk for the winter where they could make a living of sorts and put the boys in school, Mitchell being ready for high school. He wanted a good education. Thomas, Jr. would rather ride horses and drive cattle.

Tom Bell said, "That boy will make a fine rancher someday. Got the makin's of a bronco buster, too. Will give him a light job on the ranch next summer."

But Tommy went to school. My father quit the section, spending his time between boarding house and claim.

Instead of being run out of business, my little newspaper was on a solid small-profit basis with the Land Office publications gradually increasing and I had managed to get new shoes on my feet and a new roof on the shop without having bartered my soul for it (or at least my principles and my people). With money from the campaign, I had raised the salary of my helpers a few dollars a week, paid up my bill -- those ink bills, and had the print shop fixed up for winter which was about all the average frontier printer could expect to do in starting up. During the holing-in period which was close upon us, business would be dull but I could pull through, and next spring with the town and country growing, I would have more business than ever.

A few schools had been established among the colonies. Small, crude, one room buildings. Next year, we would have more schools and a high school in Van Tassell, if things went well.

Windmills, standing tall like oil derricks, broke the continuity of skyline. Their great round fans turned and clicked metallically with every turn. Click, a-click, a-click, marking off time like a loud ticking clock. The windmill in a homestead region was evidence of permanency.

Neil Jordan, stopping by one day said, "Well, I see the dry farmers are putting up windmills. They had better wait 'till the winter's over. Might not be here to use them. They are not fixed to survive a hard winter."

"Stockmen, too, have to run the hazard of a hard winter sometimes do they not?"

And little did I know what prophecy those words carried.

"But it looks as if the colonists were going to survive without killing the ranchers' cattle to eat," I informed the cattleman.

Whether they were run out or starved out, in the end these settlers were proving their mettle as pioneers. All through the harrowing summer I had watched with sinking heart everything that looked like a caravan, afraid some poor discouraged homesteader was taking his family and their worldly goods back to God's country.

But not one of the colonists had turned back. Despite the drought, the hardships, and the conflict with stockmen, we were all there. The "Ninety and Nine" -- and I, the one.

The government said it was an all-time record in land settlement.

I knocked on wood.

Chapter XV
AND THE ONE

Like a bolt from the blue came word of a tentative appointment in Washington with the General Land Office which first had become acquainted with my work in Dakota.

It had come through the recommendation of congressmen from the West -- Mondell had been Assistant U. S. Commissioner of Public Lands and leader of land laws in Congress but had given little thought to their random remarks about my experience fitting me for larger fields.

It was not to be a routine job but one that required an understanding of homestead problems. I do not recall what the salary was to be or if it were mentioned in the first notification. But that was of minor interest. I was beside myself.

Robert Kent sent congratulations. Said he knew I could fill the place efficiently and he had appointed himself a committee of one to meet me upon arrival. He no doubt had some part in my being offered the position and I recalled his words at the station that day, "You will hear from me again."

Had I been working with this goal as my ambition, I could have beaten my head against all the doors in Washington, I reflected, and never have broken through. Life was like that for me.

But in that position, I knew I could climb on and up, for I had a wide and practical experience of the homestead movement and an intimate understanding of the homesteaders.

I could make a meteoric flash across the horizon in that great project -- what greater was there than the disposition and development of our public domains?

As they had said of me, "Well, let it be so."

And I became a changed being overnight. My old self with its love of public acclaim and the comfort and luxuries of life was now manifest again.

One day soon after I had come west from St. Louis, a stranger passing through the homestead country had seen me out on the prairie gaily decorated with the wildflowers I had gathered. He had stopped in surprise.

"What are you, a prairie nymph?" he laughed.

145

"O, no! Just a homesteader," I had laughed back.

"What are you out here for?" he then asked, his curiosity aroused.

And I had answered earnestly, "To -- make something out of myself, perhaps."

The well-dressed distinguished looking man was amused.

"A devil of a place to do it. What are you finding out here?"

"The fundamentals. Life stripped of its veneer."

That surprised him and I found myself confiding to the interested stranger (and to myself) that I had been headed toward making too much of the superficial and how I had loved color and gayety and the poetry of life. Then I had come west and seen life where drama was made, not acted! I saw a chance out here to do things useful. Put my writing, my ambition, to concrete purpose.

The stranger who turned out to be Halbert Donovan, a New York broker and investment banker, had said, I was a Utopian dreamer. "What could a young girl like you do out here on these God-forsaken plains? And what would this country amount to, anyhow?"

I wondered what Halbert Donovan would say when he found out I was in Washington.

For those two-plus years of life in the raw, I had thought the "sounding of brass and tinkling of cymbals" dead as the proverbial doornail within me. Now I went about in a fevered dream not thinking of myself as a servant of the people or an instrument in a great Purpose, but a personage soaring to success.

I imaged myself in richly appointed offices with thick rugs on the floor where, poised and attractively groomed, I would confer with notable persons. I envisioned myself at great social functions beautifully gowned: pink velvets, pale blue chiffons (how I loved dainty things), mingling with cultured people, with men of the world hovering solicitous near. Corsages -- they should be forget-me-nots or violets ... and I was waltzing to Strauss in the arms of -- well -- Robert Kent, maybe.

I looked down at my rough, ink-stained hands, at the rough floor with the wind coming up through the knotholes, at the sagging cot in the corner. I threw my stick of type on the floor.

I was sick of homesteaders! Sick of the crude life! Of the whole business. I'd show my old friends of the social world who had thought I was crazy to live like this. And I'd show the stockmen and the petty politicians. Run me out? Huh.

No wonder people went drunk with a little power.

I went down to the station, (The Northwestern had installed an agent at Van Tassell) to wire my acceptance to Washington. But the agent had locked up for the night.

Upon what small pivots our lives do turn!

Bubbling over, I went to break the news to Mother Van. She would be my only confidant, the only one out here who knew and understood that other side of me.

I found her in her Dutch blue calico dress, making up butters and jelly. Making jellies was Mother Van's panacea for many ills. The dishpan and a large kettle covered the stove.

You know, Edith, she enthused, I always say there is nothing like good old wood stoves for making jams and jellies -- they need slow cooking. As I was telling Clara Theilbar the other day when she was wishing for her gas range -- but Clara is learning ..."

Wouldn't she ever stop talking?

"Mother Van, listen!" I interrupted, "I'm going to Washington! To stay. A good position ..."

She turned and looked at me. She did not clap her hands as she usually did over any good fortune that came to me.

"Sit down, Honey," she broke into my rapid recital. "Just a minute."

She gave the butter a stir with a large iron spoon, held up a spoonful and let it drop, and took out a saucerful and got out the bread. From the granite pot on the back of the stove she poured us each a cup of coffee and sat down beside me.

"Now try my chokecherry butter on a piece of bread."

As I ate, not knowing how the butter tasted, I told her all I knew of the tentative position with the government; mine for the taking now, I had been assured. A splendid chance for success, for making my mark. It would bring me in contact with people of influence and finesse ..."

"Yes," she laughed. "You'll get there. You were always good at that. But – you've made your place without all those things, didn't you? I thought you were carving out a career all your own."

"But this would be along the same line of work, settlement of public lands," I flared up because she had not said just what I had wanted to hear.

"I cannot be expected to stay down on the ground always, and live as I do."

"No." she agreed. "But it won't be the same. I don't know how you will like it. For myself, I like to be in the thick of things -- see things moving, places growing. We haven't any of us finished our jobs here -- O, you've done a lot, Honey. But there is plenty to do yet."

"I was not supposed to stay out here with these settlers, in the first place."

I hoped she wouldn't say, "Well, you brought most of them here, you're responsible in a way."

I was sick and tired of hearing myself say that.

Mother Van got up, pushed back the dishpan and poked a stick of pitch-pine into the stove. It smoked up, black.

"That's the only trouble with this pitch wood," she said, "it makes a roaring fire but its smoky -- blacks up everything."

I walked up and down the kitchen ignoring the virtue and vice of pitch wood, "I don't care. I have worked and struggled, haven't I? I've gone through Hades since I came West," I cried in an outburst.

"Fire and thirst and hardships in Dakota. And out here, God! What I've been through, come to think about it. Drought, drudgery, penury, fighting the big powers ... I'm entitled to things, am I not?"

"Yes, we'll all agree to that. But we've had some good times, too. And compensations. As to success, you have done whatever you've attempted. Done what no other woman has done toward developing the West, I guess. That will be something to leave behind you. What does your Papa say?"

Treating me like a child that should ask its parents what to do.

"I'm not telling him, not until I get things all set -- look how I could help him out -- money for improving the land and getting stock. This is one of the reasons I should go."

Mother Van was pouring up the jelly and made no comment. But I recall that moment of something falling flat. I turned the subject.

"You are going back to Peoria soon, aren't you?" I asked.

"For the winter, yes."

The old kitchen table was filled with glasses of rich, red chokecherry butter and wild grape jelly.

"But Brother Dick and Brother Nick are staying, and Elmer and Jean."

So those two young ones were still sticking it out on their claims, and I had predicted they wouldn't stay a month.

"Well, I have to get affairs straightened out here before I leave. I am going to Lusk tomorrow to see about selling the newspaper. And there will be arrangements to make with the Department ..."

I kissed her on the cheek as I left.

She followed me to the door.

"I just want you to be satisfied, Edith. Not lose what you've worked so hard for."

Lose it! Why, the Van Sants all liked ambition and success.

"But you are the kind of person who has to decide things within yourself."

Together with the landseekers, many others were rushing into the West. People from many walks of life and of various classes hunted new opportunities.

The train to Lusk was filled with passengers. The conductor stopped for a little chat as he punched my ticket. The brakeman came by.

"Well, here you are again."

He said that to me for a year, surprised each time that I was still in the cow country.

A short, stout, middle-aged woman flopped into the seat beside me.

"You know this country pretty well, don't you?"

She had heard the trainmen talking to me.

"Fairly well," I replied paying little attention to her.

But she talked on, asking questions about the country and the towns and at last said, "I'm looking for a location. Want to get settled for the winter. Back in Omaha people say this is a man's country and things booming."

I leaned my head back against the seat and looked out the window, absorbed in my own affairs.

149

"I'm bringing out a bunch of girls," she said finally. "Fine girls. Rough-and-ready for the wild west."

"O, a colony."

From habit, I was at once alert.

"That would be nice. There are many women out here now. Many girls taking up claims. But -- it will be difficult to find open tracts here for a colony."

The woman leaned closer and lowered her coarse voice almost to a whisper.

"Not a colony, dearie," she said confidentially, "a House."

"A House?"

When it dawned upon me as to what she meant, I turned and stared at her, at the frowsy, dyed hair under a broad, black, picture hat. That hat was floppy and fussy and like her dowdy clothes, indescribable. Her hard, lined face was painted like an Indian's. Cheap, tawdry jewelry flashed conspicuously. And under close scrutiny she looked old. Sixties, I judged, but aged for even that age.

What about that town of Lusk, she wanted to know. She had heard it was a lively place, lots of cowboys and sheepherders and -- maybe gamblers? Gamblers were always "good." I looked down the coach for another seat. The only empty one was her own across the aisle.

I was amused at the very idea of a red-light district in Lusk. There was not a public gambling-and-dance left in the little town or any other of these small trade clusters. They may have flourished in the old days but were there any now I should surely know it. Nothing like that could be kept hidden, I was sure.

The Madam was hunting for an oil or mining town with sheepherders and cowboys; and easterners coming and going. That was a large order. Back east, there was lots of talk about oil in Casper, she said. If only she could strike an oil boom. She had heard that Casper was a wide-open western town.

Casper was a live place, I replied. A mecca of sheepherders and stockmen; and there was a good deal of excitement over the oil. But I was not interested in oil booms, I gave her to understand. Nor Houses.

At Node Siding, a man got on and took her vacant seat so there was no escape. For a time, the woman sat silent, listening to a group of homeseekers in front of us.

Then, "Seems like everybody you meet is taking up land. Now – I'm just thinking. My girls might get land on the side, if they could find claims near a good town. Rest out there in the day -- nice and quiet -- and come to town at night. A lot of people have claims, a man on the train told me, and work in town."

That would be a reversal of the regular procedure in which staying on a claim nights constituted making it a home. I fell to thinking of the technicality and how it would be interpreted under the Homestead Rulings.

"You know, dearie," the woman decided, "I'd like to have a piece of land myself -- for a home. Got to look out for the rainy day, you know. Running a 'house' for twenty years is no snap."

She would go on to Casper. If she did not like Casper, she may go to Deadwood. Deadwood was always "good."

I advised Deadwood. Deadwood, South Dakota, the bonanza of wide-open gambling, of saloons; of prostitutes and dance halls, the bonanza of Parker Alice and Calamity Jane that would make those of Alaska in the gold rush look like a Sunday school. E. L. Senn, the newspaper king for whom I had run my first newspaper, was publisher of the Deadwood Telegram. He was throwing all his money and influence into cleaning up Deadwood. I suspected he would make short work of a new House with "a bunch of rough-and-ready girls."

"Well, goodbye dearie," the Madam said as the train pulled into Lusk, "Good luck."

I gave a righteous lift of my head and drew my chaste skirts close as I squeezed past her to the aisle. Then impulsively I turned back. The woman sat lax, a tired, pitiable looking object.

"You can find free land around Deadwood," I told her. "In the Black Hills. A lovely place to settle down."

The train was starting up.

"Bless you, dearie," she called after me in her hard coarse voice.

Out on the frontier one was prone to look upon life from a broad viewpoint. Just another soul, I mused, whose trail had crossed my own and led on, out of sight. Per chance -- who knew in this strange land -- they may cross again someday. Or never.

In Lusk, I went straight to the boarding house to tell my father of my new plans and to see how they were getting along in their new venture. But he and Carrie had gone to the homestead that day leaving the Roszells (of the Peoria settlers) in charge. The Roszells were old friends of the family. Charlie had contracted a plumbing job and his wife Emma was helping to run the boarding house. The folks were doing pretty well so far, she said.

I found no one to buy my newspaper. I may have to discontinue it. When I got home Angel was waiting for me. People has been coming and going all day, she reported.

"What did they want," I asked, "anything important?"

"Several women dropped in while they were in town just to see how we were getting along. A man wanted your opinion about a certain point in the land law -- he can't get any plowing done the first year, and could you tell the government how it was? He'll make it up next year. And -- O, yes! There's a group that want to talk to you about getting the Commissioners to make a public road through here. They're tired of following cow trails to town."

"Just one of those days, Angel," I answered.

"I think it's wonderful though, don't you? People coming to you for things?" Angel said brightly and I did not have the nerve to tell her that night about Washington.

I wrote to the Department in Washington accepting the position upon which further information and usual red-tape would follow.

I was working at the press when suddenly I heard a wild baying of dogs and the next moment, a pack of greyhounds came over the ridge like a bunch of antelope. They ran off the trail leaping, baying, scaring a bevy of grouse along the fence. In due time, Tom Bell appeared riding leisurely out of the draw on a small, bay cowpony the white angora chaps, twenty-gallon white hat, and silver spurs dazzling against the gray-brown plain.

Watching the approach of the squat rotund man in his royal cowman regalia I remarked to Angel, "Behold! Napoleon rides."

He called me to the door, whistled to the hounds. I went running. The hounds came back leaping. We all stood waiting, I in the door, the hounds in a semi-circle around their master.

"You gals seen anything of a couple of stray cowpokes? Supposed to be loading cattle down here at the pens."

I turned and relayed the question to Angel. She had not seen them. I assured him we had not corralled his cowboys.

"Well, I'm not sure -- a couple of them are pretty badly stuck on that girl you got in there."

This, so Angel could hear.

Then in a lower voice, "What's this I hear about you vamoosing?"

I ran the word rhetorically through my mind.

"To decamp."

"A forced get-away."

It did not fit the dignity that should be accorded my departure.

"How did you find out, Mr. Bell?" I asked him.

"O, things leak out. Trying to sell your paper in Lusk, weren't you?"

Stockmen seemed to know about it.

I told him about the government appointment. Why was I going? Need one ask? A higher position, more room for achievement and recognition.

"And more money," he interjected.

Was he thinking of the day but a few months gone when he had solicited the few paltry dollars in subscriptions among his cowhands to keep me going?

"I like you, Miss Printer," he had said that day, "because you're not a quitter."

The dogs lay down with their front legs outstretched, heads up, alert, waiting for their master to move on.

"A higher position? Washington is not so high," he said in a droll humor mixed with irony, "a few hundred feet or so. You're a mile high here. More room for doin' things. That town of Washington is only a little corral compared to the range. And doing what a fellow wants to do is the main thing. Hell, I wouldn't trade places with Rockefeller. Nor the

153

president. Well, I got to get these hounds after them damned punchers if Angel in there ain't got 'em lariated."

He picked up the rein from the saddle horn. The dogs were on their feet. He gave another whistle. They gave a leap over the barbwire fence back of the town as the cowman rode around it, and went running over the prairie, the two vicious-looking bloodhounds scenting ahead.

The most profane talking man on the range, folks said of Tom Bell, and the biggest hearted.

I was making preparations to get away, hoping to the last minute that I could dispose of the newspaper. As I gathered up my personal belongings, my resolve to make the change was strengthened by the realization that I had nothing worth taking anywhere. No gewgaws.[11]

My worldly possessions consisted of the dinky shack, a dinky printing outfit, and a mortgaged homestead in Dakota. With good crops there this year, I had been offered three thousand dollars for my hundred and sixty. But I had not sold -- it was a nest egg.

Someone was in the office. I stepped out, drawing the curtains to the little room behind me.

"Hello, Mr. Miller," I greeted the dry farmer. "How's the sick wife?"

The Millers were such solid folks -- had come from Canada -- good farmers.

The elderly man shook his head.

"She's a very sick woman. Just doesn't get any better. A decline the doctor says. Come to ask about that leave of absence. May have to take the wife where she can get better care."

"I'll send in the application," I assured him. "I'm sorry about Mrs. Miller."

I remembered the day a group of landseekers and I had stopped at the Millers and the friendly couple had persuaded us to stay to dinner.

While we were talking another settler came in.

"Thought I'd ride up and see about getting that school down by Prairie Center. We do need it."

---

[11] Geegaws are cheap, showy jewelry or ornaments on clothing.

I invited him to sit down. He looked at his soiled overalls and jumper.

"Well, I'm pretty dirty. Been putting casing in the well," he said.

"O, never mind that, Mr. Gray. Why -- yes, I have been working for that school but the county is low on school funds."

The two men talked together.

"We got to push harder for herd laws, too. Sheep ate my stack of oats last night," Gray remonstrated.

"Our only chance, the older man replied, "is to get a county, and county officials of our own!"

"But you settlers must get out and fight for those things," I carped.

"Of course," Gray agreed, "we are ready to put our shoulders to the wheel, any way we can. But we have to have a leader -- like The Progress. And the settlers have had no time with their noses to the grindstone twelve, sixteen, hours a day."

Miller spoke to me.

"O, yes! Some of the neighbors want to know when we are going to start a protest against the high freight rates -- gosh, the money we've paid to these railroads."

Abruptly I turned to the man. "But -- I won't be here!"

There, that was over.

"What! Why what's the matter?"

"Nothing. Only I'm going with the Land Department in Washington. I can do a lot for the settlers there."

They looked at me as though I were a stranger, trying to comprehend.

"Washington!" Miller said with finality. "What do those fellows in Washington know about our problems out here?"

Washington was at the other end of the world from Wyoming.

They went out together. With folded hands (rough ink-stained hands), I watched the two men ride across the railroad track, across the Running Water beyond, and move on to the south. Salt of the earth, those men, and of the blood which had made America. My own father, too, was of the salt and the blood. And the two young boys and all the younger folk who must stay because there were no more frontiers.

I sat by the window gazing fixedly across the great expanse. The moon came up, a great golden disk, while the sun's rays still lighted the range enveloping it in an awesome glow. The two settlers parted on the trail and passed from sight over the hill. A bunch of antelope grazed peacefully along the gentle slope.

Beauty? Art? What would an artist not give to catch it all on canvas. And what could be more romantic? Homes in the making, new worlds in the building. The whole scheme fired by that Infinite spirit which held families -- and countries -- together.

Thick soft rugs -- who wanted thick rugs with miles of earth softly carpeted in green; or snow white; or in the Fall tones of yellows and browns, with grass that gave life and strength to its herds, and to its wild life, even in dead of winter.

Blue velvets, pink chiffons? Look at those skies. And in the spring the wildflowers of every hue! And blue and pink ginghams to adorn oneself were freshly pretty after all.

Who wanted rites and artificial lights which oft times blinded one's eyes to the light; and to real values. And could I -- after seeing the financial struggles of pioneers -- could I ever live among those who spent lavishly, extravagantly, for things that were not needed for preservation, or for comfort?

I tried to make myself believe that in this new position I could accomplish more than I could with my frontier newspapers. But at heart I knew the work would be too impersonal and not at sufficiently close range.

Lone Star had said, "You won't do as much harm in bigger fields, won't be herdin' at such close range."

Here I knew every man, woman and child for miles around. Knew their struggles, their joys, their achievements and how much money they had, almost to the dollar and how they were going to use it.

And what a picture those settlers were making on the background of the once empty range. I had watched every stroke of the brush of Progress put there. Each day the landscape had taken on new body, new color, added touch here and there. How unceasing, untiring were their efforts to make of the work a masterpiece. A masterpiece for the Creator.

I wanted to see the picture finished.

There were many who would be glad to fill that Washington post. Few, if any, who could (or would) take my place here.

The night came on and the stars came out, still I sat motionless, hands loosely folded in my lap, until I heard a loud, drawling voice across the plain singing:

"Bu-ry me out on the lo-o-ne Prair-ree ...
Where the dewdrops fall and the butterfly rests
The wild rose blooms on the prairie's crest.
Where the coy -- otes howl and the wind sports free
They laid him there on the lo-one pr-parie."

It was Lanky, coming to help turn out the paper. And the form not on the press. I jumped up and lighted the lamps. I'd have to get things percolating.

At midnight the paper was printed. Physically exhausted, I threw myself on the cot with half my clothes on and all the printers' ink that would not come off with cold water. But I was filled with a heavenly sense of peace. Out here on the Great Plain, the flock was still safe in the fold. The Ninety and Nine.

And the one!

Next day, I wrote to Senator Warren.

And so, I let the golden Star of Opportunity float by -- and set -- while I turned my eyes once more to the sod.

Senator Frances E. Warren once had written me as a proponent of the homesteader, "It is a great field in which the laborers are few."

I wrote to him, stressing my appreciation of his efforts in my behalf -- most of all his recognition of my work -- explaining my decision in his own words.

Chapter XVI
HERE COME THE WOMEN

I was alone in the printshop when a settler from an outlying district came in. He was so excited he could scarcely talk.

At last, he stammered, "My shack is gone!"

"Gone?" I exclaimed, "What do you mean -- burned down?"

"No. We were in Harrison last night and when we got back our home was gone."

He is probably drunk, I decided as I asked, "What became of it?"

"That is what I have come to find out -- if anyone has seen my shack moving across the prairie."

No one had. It had mysteriously disappeared in the middle of the night with everything in it. There were fresh wheel tracks around the place, but they had been lost in the crisscross trails.

I was as puzzled as he.

"You never had trouble with the range men," I parried.

"No -- but we all have good grassland out there. It breaks off quite a strip of winter range."

Another settler, the report came, had returned home after several days absence to find his fence down, his stock missing; his shack torn to pieces and scattered over the prairie. Shacks disappeared like magic in the middle of dark nights while owners were absent, particularly those who had gone on their leaves of absence, boarding up windows and doors before leaving. It was generally said that the missing abodes were put on wheels and rolled onto the range pastures to "cover up" open land. A furnished shack on it would lead a home seeker to believe that piece of land already had been filed on.

A seeker may have found a choice claim with a waterhole or with a creek running through it, but next day there would be a shack on it. Large areas of open range were being "covered" by emergency filings or without being filed upon at all and thus shacks, ready-built, came in handy.

There were many others than range men in that heyday of settlement who needed shacks. Homesteaders proving up or building larger homes sold their original shanties to newcomers. And -- shacks were shacks, thousands of them built so similar that even the owner could not identify his own except at close range. The more cautious appropriators left the household goods behind. Too, there were poor settlers desperately needing shacks to hold the land who might take one if he could get it without being caught. But they were few and regardless of inclination they would not dare to take the risk, being surrounded as they were by other settlers.

We knew the more reputable stockmen of that section had no part in the thievery that had broken into mayhem. They, also, had begun to suffer encroachment from outsiders who popped up in the West like mushrooms to get into the stock business before the last of the free range was gone. Employees of cattle and sheep growers were trying to get a start of their own and not a few were reputed to have gotten it with their employers, sheep and cattle.

However, with self-preservation, the law not only of nature but of the range, there were stockmen of good standing who considered it their right to devise their own means of ousting the usurpers.

Law? The range was its own law. The outlawry had been committed largely in outlying districts not so thickly settled but the homesteaders had gotten together and were talking of forming a vigilance committee. The Progress published the notice and without our knowing what effect it may have had or if it had brought investigators in, the outlawry gradually died down.

But, as the Cheyenne Daily had said of my name, "That Eudora gets our goat," Wyoming was about to get mine.

One night I lay meditating and somehow my thoughts turned to Grandma Ammons. She had been a pioneer woman. She could neither read nor write but she was intelligent and filled with the wisdom of life. I remember her as a strong and placid woman with her silver hair crowning a character-lined face, her hands lying calmly in her lap or pushing her knitting needles in and out of the yarn. As young Maria Lockhart, she had been a belle of the countryside down in Tennessee where she had married Thomas Jefferson Ammons and she had followed him into the timbered wilderness of Illinois – "the Mississippi Bottoms." She had died at eighty-four with the admonition to her three young granddaughters -- Ida Mary and me and our cousin, Belle Maddux -- that the greatest achievement for women was a good husband, a home and a family.

"It was meant to be that way."

I was thinking now of the peace and security that this would bring. A remote homestead, perhaps, with a gurgling creek and the love and protection of a staid man. A quiet calm affection that ripened with children and with the land. Like these thousands of settler women. Ida Mary was happy and content.

But any alliance for me must not be passive nor commonplace. It would have to be as all-possessing as the land, the earth, itself. That loose tar-paper on the roof was flapping again, like spirits knocking -- I must have a new roof put on after election.

Then one day, of all things, I was informed that my printshop had been made the polling place. It was the only available quarters for that precinct. And on Election Day, it had become a Tammany Hall.

Everybody in that part of the range had turned out. Settlers not qualified to vote could talk. They met in groups, men and women, conversing earnestly. The votes were heavier than we had counted upon.

Angel, trying to keep track of the voters, was flushed with excitement, her eyes shining. I seemed to see her for the first time in long struggling weeks. Burleigh Blanch Humphrey was beautiful.

Mitchell, reporting news from the outside was elated over the settler strength. This day of commotion and tense excitement was worth to him and Angel all the weeks of hard work during the campaign. It stirred their young blood -- they, their people, were a part of all this.

Women's Suffrage was piling up settler votes in Van Tassell and in all the homestead regions of the state.

"If it were not for the danged women -- " petty politicians were heard to say.

Cowboys shambled in, a few voting conscientiously for their bosses, others making crosses hit or miss as though it were a punch-board game while they ruminated on the uselessness of ballots.

"Wear a fellah's fingers plumb out, all this cross-makin'. And Jahosophat! What difference does it make who sits back in some office? Couldn' fix the weather could they, or make the grass grow! Took the 'Big Boss' to run the range."

The cowpoke's business was to haze the critters. They performed their duties faithfully, come day, go day, and thirty dollars or so on pay day. They would still go right along with the cattle, and herders with the sheep and the idea of running a range country with little crosses on paper was too belittlin' for a cowpuncher's outlook.

Stockmen of that district came in, voted, and went home leaving their range bosses or other employees to cast any aspersions. Petty politicians electioneered in the corners of buildings and fences. Candidates mixed with groups in the store or out in the open arguing the stockmen-settler issue, a few discussions coming to blows and no peace officers to stop the show.

For the first time in the new town I saw whiskey bottles openly flourished, as inducement. It if were not for the pesky women mixing and mingling with the men (but the wild west would have been shocked to see women "swigging" liquor), the whiskey vendors might have gotten somewhere, they ranted. But with a law forbidding electioneering within a certain distance of the polls they never got much closer than the hayshed.

While some settlers may have been tempted (for liquor was out of reach in distance and price for the average homesteader), they were not bartering their new heritage for firewater.

That evening the little Tammany Hall on the range was deserted and a group of cowboys started home singing:

"The old gray mare ain't what she used to be
Ain't what she used to be
Ain't what she used to be
The old gray mare ain't what she used to be
Ma -- ny lo -- ong years ago."

Each verse became louder until gradually the rollicking voices died in the distance.

The Fall elections were over and the imperial range country knew that the days of stockmen control were numbered. In Colorado, in Montana, and, yes, in that last and wildest frontier and one of the greatest of all cattle kingdoms -- Wyoming.

We did not expect to win sweeping tangible results. But we had been instrumental in defeating a few adverse candidates and in electing several farm supporters to office. Joe Horton's clique had been defeated.

He was not so pompous now but he gave vent to his fury.

"When it came to a sheep-and-cow country being run by petticoats, it was a damn poor place for a man to stay."

I could not disagree with him wholly. I was not enthusiastic about Woman's Suffrage. It was a godsend to the West in the launching of the new regime, but whether on the whole it would make for better government I did not know. Joe Horton would stay and come out next year, I wagered, on the dry-farmer ticket.

The real victory, and the one for which I had made the fight, was to establish the dry-farmer firmly for County Division and as a future influence in public affairs.

Despite the fact that my father was Thomas Jefferson Ammons III, I still was a non-partisan. And I cannot remember that he talked about Party affiliation in that day. Gradually, however, through my broader experience I became an Anti. Anti-political. I found the farmers could build straighter line-fences by supporting whatever measures were best for the people and for the country regardless of their Party brand.

I had learned that the great majority of our frontier statesmen (men like Warren, Mondell, Smoot, Borah) and the West itself were strongly Republican.

The strength of the Party in the West was an outcome of the Civil War of Unionists and Non-Unionists, with the Northerners, Republicans and with the Southerners, Democrats. But it was more than that. It was the Republican leadership which largely had promoted the West's growth and its policies and laws -- among them, the Protective Tariff, especially on wool, which had done much toward promoting the livestock industry.

President Theodore Roosevelt had great faith in the West and had done a great deal to promote its growth and protect its interests. Taft and other Republican presidents had fostered settlement. Anyhow, so far as the subject relates to this epoch and epic, the most phenomenal development in our history came under Republican administration. And the World War I under a Democratic regime -- which may have been a happenstance, or was it?

After all, parties were only men who make them and statesmen must come first, for upon them the fate of a country hangs.

The State Chairman of the Committee on Public Lands notified me of a meeting to be held at Douglas, where certain phases of the Homestead Project were to be discussed.

He said, "Senator Warren and other of your friends hope to meet you there. In the meantime, let's forget the political abuse."

The range was beginning to accept me, like blizzards and cactus -- things that had to be endured. But, a part of it.

And now I knew innately and without analysis of the fact, that I could lead homesteaders to victory. It was as intangible as the forces of nature about me. Like knowing the grass would grow and the sun set.

But I knew that I could lead a people.

This is one of the original photos Edith had taken of the "Sodbreakers."

Chapter XVII
THE STARS IN THEIR EYES

I had worked hard that year and life on the high and dry Wyoming plain was drastic. For weeks my nerves had been keyed to high pitch and I had mistaken the tense, exhilarated energy and strength. With the letdown came physical reaction. I was like the old flivvers that came through loaded down with homestead baggage and couldn't pull through -- chugging, stopping, spurting on again, at last stalled -- out of gas.

I stayed in bed several days at Mother Van's homestead with Jean and Brother Dick's girl to wait on me and Mother Van to fix her good, old, German dishes. When I was called back to the office on an urgent matter, I was so light-headed, I had to lie down in the back seat of the car. Those light-headed spells? Must be the altitude, I explained them away.

Angel in her cheerful way relieved me of every possible detail and Catherine dosed out her nux-vomica, "best tonic in the world. Six drops before each meal and if you are not stronger in a few days we may increase it to eight."

"Like getting a race horse ready for the ring," I laughed as I accepted all the coddling.

Dr. Priest of Harrison (Nebraska) came.

"Sound as a dollar, just not built for the rigors and hardships of a raw country," he said.

Dr. Priest was one of the most able, young, country doctors in the West. He covered a large territory and spent most of his time on the trail. I did not have to give him my life history and pedigree and he knew what I had been doing out here.

"You burn up too much energy," he scolded.

But I argued that I conserved my energy as I went, did not work hard like a homesteader's wife. Why should I be lacking in stamina, with no physical ailment?

"That is only physical energy you conceive. You need ease and comforts. Better give up this kind of life."

Where would I go to find leisure and ease and comfort? I had no green pastures to graze around in. I should have to fight this out right here. I would not be defeated. Give up as a weakling now, when I had come this far? After I had fought so many other forces? I had come west largely to gain health and strength and I had more resistance now than when I came.

"No, Doctor, my place is here. Where would I go?"

Well, that was a problem to be considered.

He ordered rest. A tonic, good food, sleep. Same old story.

I slept long nights from utter exhaustion and woke up unrefreshed. I was lying on the couch one Sunday morning in the small living room of the shop when my father came.

He sat down beside the couch and said, "How are you, Edie?" in that compassionate tone he had used when I was a little girl down on the Illinois farm and had just lost my mother.

"Heard Doc was here. What did he say?"

"That I will be all right. Just overdone, I guess. But (I must have been sick to have said it) I feel sick like that time I kept walking around with typhoid not knowing I had it. Same feeling in my head."

"Could you drink some good fresh milk?"

Milk! I had not tasted fresh milk since I came to Wyoming. In that land of a million cattle fresh milk was as scarce as sea food. Other than a very few settlers who had a milk cow or two, the people used condensed milk. I was not fond of milk to drink; but now I felt a longing for good, cold, nourishing milk. I turned to my father.

"Yes, I would like to have some. But that's like asking a child if he wants the moon, isn't it?"

"I'll bring you fresh milk. You didn't know we had milk cows, did you?" he said in the expansive mood of one bringing a happy surprise.

"Milk cows? Why -- Dad!"

In the spontaneity of the moment, I had called him Dad instead of Papa.

"Tom Bell came over the other day; wanted to know if I could take a few of his cows for the winter. He will pay me to feed them and we can have all the milk we want. Bell says the Running Water Divide out here is the best winter range in the state."

"I think we are well located," I replied.

"I've made a deal to run a bunch of heifers for him on the halves next spring -- all I have pasture for and we can run Free's land too for he has no stock."

Bell had told my father "You danged dry-farmers took my open range and now, by Jesus, I've got to give you part of my cattle to get a little grass for the rest of them."

A hell of a note! We both laughed.

It was late afternoon when I saw him coming down the trail walking in his brisk gait, carrying a gallon pail.

"Now this is fine milk, Edie," he enthused as he put the bucket on the table and sat down to rest.

"Papa! You walked."

There was a big lump in my throat. I never had been able to think of that simple act of devotion without a lump in my throat.

I had eaten but little food that day. I poured out a glass of milk and sipped it. It was fresh and rich and delicious.

"This should give me strength. I'm so glad to get it," I said gratefully. "But you should not have walked all that way to bring it. A four- mile walk for a gallon of milk."

"O, shucks. I've walked it before. The boys had to go to Lusk with the team to be in school tomorrow. I'll catch a ride home."

"I've just been thinking," he said. "Next spring when these heifers come fresh, I am going to milk some and sell the cream. I was looking today in a mail order catalog at a cream separator, I can get it on payments."

There was constant demand for milk and cream in the new West. It could be shipped to Omaha or Denver, so my father said. I know nothing about markets.

"Could it be made profitable?" I queried.

"Of course it can," he declared. "We have plenty of good water; and any grass that will fatten beef will produce milk. The settlers can raise enough grain at least to feed a few cows through the winter, and have a little money coming in regular."

"Well, I must be going before it gets dark on me. I'll be back in a few days with more milk."

Perhaps Tom Ammons had served his country, too, that day. He had brought not only milk but the idea of a dairy industry for the colonists. Fresh milk for the people. Money for the homesteaders to buy groceries and other necessities. Why, that was wonderful! I effused. Could be promoted right along with the following plan! I got up, and grabbed pencil and paper. Laid them down. Some other time. I was too weary.

Milking cows on the range! What would the stockmen say? That would be adding insult to injury.

My sharpest battle still lay before me -- that between will-power and physical lack, and the conflict was wearing me out. In my dealings with strong men and hard counties, I must not be branded as a weakling – if a critter could not keep up with the herd, it just lay down and died. Not only critters but women had to keep going. It was the law of the range. Nervous breakdowns in those days and especially on the frontier were looked upon as a luxury if not a disgrace.

So I was hiding and denying my physical debility as a woman her moral shame, girding myself up to meet the public and to perform my duties. And in the final analysis, who shall say which is the greater sin -- violation of the physical, or the moral laws? But I had not wantonly wasted strength nor used it for self-indulgence, I excused myself. But conflict within oneself, I decided, wore one. I would let myself go with the tide.

One day, a cowboy came into my shop to "have a palaver[12] with the skirt printer," and as I emerged from my inner sanctum, he took one look at me and said, "Maybe you oughta send for the soul-saver."

"Never mind about a soul-saver, Shorty. What's the palaver?"

"A shindig out at the Box X. Maybe the folks round-about would like to come. Going to have all the trimmin's" (which meant music and plenty to eat.)

I hesitated. "How come the settlers to be invited?" I asked.

I was afraid of trouble. The Box X was one of the most noted outfits in the state.

"O, no, Ma'am," Shorty said. "We are not invitin' anybody. We're just tellin' folks. Everybody in the county comes to Box X doin's -- dance all night in the big barn loft with plenty of eats, and come home day after, so as they won't get lost.

---

[12] Prolonged discussion, idle talk

The owner of the Box X lived in Montana. It had become a Montana corporation -- and the "corporation" wouldn't be on hand to make trouble at a hoedown, I decided.

"You see," Shorty explained, "we're short o' women out that way and all these homestead gals would be more than welcome."

I had been to many such affairs but it would be something new for the colonists. Angel, Catherine, and all the "girls" from sixteen to sixty were to receive a howlin' welcome. Families, too, hitched up and started out before sundown to the old Box X to "shake a leg" to two fiddles, and a guitar, and a banjo -- and of all things an accordion! One would think it was the covered wagon days, the amused city folk said, dancing to an accordion! But the colonists had the time of their lives.

No range war nor enmity toward settlers could keep social fences up between young folk, and the range country was not one to maintain social barriers of any kind for long. The settlers began to have neighborhood parties and dances when the fall work was done and the dull season came on. But community gatherings were of little interest to me now.

At the boarding house in Lusk, I lazed around, ate three square meals a day, and spent hours in the warm sunshine that became piercing in midday. Mitchell and Thomas Jr., going off to school, looked like little boys with their fair skin scrubbed and light hair combed sleek. In the caps and knickers they had worn in St. Louis, they appeared quite citified I told them. They would like to have long pants now, but they must wear out the short ones.

"You see, Sis," Mitchell explained, "There were two pairs of pants with this gray suit I got when I graduated from eighth grade last year."

A two-pants suit did have its disadvantages, I decided. But clothes were clothes on a homestead.

"When I go onto The Progress next summer," the boy said proudly, "I'll have me a long-pants suit with a vest."

"And I'll make you assistant editor," I added, encouraging his youthful zeal.

Back at the printshop I sought quietly for a physical energy to keep up with that of my mind and spirit. Fighting often weakened the resistance of a man -- or a nation.

169

I wondered if there were any place where the Autumn smiled so broad and bright as on the frontier. Those days of warmth and sparkle turned one's thoughts to life as Spring to love. In harmony with Nature, I turned my own will to life, and followed the stars in their course.

I watched the herds of antelope round themselves up for the winter, the flocks of geese fly south. Even the stray cattle voluntarily came in from the isolated spots to face the winter together. Stockmen knew that straggling critters missed in the roundups would come in of their own accord when winter came. Both wild and domestic life in the animal world moved in unison, and in concord with the universal forces of preservation.

From this basic principle for all life, my own idea of cooperation among settlers was strengthened, not dreaming it would be applied to great bodies of men through the Cooperative System which was to become a gigantic factor in the West's development.

I returned to the shop one day to find Angel talking to an attractive, clean-cut, young man. Her face was radiant. Her fiancé of whom she so often talked, had come. They were school-day sweethearts and the young man (I do not recall the name) was attending college. I was almost as elated as the girl herself and it was plain to be seen they were deeply in love with each other. He was taking up a claim in another district.

He stayed a week and after he had gone, I noticed the girl was brooding and one night when I asked her if they were to be married soon, she had answered, "No. Not soon. And maybe -- never!"

Her face was drawn and her lips tight-set.

What could have happened? Had they quarreled, or had he jilted her? I put my arm around her.

"Angel dear, tell me."

She leaned her head in her hands and wept. He was ill, she moaned, suffering with a chronic stomach ailment for which he had found no cure. He had been ordered to quit college and his finances soon would be exhausted. There was but little chance for his recovery she feared.

"But -- I will wait and pray," she declared.

If he improved, they would be married next year and go on to the homestead together.

Mother Van was going back to Peoria for the five months leave of absence and the man from the Land Office who had paid her a farewell visit was at the train to see her off. She looked quite regal in her black traveling coat and hat and the diamond-drop earrings. Her hands were roughened by work but her eyes were bright and her hair still brown and soft as silk. I caught the admiring look of the staid official as he helped her onto the train. And suddenly, I wondered if his visit had been entirely in the interest of public lands.

Mother Van leaned out the coach window. "I'll be back in the Spring. Who said I'd never prove up on a homestead?"

Son Leport had gone back to run his dental office. The Wattses and others who still owned homes or businesses back east returned for the winter and many of the tradesfolk at Van Tassell went to live on their claims in the dull season, either closing up shop or curtailing operations.

It was a Sunday afternoon, unusually warm for the time of year. (It was that year I think when the settlers ate Thanksgiving dinner with shack doors open.) The little town was deserted. I had eaten dinner with Catherine at the Chow Palace and she was washing clothes. We were wondering what we could do to break the monotony when I looked up, startled, to see a Gypsy girl in a bright, paisley shawl standing in the door.

"Tell your fortune, lady?"

She had seen only me from the doorway. She took a step forward, her full-gathered skirt swishing. Catherine turned from her dishpan.

"Your past, present -- and future. Feefty cents," the Gypsy pleaded.

Where had she come from? There was no one, nothing, in sight. It was as though she had dropped from the skies.

She wore a bright, silk scarf wrapped tight around her head and tied at the back, Gypsy fashion, and large circular earrings dangled from her ears.

"Cross palm with silver piece? Bring you luck -- " she held out her brown hand to Catherine.

We were eager as two children. This would be fun, to break the loneliness. She was a fake, of course. No good fortune teller would be traveling through a poor homestead country, and fifty cents was too much, Catherine argued.

"You got no feefty cents?" the Gypsy frowned. "A quarter?"

Catherine wiped her hands, took a quarter from the tin can in the cupboard and laid it in the girl's hand. Looking around the corner of the house I saw a band of gypsies waiting down by the corrals -- two covered wagons, a rusty dilapidated car, bony horses. They were headed south -- probably trading horses along the way.

Catherine's fortune was nondescript, each of us bantering, asking questions, trying to place the light-haired woman who would "make trouble." She would get her land proved up, the Gypsy said in answer to Catherine's question and there was money coming from a distance. At that, we broke out laughing for every month Catherine received a check through the mail, refusing to divulge the source, or amount -- which must have been very small for she was always hard-up. The "mystery money," Angel called it; and I, "the alimony check." We knew, however, as the land office records showed that Catherine Lemmon had not been married.

Catherine's fortune finished, the girl turned to me.

"You got feefty cents? Tell you more for feefty cents. Cross my palm with half-dollar. Bring you good luck ..."

"No," I said. "Only a quarter."

I would pay when she was finished. Crossing her hand with the silver could not bring luck, I declared. She muttered something in native tongue and shook her head.

Then suddenly, she was kneeling beside me, tracing the lines in my palm. The frigid ends of the vari-colored scarf hung long over her left shoulder, the full-gathered skirt making a circle on the floor around her.

"Long lifeline. See!" She traced the line around the thumb to the wrist.

"You will travel – far ... People. I see people."

She shut her eyes as though envisioning things not in the palm.

"You will lead many, Senorita, -- so ver' many. In bands, like the Gypsies."

There were other, trivial, things I could not remember.

"And meet a dark man, and have lots of money," I supplied satirically.

She was bent low over my hand again and with no sign of having heard me she looked up with a darting flash of the black, beady eyes.

"Death! I -- see death!"

I pushed her aside.

"You expect me to pay you for telling me that? Get out."

She was doing this out of spite because I had refused to cross her hand with a half-dollar.

Angrily she grabbed my hand again, pressed my fingers back in her strong grasp to scan the lines more closely.

"You'll see Senorita! You -- see! Ver' love one. Ver' dear. Before flowers bloom again ..."

I gave her the quarter. Inclined to be superstitious, I was depressed and it was with relief that I watched the caravan move on.

"She just told you that because she was mad," Catherine said.

"Of course," I agreed. "But I wish she hadn't."

Then like a bad dream that haunts one for a few days and is forgotten, the Gypsy's warning faded from my mind.

A gray sky hung low with a threat of snow in the air. I threw on a sweater and took a walk along the white cliffs back of the town. I loved the feel of moisture in the air, the sting of cold around my ankles. With presage[13] of a storm, horses went capering, kicking up their heels, calves went frisking; a big buck antelope held his head high shaking his long antlers. My blood tingled and I ran, trying to keep up with my <u>vagabond</u> spirit, until I was out of breath.

I sat down on a sun-warmed butte to rest. An early dusk would soon be settling from the cloudy skies and the range seemed deserted. It was there that Lone Star found me. He was so much a part of the surroundings that I felt no surprise at seeing him. Our greeting was casual, as usual. He had seen me as he came to the village and had ridden on.

He dismounted, and stood beside me leaning against his horse, his arm hooked over the saddle horn.

"You are late going south, aren' you, Lone Star?"

"I'm not takin' a herd south. Joinin' up with one of the big spreads in Texas for the winter."

"I expected you sooner. The geese already have gone through," I jested.

---

[13] An omen, a foreboding

He left his horse and sat down beside me, explaining his prolonged absence. Tired of the hub-bub around him he had ridden on to Canada only to find people flocking to the land -- not so fast, maybe, as in the states but they were plowing up the Canadian Northwest, he told me.

"The landgrabbers are taking the West – there's no use ..." he sighed resignedly.

"It's progress, Len. The Lord would not have made all this productive land to lie empty," I said soberly.

I gave him back his advice to me on what to do if caught in a stampede.

"When you are caught in a stampede, Lone Star," I mimicked his solemn mein, "the thing to do is jump on a critter's back and go along with the herd."

He slowly rolled a cigarette, moistened it with his lips -- held it in one hand, the unlighted match in the other.

"I -- did. I filed on a homestead."

He said it with the finality of a desperate man confessing a crime to which he had been driven.

"Len! You didn't. Where?"

"Montana. Snowy Mountain country. Two days' ride from railroad. An isolated spot in a green valley -- with springs gushin'."

I envisioned the country as he described it. The Snowy Mountains, secluded valleys, sweeping plains.

"I may go there someday," I said idly. "A lot of development going on in Montana."

"Well, don't take that newspaper shebang to Montana! It's a hard country. Guess you've had enough trouble, here."

I turned to him and in the earnestness of appeal, I laid my hand on his arm, felt the muscles strong as whipcord raise under the touch.

"Len! Prove up on the claim. While you can get free land. You must."

"I'll try. But there are landgrabbers strayin' in close already. It'll be mighty lonesome hemmed in with people --"

With the dusk, early stars broke through the black sky and a pale moon pushed through the clouds and cast a silver band of light on the upper shelf of the cliff where we sat, lighting our faces like a soft spotlight, leaving the lower shelf below us in shadow. We sat enrapt. This time it was he who broke the silence and there was a plaintive softness in his voice.

"Sometimes I ride all night -- just the moon and the stars and my horse, and me. I can't explain it but just seems like the world is a part of the sky -- or Heaven, as you call it."

"O, yes, I understand. I felt like that at my first sight of the West with its spaces stretching to the horizon. I have felt it many times, this Oneness. But you -- you don't believe in Heaven, do you?" I asked.

He pondered the question.

"Well, this frontier and the open life is all the Heaven I want – it's good enough for me."

"I love it, too, Len. The bigness, the solitude, the -- the divinity."

"Yes, but these landgrabbers are a ruining it."

I had often heard him lament this fact.

"Oughta be some place left like the Big Boss made it," he remarked.

Filled with desire to know what had developed this unusual character, I pleaded with him to tell me something of his life and himself. I wondered what name had gone into the land records when he filed on a claim. But that did not matter. "Lone Star Len" was good enough for me.

He took a few extra puffs of the cigarette and threw it away, crushing the fire out beneath his boot heel as he sat with hands loosely clasped around his knees.

"Nothin' to tell," he said simply. Born on a Texas range. My father killed by a gang o' rustlers for squealin' on 'em, -- I was just a little kid. And my mother died soon after, from poverty and grief, I guess. She cottoned to the open spaces, too. After she was gone, I found some right pretty clothes, and old letters and painted pictures in her trunk. She was an artist. Had come out from the East a young girl to marry my father."

He stopped, apologetic.

"You're the only one I've ever told these things to -- "

"Yes -- go on. Then what?"

"Lived among the ranchers 'till I was big enough to ride. Rode the plains ever since. Never any trouble to get a job with the cattle outfits -- "

He straightened up. His voice became hard and bitter. "Then I set out to get all the horse thieves and cattle rustlers I could find. Worked for the big outfits that were losing cattle."

Now I knew he was the man whom the cowboy, Tex, had told about.

"Quick on the draw -- rustlers don't fool with him," Tex had said.

"One time, he lassoed a couple of rustlers and dragged them in."

And so, I said now, "And you generally get your man."

"Well, the outlaws don't trouble to get in my way."

I looked at him and saw only a quiet young man who liked to ride under the stars. In the dim light, his face expressed a great calm and a loneliness.

There was a biting cold in the nightfall that stirred one's blood. I shivered and Lone Star took his leather coat from the saddle strap, put it around my shoulders, and at his touch a tingle ran through me that was not from the cold and the vibration carried me far away.

Was this the magic of the spaces -- or of the man? I was ever asking myself that question when his nearness put into me some strange emotion that left an emptiness behind.

A man and a woman in a primeval world. Such would be the love of this man beside me. Isolated spaces, camp fires gleaming, stars hanging low, the caress of the night with the struggling world shut out and only the man and his mate -- and God. That might be all the Heaven one could want.

I rose and shut out the vision. Lone Star walked back with me, Black Indian following behind. The air was vibrant and heady. I stopped, raising my face to the star-studded sky and reached on tiptoe.

"Look. Almost I can touch them."

I pointed to the evening star, big and bright, moving steadily and without a flicker in its course. But the old moon was ominous. Suddenly, I felt myself drawn close, my arms held tightly in Lone Star's grasp. His face bent above my own was tense and the sensitive lips were quivering. I raised my face to his as I had to the heavens and felt the power of his emotion. It ran through my own being like a flash of lightening that blinds

176

and stuns. Then I spoke his name softly, unafraid, and he had pushed me from him.

"Go!" he said, his voice loud and commanding.

"Go -- I tell you!"

In the dim light, the strong lean face was drawn as the lonely look was there.

I heard the sound of flying hoofs. Lone Star had gone and I stood looking after him until he had disappeared into the distance. He would ride all night -- the lone eagle of the plains, going south with the wild geese but he would be back when they flew north again.

He had not kissed me. For two years, I had hoped and wondered if someday the strong, diffident plainsman would kiss me.

I walked slowly the short distance to the little town asleep in the early night, its last glimmering light going out. Already it seemed as settled and civilized as the small, Illinois community where I was reared, and as Ma Wagor back on the Brule would say "monopolous[14] as Blue Springs (her home town) with its Ladies' Aid."

Some new strength pulsed within me. After all, what did we of the superficial world know about living, about life, as they who live with Nature know it? As the lone plainsmen knew it?

I made no attempt to analyze the strange emotion I had felt. It may have been as raw as the earth itself -- but it was very near to the Divine at that.

A star had touched the earth.

---

[14] Boring as well as time-consuming

Chapter XVIII
SHE OF THE UNSUNG SOLDIERS

I was going back to the Brule for the rest of the winter.

Ida Mary had written me to come -- "I want to see you, Sis; want you with me. And you need the change and the rest. I am so happy about Papa," she had added. "He'll find a way to make good. And the boys -- they are little Trojans."

My sister and I never had been apart so long. It was more than a year now since I first crossed the Wyoming border with a band of colonists, and I could hardly wait to see her. I would build up reserve energy for the work ahead.

Next spring there would be another trek to the West with a development of new territory like which no nation ever had seen. Wyoming would sweep into agriculture with potatoes, oats and rye. Rye, the "grain of poverty," was to become a leading sod crop for Wyoming, as flax had been the main sod crop in Dakota. Montana was talking about wheat; the farmers there were sowing winter wheat. Colorado was going into wheat too, and there was talk about fruit and sugar beets and irrigation in that state. Fruit, the very idea! One would think settlers to Colorado had found a Paradise Lost.

Spring, when the great Frontier would blossom again. I was seeing new trails again.

I hired a young newspaper man homesteading across the Nebraska line to come a day or two a week and manage The Progress. Angel would run the office and in emergency Mitchell would help weekends.

In packing, I ran onto Lone Star's gun that he had left with me last summer when the shack-and-stock stealing was going on. He had heard that the hirelings of a West-end outfit was going to move my printshop off some dark night. Either that, or tear it up, so Lone Star had come one day, riding in from the West, to tell me that I'd better "graze close to home" for a while and after he had gone, I found the gun lying on my table. I had buried it deep in the trunk -- more fearful of the weapon than of the marauders.

I ran over to the combination optical-blacksmith shop where Doctor McHale sat grinding a pair of lenses.

I pushed the door open, stuck the pistol in front of him and said, "Put 'em up!"

He wheeled on his stool and threw up his hands in reflex action, stared at me with a blank expression as though he had been shot.

I laughed, "Here, take these slugs out, will you?"

"Why, Edith! I didn't know you kept loaded firearms but in your place, I think it was a good idea."

"A range rider left it one day. I'm afraid of it!"

It was his turn to laugh.

"Well, I'll be danged. You! Afraid to handle a gun," he said, and emptied it.

I put it back in the trunk. I would return it to the owner who would be back when the geese flew north and the wildflowers came again.

It was Christmas Eve when I arrived at Cedarfork where my sister lived. And what a reunion. Cedarfork on the border of the Brule reservation consisted of the old Cedarfork ranch, the store and post office and nearby school.

The old log house was bright and cozy with its wood fires and Christmas trimmings and Yuletide spirit, all the gayer because I had come. Ida Mary and Imbert were getting ready to attend the Christmas party at the schoolhouse and she had her packages done up in red and green paper and tied with Christmas cord to put on the tree for the neighboring children.

It was a real Christmas tree. It had come clear from the Black Hills, and a settler had hauled it out from the state capital, twenty miles or more. Imbert was to play Santa Claus -- well-built and square shouldered, he would make a fine Santa folk said.

Ever since the reservation had been settled (this was the third year) Christmas had been a gala event for the isolated settlers with peace and goodwill abounding. On this Christmas Eve, there were services at the little schoolhouse with carols and impressive presents; with boxes from back home filled with gifts and delicacies that had been made by loving hands. There was a mosquito-bar stocking filled with vari-colored candy for everybody, old and young.

Sleigh bells came ringing over the prairie, and the men with their shaggy, snow-covered clothes all looked like Santa Claus. There were Christmas dinners in humble shacks with friends and neighbors pooling their food and celebrating together. And the star of Bethlehem shone brightly over the virgin plain.

I did not go to the schoolhouse that night. I was tired from traveling and there was a mist in the holiday joy, in my homecoming. The stork was nearer than expected from Ida Mary's letter about it.

Ida, to be a mother! With her small figure, the burnished brown hair in a coronet of braids that framed the oval face; her round blue eyes and the nose that just missed being pug and the open innocent feature -- why, she looked like a schoolgirl. Yet she was sensible and very practical.

Those days that followed were happy ones.

I helped with the cooking and got a thrill from punching down bread dough and watching it pop up again with Imbert saying, "By golly, Sis, you would make a man a pretty good wife after all."

There were long evenings when the three of us would read or sit by the fire munching apples and popcorn as we talked. Days when Imbert was out over the ranch, Ida Mary and I would tend the store which was near the house. The Sioux came frequently to see Paleface-Prints-Paper who was back from the heap-big, hunting grounds of Wyoming.

Somehow, I could not mention the unborn child nor look beyond the hour of its birth but one day, we talked about it at length, reviewing the child's background: Imbert Miller was an only child. Our mother's family had no progeny. She had died young -- in miscarriage and her one brother, Grafton Smith, had passed on while in his prime. They were orphans. Mama had been a teacher and Uncle Grafton a professor in the University of Colorado. As a child, I used to think Uncle Grafton was the most learned man in the world, and my father said he was one of the finest characters he had ever known.

And the Ammonses -- well the Ammons family needed replenishing too. They were a solid, progressive people and the Millers were good substantial ranchers, a little above the average westerner of that district. Thus, the child would have a desirable heritage to start him on his way.

But folks out west paid little attention to lineage. This child should be a son of the Burnt Thigh (The Brule), said those settlers, and conceived along with that new empire by the woman who helped in its development.

But their patriotic pride had no place in my mind. I was anxious. At times, the anxiety became apprehension, but I must not let Ida Mary know. Had she weakened her physical resistance during that period of hard work and hardship? I wondered.

Imbert and I planned on her going to the hospital.

"You can stay with friends in Pierre where you can get to the hospital quickly," we suggested.

But she did not want to do that.

"With the telephone here, we can get the doctor here in an hour or so," she explained.

"If there isn't a blizzard or the roads blocked," I debated.

"You go on so," she chided good-naturedly. "Funny how you stew and fret over personal things -- over your loved one -- and maintain such equanimity in this land-settling business. Think how most of the homestead women are situated -- families crowded into one-room shacks, no conveniences, and out off from help at such times. Pioneer women had their babies on the road, in a covered wagon. Mother Van had a baby in a homestead shack --"

"Yes, but Mother Van was a robust woman who came from sturdy German stock," I reminded her.

"But we have things convenient," Ida Mary argued.

For the prairie country, this home was the height of convenience, even with no water in the house, no bath, no gas or electricity, and the barbwire fence serving in part for a phone line! With a well of water at the door, the house well-furnished and warm, what more did one want?

It was a bright winter morning with the sun shining warm that Ida Mary and I walked the half-mile across Cedar creek to Ben Smith, a squaw-man's ranch. (How could this weather hold out, I kept thinking -- and if a storm should come!)

Ben Smith's wife was an intelligent, educated Indian woman. She would be with my sister during her time. Mrs. Smith had that instinctive knowledge and the practical experience of childbirth which the Indian women possess.

Sauntering home slowly because Ida Mary could not walk fast, we talked of things around us and of more intimate things and of my experiences in Wyoming.

182

"The trouble with us," she deliberated, "is that you undertake too much -- both of us have."

"I know. It just came upon us. There is no order for things in these new countries. I was to run a little newspaper on my claim, and you a post office where we could mail the paper -- and folk would come in after the mail. It was to be an interesting venture. We did not know ..."

"Of course not. How could we!" she finished for me.

"But you did not want to quit when the prairie fires and the water famine came -- and everything."

"No," she replied simply. "We had too many things to do -- and you had your claim to prove up."

She had done what she saw to do under the circumstances and she voiced no regret that she had followed through.

But she cautioned me against overdoing or throwing myself so deeply into my work that I would forget all else.

"You are not the type of woman that a career can satisfy," she said positively.

"Don't worry, when I find the right man we'll go right down the same trail together," I laughed.

Then soberly, "It is you we must think of now and I wish you were going to the hospital."

I might be able to boss a colony of homesteaders or to assume a small bit of authority in Washington. But to Ida Mary, I was the same visionary, high-strung sister who had to be scolded and curbed now and then.

She had felt pretty well through this period and had taken care of herself she assured me. If she felt any uneasiness, she did not show it.

The next morning there was a piercing hard cold but no snow. The Indian woman was working efficiently, stoically. "Doc" Newman of Presho had arrived at daylight and was sending to Ft. Pierre for another doctor and for nurses.

Doctors, white uniforms, the agonizing cry of travail ringing through the house. Why did that little Indian boy keep sitting under Ida Mary's window like that? His mother had tried to get him home and here he sat in the cold, flat on the ground Indian fashion, immobile as stone.

"Go 'way, Buford!" I shrieked. Then, kindly, "Run on home."

183

But he looked at me with that obstinacy of his race and sat there against the wall like an omen -- like the proverbial dog howling a death warning.

Blindly, I ran up to the old attic over the log store and stared out over the land. It was from this old trading post of Cedarfork that I, a stranger, had stood with a crowd of landseekers who were looking over the vast uninhabited region being opened to the whites. Here on this very spot, said to have been a fort in the Indian war days, the homeseekers had stopped for food and lodging and here it was that I had stood gazing upon the golden empty expanse and said, "To convert this tall-grass domain into homes for the people surely would be a great work."

And the two young girls from St. Louis had broken a trail into it with a homestead shack on wheels and a printing plant, with ambition and hope and youth flaunted high, their heads raised to the far horizon and to the future.

And during this hour of Ida Mary's travail -- that hour when woman goes down into the shadows; that hour in which she becomes a Creator, I besought the Lord to spare this one who had so faithfully labored in His Vineyard. Out here where the world and the heavens ran together, I sent my plea through the Omnipotent spaces.

O, God! Did not she -- and I -- have a right to demand something of this country for all we had put into it! We had hungered and thirsted and, weary, still had gone on.

I asked nothing for myself, only life for her who had consecrated her youth.

"Dear God! I'll work on and on for your multitudes, for your good earth, if you will but spare her. O, God, You are so close! Just over there beyond the sunset, where the Reservation touches the sky. Or take me, if you will -- but let her live. Heavenly Father, take away this cup!"

Bargaining with God again.

And then the doctors saying, "Yes, Ida Mary came through. But the baby is dead."

The baby which was to have grown up to become a trailbreaker of one kind or another was a beautiful, blue-eyed girl.

But -- Ida Mary was here! What else could matter? And after she had rested, she talked to Imbert and me. Ma Wagor was there taking charge of the household. And with every breath my heart sang, "Thank you, God!"

It was late afternoon two days later and Ida Mary was sleeping. Ma Wagor had gone home for a few hours rest; and the nurse was dozing. I sauntered aimlessly down to the henhouse and gathered the eggs. I hadn't gathered eggs since I was a small child. I slipped into Ida Mary's room and she looked up and asked me how many eggs I had gotten and when I told her she seemed pleased over the increase.

As the slanting sun stole through her bedroom window, there came an ominous hush. Then wild incoherent action. The nurse giving orders. Get hot water, quick! I ran to the kitchen. O Lord, make the fire burn quicker -- the water, hotter.

The nurse shooting a needle into my sister's arm. Ammonia! O -- where was that ammonia?

And Ida Mary's voice, faint, breath fast leaving. "On -- the kitchen shelf – Sis ..."

Calm and game and fighting to the last.

I no longer stretched my arms to God. There was no God who would listen to a mere speck of humanity!

On my knees, I wiped up the kitchen linoleum -- with skin milk "to make it bright and shiny" as she had done, and cooked something for the nurse to eat. In a daze, I felt Ma Wagor's sustaining presence, her usual humorous banter hushed.

Weeping, people gathered around as they had done when the trading post had burned down leaving us homeless and I had said to Ida Mary, "We have each other."

And she had added, "And the land. You can't destroy the land. Land is solid."

Kindly Father West was here now and Huey Dunn, our first neighbor in the homestead country, whom I had not seen since the day during the water famine when he had hauled us a barrel of fresh water the long way from his claim at McClure. Huey Dunn had looked after us those first months as he did his own family.

The next Monday morning, a week from the hour Ida Mary and I had sat talking on the bank of the creek, a long caravan headed by a black covered wagon made its way slowly across the Land of the Burnt Thigh.

Like a flash, I saw that Gypsy girl kneeling beside me and heard the echo of her voice: "I -- see death, Senorita. Death. Var' love one. Before the flowers bloom ..."

Was this the wind of destiny again, before which one was as a tumbleweed? Were all these trailbreakers part of a Destiny? The destiny of a Nation?

Ida Mary was going on to the Last Frontier, leaving the land where we had known so many hardships and tribulations. This land to which she had consecrated the work of her hands, the strength of her small body -- and her magnificent strength of soul. Those small hands which had labored so faithfully -- I closed my eyes to shut out the sight of them putting up the mail; hitching up the team on occasion, hauling water, cooking -- always busy, and that white scar on her wrist. The motherless child trying to help with the cooking had burned her wrist. A little thing maybe but it burned a scar into my memory now.

It was she who had initiated the trip west and our taking up land but it was I who conceived the venture on this reservation not dreaming we should be caught in such a maelstrom of events. Should we, who could help the settlers, have thrown up our hands in the crisis they faced? Or stayed as we did and keep the newspaper and mail going, and help to win the fight?

I did not know. I never have known.

It must have been right along here, in this gully, where the wagon had turned over that dark night in a sudden spring freshet when Sister had gone to Presho with Dave, the freighter, to order her first bill of goods for the store and a crate of expensive oranges, and of apples (bought on credit) had broken and the red and yellow balls gone floating down the flush. And I on the claim waiting alone, frantic. But next morning, we were really happy because she had gotten home safe and Dave had rescued most of the fruit. How we had laughed as she related Dave's contortions in the rescue.

Yes, there had been some compensation. The interest in worthwhile achievement and the many pleasures we had found along the way. But with all my attempts to console myself, I knew Ida Mary had gone through too much. She should have been carefree, as other young girls we had known. Many girls lived on homesteads but merely living on the raw prairie was not to be compared to taking part in taming it. And there was no use pointing out what women of the old pioneer days had endured.

As the procession passed the Ammons trading post which the settlers had helped to rebuild after the fire, I turned my head away. Then looked back. Standing like a statue by the deserted printshop was a small boy, cap pulled far down over his eyes. Little Heine Christopherson, who had been so much a part of our lives here, was waiting for us -- for her -- to pass. Farther on, two Indians appeared on horseback, riding from the Sioux settlement. At the top of a ridge they stopped, making no sign nor motion. Straight, austere and in tribal dress, their presence was like an impression carved on the subconscious mind. I remember only that impression. As the caravan passed from sight, they turned and rode slowly back. According to some ritual of the tribe, they were sending the Good Spirit with Little Paleface to the Happy Hunting Grounds.

In Presho, our father was waiting, standing alone on the hill watching the long, black line move across the white plain toward him. He had last seen Ida Mary in her wedding dress when she and Imbert had gone back to St. Louis to be married -- the girl he had called "Dick" when she was a healthy romping child. I remembered how disappointed she had been last year when he could not come by on his way to Wyoming. She rarely cried but she did then.

Looking upon his white face, I knew how wrong it had been not to prepare him for this shock.

"Don't tell Papa," she had admonished, "he will worry and he has enough to contend with just now. We'll surprise them all."

Strange that little Ida Mary should be the first among the several hundred settlers there to be taken. Why should she alone have been called for the sacrifice -- she and her child - like "the pound of flesh?" The Primitive had taken its toll.

At the minister's words, "Greater love hath no woman than that she lay down her life for another -- for her country ..."

I turned away, rebellion in my soul. For her country!

O, God! Where are you? I -- can't see you anymore. This cross was too heavy.

And there in Presho, we left Ida Mary, the little torch-bearer who had kept her lanterns lighted in the windows at night to guide the traveler on his way. Who had kept her touches burning in the march of these settlers to victory.

My father went home with us that night, getting his first view of the Dakota land of his two daughters who were the only two women ever to operate a post office and mail transport, a trading post, and a newspaper on an Indian Reservation. In the cold winter sunset, it looked like the end of creation. Ma Wagor and the Sioux woman stayed with us that night, and the next morning we shut up the little house. Imbert went to live with his aging parents on their nearby ranch. And without looking back, I left the Land of the "Burnt Thigh" behind.

The Sioux had named the region Burnt Thigh because of the Big Fire that had swept the prairie and in which the Indians wrapped in wet blankets had thrown themselves to the ground. But the earth had become so hot, they had been badly burnt on the right thigh, many of them carrying the deep scars always. A French Missionary had given the Reservation its official name of Brule -- "burnt."

This is an original photo of the "Trading Post."

Chapter XIX
THE COUNTY DIVIDED

I counted all the sheep in Wyoming jumping over all the barbwire fences in the state a sheep at a time and I could not sleep.

Homesteaders gathering around, sympathetic; stockmen who had been conciliatory, and a few who never had spoken to me before now stopping in at the printshop with a kindly word but saying little of my sorrow as was the way of the West. And my grief-stricken father still walking with quick step, shoulders back, trying to divert my mind to things going on around me.

The West Land Company opened up offices in Lusk expanding its operations and would I consider colonizing another large range further West? No! No! ... There was a new onrush of settlers coming in next spring. It would increase settler strength. Well -- let them come. Van Tassell was going to boom? Who cared? There were hundreds of these new towns over the frontier.

Joe Horton, the petty politician who had sworn to run me out of business came one day. He too tried to be kind in his gruff, blustery way. He had turned over a new leaf, he said. Next year he was going to run for office on the dry-farmer ticket. I laughed for the first time in many days. He was a maverick who would brand himself with whatever group could get him into office -- and the settlers now carried more votes than the stockmen.

Tom Bell always had a jesting, cheerful word though he had trouble of his own that winter, trying to find sufficient pasture for his cattle. There was an unspoken sympathy between us for I knew that not long since one of his sons, a sixteen-year-old youth, had been instantly killed when he was thrown by a vicious bronco.

Kearney, the salesman, who had been away for the five-month period allowed off the claims, returned for another seven month period.

"Hello, Moses!" he greeted me. "How's the Promised Land? I have a new job -- selling machinery to the dry farmers, what do you think of that?"

Without response to his enthusiasm. I made a news item of it.

After the first shock of my grief with its tearing remorse and the pangs of what I thought might be retribution, desolation engulfed me. Desolation as hard and dry as the primitive spaces.

From every side, the homesteaders had begun to feel the pressure of stockmen or politician influence in the county administration and the Division question was brought before the legislature in Cheyenne. But I had done my work on it last fall. To the proletariat, the "Legislature" was some august power as impermeable as the House of Lords. It had not occurred to the settlers to demand voice in the Assembly.

It had been a surprise and a shock, after all the fighting I had done in the campaign on County Division, to find the stockmen of the East End were for it; they, too, were victims of the dominating West End where sheep men and office-holders ruled the entire county. Thus, I had been playing along with the stockmen of this region without knowing it.

Then one day, Neil Jordan came. Much water had run under the bridge in those last few months since we had quarreled bitterly over settlers taking up land.

"I came to have a little talk with you, Miss Ammons, he said crisply. "Most of the stockmen in this part of the county are for dividing it and we know the fight you have made for it. Now we need all the influence we can get down in Cheyenne."

"So you want to use the settlers to help put it over. Then you stockmen take control of the new county, is that it?" I said, weary of the whole thing.

"Yes, of course, we would control it if we could. But we can't unless, and until, the dry-farmers get out. They are now a vast majority. As it stands, the settlers have our range and the West-end politicians and sheep men, the power. As long as the county seat is in that end -- I wondered why you weren't doing something? The Progress gained a lot of prestige on that issue."

This, from the man who had said to me, "You can't expect any support in this cow country. We'll lick the settlers."

Indifferently, I, too, wondered why I was sitting by, dismissing that vital matter with, "O, this Division fight is up before the Legislature."

It was reported that the West End had held a big meeting to block Division. The fight was becoming a war in Cheyenne and the whole

190

county of Converse was like a beehive in swarming time. The West End people had the largest towns, strong newspapers, and money back of them. And the political set-up. Had the settlers established enough influence to count against it?

Mechanically, like turning on a switch, I went into action with the homesteaders back of me. We appointed official committees and The Progress came out with: "The Sodbreakers Demand Converse County Be Divided" and a brief review of the reason which had been given in the fall campaign.

Other headlines were: "Sodbreakers Mean Power and Permanency." And "Remember the Women Can Vote."

That last was a sort of warning to legislators who may want to be re-elected. Copies of the newspaper, together with resolutions of the settlers, were sent to the Legislature.

The colonists said, "Now we are getting somewhere," and they were elated over my taking hold again.

In the East End, there were more cattlemen than sheep men. So, Division had become a controversy between sheep men and cattlemen, both wooing settler support. Russell Thorp, Jr., upon whom I had looked as caste among the range men, was in Cheyenne representing the Divisionists. The Legislature was close to adjournment and the measure not passed.

Then one night Thorp wired the Committee in Lusk, "Converse County has been divided."

The news was carried from one county to another. The settlers took it soberly. Forming a new county was like setting up an agricultural sovereignty. And we now had a county seat at our very door -- only twenty miles away.

The new county was called Niobrara (the Sioux name for Running Water.) It covered only two million acres. That was surely cutting down boundaries.

"Yeah, they'll have the counties cut down to truck patches pretty soon,." a few old-timers complained.

The colonists, the farmers on the old Ridge and the outlying settlers of the Van Tassell region had stood unanimously for division and for Lusk as the county seat.

The old cow and sheep town held a celebration. There were a number of sheep men in that part of the county and "Old Jackie Mills" had enough woolies of his own to call Lusk a sheep town. The place was percolating with stockmen and homesteaders and punchers and herders. There were brass bands and a rousing hullabaloo.

When I arrived a delegation of Division leaders, mainly stockmen, was at the depot to meet me. Just how much influence my paper had in the victory, along with other and older newspapers, I could not be sure. But it was the only paper in the county, east of Lusk, and it had the largest and strongest settler representation. Anyway the people said The Progress had "ridden 'em cowboy."

But I knew that had the Legislature failed to do so, the settlers were now strong enough to divide the county through a poll.

Businessmen of Lusk were so elated over the county seat victory, they hailed the settlers.

"How're you? Mr. – Ah …"

"Coburn is my name. George Coburn. And this is my wife."

The banker shook hands with the Coburns. He did not know the Coburns had guest "chambers" on the homestead and plenty of money stored away to last their lifetime.

Stockmen spoke to dry-farmers. "Well, we put it through."

They may fight tomorrow but this was today. There was talk about electing a new mayor, of building a courthouse.

The cowboys in their gaudiest regalia held bucking contests and put on horse races down that rough Main Street which ran into cow trails at both ends, with the town's few dignitaries protesting that such wild-west revelry was not becoming to a new county seat.

But Tom Bell being mayor pro tem shouted, "O, Hell! Let 'em buck. We don't want any tenderfoot stuff in this town …" and waved his twenty-gallon hat to egg on the show.

And no one dreamed that in a short time, the little Main Street would be a Wall Street with financiers, with hordes of tenderfeet pushing, milling, staking and making fortunes on oil, and the trail leading north, a crowded highway in one of the biggest oil booms in the country -- the Lance Creek fields.

Or, that capitalists and scientists would be flocking into the town, pressing, shouting "Radium!" to the world, "We have found radium here!"

Russell Thorp, hemmed in, was putting cattle out among reliable settlers to get range. Tom Bell began renting land around him. He leased all the pasture he could get hold of on the North Table.

And Spring came again to the range. The Spring which a few weeks ago I had so joyfully anticipated. New cavalcades marched farther into the wilderness, thin threads of trail stretched farther out and the trails of yesterday broadened into roads but I did not proclaim: "A Greater America!"

Yet for the future strength and protection of our Nation, we must make this a Greater America!

The birds sang in the early burst of the season and the grass popped up green in the warm sunshine. Early wildflowers colored the landscape. A flock of geese flew north with their cawk, cawk. There came new life, new activity, and the picture of Progress being painted on the range put on finishing touches.

But I took it with a listless acceptance. The gay swell of spirit of the year before was gone. I knew now that it was the spirit within, that had led the pioneers on.

It was the middle of April when the "lone eagle" of the plain came back.

The elation which the reunion might have brought to either Lone Star or me was tempered by the news I had to impart. He had known Ida Mary at the old trading post. The undemonstrative plainsman had no word to say but I knew he was deeply moved and surprised.

When at last he asked, "What happened?" and I explained, "She had a baby. They both died," he seemed embarrassed and shy, and resentful at such a fate.

"This raw country is no place for girls like you and her. Nobody but hard strong men have any business here."

So Lone Star Len would never sacrifice a refined, delicate woman on its altar!

On this soft spring day, the environment of the printshop was stifling. Lone Star was on his way to Montana and I pressed him to hold onto his homestead and was amused at the "sentenced" look which mere mention of it caused.

"Living on a homestead would go against the grain," he protested. "Like being in prison."

But his place was the farthest from the homesteading herds of any he had found.

"I might run a little bunch of cattle of my own up there if I can keep the landgrabbers out," he said and I encouraged him to do that.

Could it be that I had had a subliminal influence in this departure from the migratory life Lone Star had led?

"Len," I said, "We may never meet again. But you have taught me beautiful things; and you have served me in many ways -- even to rescuing me the day I fell off my horse."

It brought to mind our first meeting and he remarked naively as if to himself, "Sometimes I wish I'd never shot that eagle."

Which meant that if he had not scared my horse that day, our paths may never have crossed.

Lone Star hated mushy sentiment. He had kept himself armored against the Eastern girl out on homesteads for whom the quiet plainsman held a strange fascination.

So I did not know how he would take it but I said, "You will always remain a part of my life on the trail. Some people, I think, put root into our own being like vegetation into soil and in the end we find our character made up largely of what they have put into it."

He looked at me trying to comprehend.

"I guess you won't grub out easy, either." His voice was deep and set. "But our trails will run together again sometime."

I did not know. He was going far, declaring his intention to stay; and my own trail breaking was over.

Characteristically, in that parting, he did not say goodbye. Instead, he remarked that we were in for a storm. It was brewing and it might be a whizzer. Spring had come on too suddenly and too hot, for the Northwest. He admonished me to prepare for it.

As he was mounting his pony, I ran out and called to him.

"Len! Wait," and I reached up and kissed him on the cheek.

It was a bold thing to do to him. He was startled. A slow flush spread across his face and a soft mist came into his eyes. Could it be a withheld tear? And then with all the strength and fervor of his virile nature, he lifted my face to his and kissed me. Right in broad daylight where anyone happening to pass might see.

"Goodbye, Lone Star. Bon voyage."

With no attempt at being the picturesque cowboy he made an arresting figure. He wore a gray flannel shirt with a dark neckerchief, black fur chaps and black boots. His gray sombrero was warn at a careless angle that marked his individuality and there was an agile grace about him.

For the first time, Lone Stat had left me with a serene, contented feeling. He had kissed me. (Some things do come to those who wait!) In his protective strength, I felt a comfort. And I knew what he was thinking; that our lives ran far apart. That never could he belong to the civilized modern world. And who could want to tame and break Lone Star's magnificent spirit! But as he rode the plane tonight, I was sure that his horse and the stars would not be all the heaven he wanted.

Chapter XX
THE WHITE FURY

I watched Lone Star until he dropped from the rim of the plateau, a solitary form against the red sky.

The day had been warm and mellow and now foamy fleeces of sky hung like orange-colored mountains resting upside down on the horizon that turned to a mixture of reds and yellows and then to gray. That evening my father stood looking out the kitchen window of his claim shack.

For some time, he stood there admiring the scene before him.

"That's as pretty a sight as I ever saw," he remarked to his wife, Carrie.

The broad, smooth tableland of green grass with the brilliant sun setting on it; the peaceful homes, the livestock grazing on the slopes.

A herd of yearlings (the Tom Bell cattle), in scattered groups were still feeding in the quiet balmy evening. Hundreds of whitefaces, content, their red bodies filled out from the new grass. The little herd pasturing on the Ammons claim was drifting toward the corral. Star and Si having eaten their fill were standing on a ridge swishing their tails. And so it was with a sense of well-being that Tom Ammons looked upon this benignant[15] land.

But that night, the wind came up, a late snowstorm broke and turned into a blizzard. It had come from the North and by morning, Tom Bell's cattle had been swept off the Table, driven by the storm to the south through Van Tassell, and on to the Running Water where they were stopped by the long ravine.

The wind drove the snow before it in great white sheets that filled the cuts and banked into drifts from five to ten feet high. The next day, shut in alone, I set aside the ink-roller and the type. Who could keep eye or mind on type with a blizzard like that?

It became worse that morning and raged on through the day and the night with a force that lacerated and whipped and blinded. One could not see ten feet, at times not a foot, in front of him. And it was lambing time with thousands of wee lambs out on the range! Ewes perishing with their born and unborn young. Calves by the thousands, cows ready to

---

[15] Kindly, benevolent

197

calve, trying vainly to find shelter against a storm that drove even the strongest animals mercilessly on.

The majority of settlers were not prepared with their flimsy shelters. They were not experienced in meeting these blizzards and they had been caught napping in the promise of Spring. They may not have fuel to meet this emergency.

But there was nothing I, or anyone, could do but stay under shelter. With fuel to keep from freezing and enough food to keep soul and body together, we would survive.

On that first morning before the storm reached its height, they bundled themselves up and tied ropes, one end around their waists, the other to the house and made their way to sheds or to open piles of fuel making one trip after another with wood or coal -- most of them had tried to keep a jag of coal on hand -- carrying in a supply. With some, that supply was pitiably low.

They fought their way against the blinding snow to save their chickens and livestock. But where was the shed? Or the barn? They groped, trying to find it. They wandered in opposite directions, made circles around their own shacks until their frightened family pulled them in.

Others made it to barns to feed their stock, and to caves to get food from the meager supply they had on hand. In a few homes, the food stored for winter had been eaten long since, and only a few shriveled potatoes were left. My family, I knew, could find food for a few days to keep from starving.

The Ammonses like many of the settlers, had turned their horses loose to graze that warm April evening. During a cold, mid-winter snowstorm, before they had their hay barn, my father had gotten up in the night, brought the team inside and tied them in one end of the shack to save them.

Now in this blizzard, they were sure the horses had perished but when they got up on the second morning, they saw two dim shadows standing beside the shack. It was Star and Si making their way to the nearby hayshed. They had fought their way home against the storm.

The snow piled to the top of snow fences along the railroad, swirled around and over them and filled the tracks. A stalled freight train that had pushed its way into Van Tassell the night before stood half-buried. A few cowboys who had started out to find their stock and could get no farther. Trainmen and townsmen were marooned. They could not see their way to the next building.

That night, I kept my lamps burning in the windows as Ida Mary had done, to guide some poor soul who may be lost within ten feet of my door. Sometimes a tiny flicker of light can shine a long way on the desert of space -- or of life.

But the storm was shutting out all things, all light except the white curtain of snow. There was no sleeping. The wind howled and shrieked and lashed against the buildings. Thin walls creaked and popped like bursting shells from the force and the contraction to sudden cold.

A barrage of snow beat like hard pebbles, blew through the cracks and lay piled in corners and around the doors and windows inside houses, and on the outside it banked high against walls and doors and the flakes splashed and froze against the windowpanes. Fires must be kept up against the increasing cold.

I met this ravaging disaster with a stoic, steadfast calm as my sister had said I met all obstacles in the settling up of the West. I had been through blizzards and came near perishing in one. Yet, had there ever been a blizzard equal to this? I marveled at this elemental force. There was a challenge in it -- and a magic. Soft snowflake carpeting the world and not a sound except that of the wind. A silent, pure-white world became a demon of wrath. That anything so beautiful and so majestic could be so cruel and so destructive was incredible.

I was neither hungry nor very cold. I had enough food and coal in for another two days. I sat near the stove turning first one side and then the other like basting a fowl, keeping as far from the cold north end of the shop as possible, where the wind and snow were whipping in. And when the storm pushed into the very walls and the windows became frozen over and I no longer could see out, I went back to work. It would pass.

Coming in the night as it had, surely my folk and most of the settlers were at home, inside. Doubtless they would have rice or coffee. They could grind and parch grain for it, if they had it. They could reach outside the door and dip up snow to melt for water. But fuel? (I almost said, Dear God, what will they do for fuel?) With this frenzied, freezing havoc, they may have to burn furniture as I would have to do in another two days, or freeze to death!

But we had to go through it! Like a woman, her travail. This was the way we settled the West.

Another morning, and the blizzard had turned into a mad raging fury. Cut off! The range completely cut off from the rest of the world. The people shut in from everything outside their four walls.

It was the vastness of it that gave it added force and velocity. An eternity of cold, of snow, of wind, with nothing to turn or break it.

Across the boundless frontier the storm swept, with those tiny flimsy shacks, the settlers' only refuge against the onslaught. With snow banked high against their walls, the low roofs buried under snow, the homestead shanties were but white mounds lost on the white earth where men now and then burrowed out to shovel the heavy snow from thin roofs to keep them from falling under the weight. And they were the only fortifications against the Primitive for these colonists and for thousands of homesteaders on the desolate frontier.

And across the shelter-less range, the vast herds could find no refuge. The storm drove the wet heavy snow like needles of steel into the fur of animals, filled it, packed it, wrapping them in frozen blankets. It filled their eyes and the cold wind and snow still beat and cut and drove them on as they huddled together, or held them back like a mighty moving wall. Weak from lack of feed, they were in no condition to survive the cruel suffering and exposure.

The breeding stock had been turned onto the range at the critical lamb-and-calf cropping season because stockmen had run out of feed. Their hay supply had been drastically reduced that year by the homesteaders and along in January (and February as I recall) there had been weeks of deep snow with pastures frozen and buried.

Cattlemen, flock masters, sheepherders and cowboys fought their way through the blinding storm, risking their lives to save herds and flocks until there was nothing more they could do. Man and beast were held powerless against the unleashed demon.

People caught away from shelter would die, freeze to death almost instantly. Those who were sick (thank goodness there was little sickness) must suffer, or die, without aid.

My folk had moved to the claim to start their spring work and Carrie's aged father had come to live with her. Her brother, Everett Perkins, and his family had moved out from Illinois onto a homestead ten miles from my father's claim.

Grandpa Perkins who had been failing for some time, became ill during the blizzard and the family knew it was his last. The feeble old man lay suffering and no earthly way to get a doctor. My father had built a lean-to on one end of the shack as a bedroom for the two boys and their grandfather. And there, they nursed the sick man with every home aid on hand, and tried to keep him warm.

By the second night and throughout the night, the cold froze one's breath, penetrated into one's blood, through the walls of the houses, clamped down upon the earth, and the snow came like sheets in the wind. Then the blizzard broke, and died, as suddenly as it had come.

The people began to shovel their way out of the houses, their stock out of the sheds; and while my father and Mitchell shoveled away drifts, cut wood and performed other emergencies, Tommy saddled a horse and bucked the deep snow to Van Tassell to get word to Dr. Priest.

The snow was packed, frozen with a hard-deep crust that would hold up a horse in most places. Going through a draw where the snow had filled to a level, the boy found he was riding over the top of a barbwire fence. He broke the post and forced his horse across. It took him a half-day to make the five miles. When he got to Van Tassell, he found the telegraph wire down but at long last, we got a message through to Dr. Priest at Harrison.

Engines with huge snow plows cleared the railroad tracks and pulled the stalled freight train out and went on, engines and section hands shoveling through the cuts and curves, making way for trains to follow. All traffic had been blocked and the West held in the vise of the storm.

With horsemen breaking the way ahead of him, Dr. Priest started out, stopping at farm homes along the way for rest and food and change of teams. He reached the claim the following day and waited through the night -- for death and for daybreak so he could make his way back home. Grandpa Perkins had passed away and the exhausted doctor had taken a short nap and eaten his breakfast before starting out. That was on the nineteenth of April.

201

While the rest of the family with Everett's wife and children waited in the shack with the body, Mitchell and his Uncle Everett hitched up the team and started the twenty miles to Lusk for the casket.

Snowbound neighbors had all they could do to dig themselves out and look after their own families and property. Two or three men had plowed their way across the prairie to see if they could lend any actual assistance. In that crisis, there were more vital things than loneliness and so the family stayed alone. The dead needed no more help. The living did. No one knew yet who of the settlers might be dead or suffering.

The Ammons family did not know whether Mitchell and his uncle, who was new to the country, could get to Lusk or not. The team was weak and gaunt from the ravages of the blizzard, from poor shelter and little feed; and the horses would have to break the road.

The snow lay from two to three feet and more on the level with windrows of high drifts, and the man and the boy took turns about walking ahead, trying to keep to the road. They shoveled through the windrows, they struck drifts six to ten feet high and drove around them. In the lower levels and the draws, the horses became bogged, lunged and plunged their way out.

Every little while, the drivers stopped and rested the panting, sweating horses, blanketing their wet bodies against the cold.

They met the mailman coming from Lusk to the Ridge post office, on horseback. He had three letters and a seed catalog that had come in before the storm, in his sack. It may take him three days to get there but Uncle Sam's mail had to go through.

Keeping to the trail that the mailman's horse had broken helped them but the uncle, exhausted, said, "I don't think we'll ever make it."

He was not used to bucking the hard frontier.

"We'll have to make it," the boy replied. "The main road should be opened up a few miles out of town."

And sure enough, they found a broken trail the last five miles.

They had left home at six o'clock in the morning and it was toward evening when they reached Lusk. They found the streets deserted. They tied their horses in a shed at the Square Boarding House and started out to hunt feed for them.

"We want to buy a sack of oats," Mitchell said at the feed store.

"We're out. Not a sack of grain left."

He went to the Mercantile Company.

"Can you let me have a sack of feed? My team is played out. And I have to get back home."

"How you ever got here is more than I know," the merchant said, "but we have no feed of any kind left."

Mitchell told the story of the trip and why he had come.

"I'm sorry, my boy, but there is no feed in town. And no way of getting any very soon."

The haggard, shaggy-looking boy kept going. He went to every person who might let him have enough grain to feed his horses.

"Hay? Have you any hay?" he'd ask.

"Hay! Don't you know there is no more hay in the country. And we don't know where to buy hay nor how to get it in here. What little we can get is higher in price than the Rocky Mountains."

A feed famine in the livestock kingdom!

Stockmen were frantic. Russell Thorp had raised money to have feed shipped in on passenger trains. They could not wait for freight. The livestock that was left from the blizzard was starving.

"You just wait," Mitchell said desperately. "We'll raise feed out here. Another year or two and the farmers will supply this country with grain. And with hay!"

He said this wherever he went, finding no feed. A few grinned skeptically, but not many. There was a look about the youth that silenced them -- his earnest face under the wool, stocking cap, red with cold; the frousled blond hair, a muffler close around his neck, shabby mackinaw buttoned tight around his slim body; high arctics caked with snow and ice and his hands encased in heavy wool mittens.

"God, he's a game one, ain't he?" A hard, old native remarked in sympathy as he looked at the boy.

"Who is he?" a storm-stranded salesman inquired.

"The Ammons boy," the dealer replied. "Homesteaders out at Van Tassell."

The word went up and down the little town that the Ammons boy had made that trip through what was now a snowbound Arctic country to get a coffin for his grandfather who had died during the blizzard.

At last, a real-estate dealer let him have a gallon bucket of oats. "My horses need it, but take it along, son." He found a bale of hay and bought it. It was half rotten but he could get enough out of it to keep the horses from starving. One bale of hay in a vast grass country where thousands of tons grew in the summer and, stock starved for it in the winter!

Mitchell and his uncle fed the horses the oats and put the hay in the wagon for the morrow. They got a hot meal at the boarding house which the Roszells were running while the folk were on the claim. Then they went to the small furniture store and bought the casket -- an inexpensive one.

Bright and early next morning, the two of them started out with the coffin that filled the wagon bed, the bale of hay and a small box of groceries set in the front-end under their feet. It was all the underfed team could do to pull the load. A ground wind that comes from the sunrays striking cold earth, lifted the loose snow and swirled it into the air. It blew into their faces and filled the trails again. The bright sun glared on the white landscape and reflected like a looking glass.

Suddenly Mitchell put his hand before his eyes, took it away and said, "Why - I – can't see."

"You – can't see?" his uncle exclaimed, taking the lines. "Keep your eyes shut a minute. Now -- open them."

"I – can't keep them open," the boy cried. "They pain, and I can't see. I'm going blind!"

They stopped and the uncle examined them. They were swollen black and water streamed from under the eyelids.

"They feel as though they are full of sand, and I can't see a thing against the light," Mitchell said wildly.

Then all at once he knew what was the matter. He was snow blind! The blond boy with sensitive skin and light hair was the type susceptible to snow blindness.

He took a handkerchief from his pocket and bound his face and eyes. He should have blackened his face with soot before he started out. He sat there on the wagon-seat while the horses plodded on.

At last he asked, "How far are we? We must be getting close to home."

He inquired about certain places and landmarks they should have
passed. The uncle had not noticed the places mentioned.

"We should have passed a little schoolhouse before now."

It was near sundown.

"It's red. You would be sure to see it."

"We've not been near any red schoolhouse -- nor any other
building for a long time."

Mitchell tore the bandage from his eyes, strained to open them.
But they were swollen shut. He took his fingers and pulled the lids apart.
He had to see! See where they were going. But his eyes were pricking and
full of water. He could not hold them open. He turned his head and a hard
glaring light pierced through the closed lids. The fiery red ball of sun.

"Uncle Everett!" the lad's voice was filled with fright. "We are
lost! We have been circling in the wrong direction. Turn the horses
around and keep them angling to the right, we are going South and West
instead of East."

He knew much more of the country than his uncle and had
developed a sense of direction.

"Mama and Papa will be nearly crazy when we are not home by
dark," the boy fretted.

Night came on and it was bitter cold. On such a night one could
become lost and perish within a few rods of shelter. They must have been
hours off the trail. They were alone on an empty range, God knew where,
with a team that may fall from exhaustion any minute, and a casket. They
hit a drift and tipped the wagon and the coffin came near falling off. They
got out and heaved it back into place.

Part of the time Everett walked ahead of the horses trying to find a
trail while Mitchell held the lines. Then Mitchell would get out and walk a
while to keep from freezing, holding onto the back end of the wagon,
dragging from exhaustion.

Suddenly, a faint light appeared against the horizon and suffused
the sky. Everett described the strange red glow to the blinded boy. A
reflection of the Northern lights! They were turned in the right direction
now!

A few hours later, they were back on the road. The team knew the
way but they could not go much farther.

"Mitchell!" His uncle broke a long silence. "There is something ahead. A square, dark object above the white snow."

It was the little red schoolhouse!

They stopped and fed the team the rest of the hay, made a fire, took food from the box; then lay down on the seat with their coats under their heads and slept until morning.

Mitchell's eyes were badly inflamed and still swollen shut. His uncle blackened the boy's face with soot from the schoolhouse stove and bandaged his eyes against the glare of sun on snow.

They reached home at noon. His mother bathed the boy's swollen face, poulticed the closed eyes and in a few days Mitchell's sight was restored.

Jake Zumbrunnen came down from The Ridge in his big sled with four horses hitched to it and they loaded the casket. With a cortege[16] of ten horsemen breaking the road ahead, the family and a few neighbors followed Grandma Perkins to the Peasant Ridge Cemetery. They rode in open vehicles that creaked and crept through the snow, taking most of the day to make the ten-mile trip.

At the cemetery, the little, half-frozen group, their feet and hands numb from cold, stood deep in snow as Mr. Zumbrunnen opened his Bible and read the funeral service. In long, shaggy, horse-hair coat that skimmed the snow at the bottom, its deep collar reaching to the light-colored, Stetson hat which he always wore, his gray moustache caked with snow and ice, the slight, scholarly man read in a slow, measured tone. He removed his hat and the others bared their heads as he said a prayer.

Before he came West and settled on The Ridge, Jake Zumbrunnen had been a school teacher back in Wisconsin.

He was the first man of whom Eben, the land shark, had said with a sneer, when my first group of landseekers spent the night on The Ridge, "Runnin' a Sunday school and sayin' grace at every meal!"

But he was not a minister, just a neighbor.

It was a few weeks earlier with the range in the grip of dead winter at twenty below zero that he had brought the big sled down to The Table

---

[16] Procession, file

one morning and taken the Petty woman up to the little Ridge cemetery, with a vanguard of neighbors and horses and the men came near freezing.

But Jim Petty's wife had lain dead on the homestead a week before a grave could be dug through the hard frozen ground and burial made. There had been no way to get an undertaker, so the body had kept in one room of the shack, frozen, while a tiny baby fretted and wailed in the other. The mother had gone down into the shadow without coming back. Their homestead was two miles from the Ammons claim.

For twenty years, Jake Zumbrunnen had performed this last earthly service for his neighbors. Once in some misunderstanding, one of them had not visited or spoken to the Zumbrunnens for months. Then one morning, he rode up to the door.

"Something is wrong," Mrs. Zumbrunnen said. "Here comes Ben."

A member of his family had died the night before.

'I know we haven't been friends lately -- maybe I haven't treated you right, Jake. But I need you now."

"That's all right, Ben," said Zumbrunnen.

He and his family were there to take hold. Jake's teams and wagon were ready -- and his Bible.

And for twenty years, Eva, his wife, had waited on her sick neighbors in addition to raising a family of nine children. No one ever called upon Eva Zumbrunnen day or night that she did not go, unless one of her one family lay ill. She helped the families of the community bring their babies into the world and but few were born without her being there. Sometimes there was a doctor, but not always. It was said that Eva Zumbrunnen waited on the fatally ill until they died. Then she came home and Jake put them away.

But those services had been for old friends and neighbors of their own remote region. The settlers out on the plateau were strangers yet that made no difference to the Zumbrunnens – "I was sick and ye visited me ... I was a stranger and ye took me in."

Tragedy had stalked in that blizzard's wake. The settlers around Van Tassell had survived without loss of life as toll of the storm but many had suffered cruel hardships and exposure with loss of stock and some damage to property. Providentially, the colonists (the Petty family was not one of them) were all left. The Ninety and Nine.

But a number of persons had been lost on the frontier, perishing with the storm. A sheepherder was found dead with his flock, another had his frozen legs amputated; cowboys had been found with frozen hands and feet.

It was the stockmen who had been hardest hit, some of them wiped out. Ravines were filled and fences lined with carcasses of cattle that had huddled together for protection where the storm had driven them -- starved and frozen.

Blizzards in lambing time are cruelly destructive and great crops of lambs lay dead and flocks of sheep had perished. Herds, flocks and range horses that had survived stood weak and bony in the drifts, rooting through the snow to find grass. They reminded one of Charlie Russell's famous picture – "The Last of the Five Thousand" portraying a lone critter after a blizzard, with a hungry wolf standing near waiting for it to die. Packs of hungry, howling coyotes and wolves now stocked the range, feeding on the dead animals.

Neil Jordan had suffered a crucial loss. And when that blizzard was over Tom Bell was broke flatter than a sour-dough pancake.

The creek at Van Tassell was filled to the bank with his cattle, piled on top of one another like sandbags damming a stream and when the snow drifts melted away hundreds of head of Carlink cattle stood stiff against the barbwire fences, crowded together where they had been driven miles across the plain to fence lines and could get no farther.

Settlers who owed Bell for horses or a few head of cattle tried to raise money to pay him. My father went to see him.

"Well, Mr. Bell, I guess you need your money. I'll try to raise it. Or – here's your team."

"Hell's Fire! Take your damned old team home. Pay me when you get around to it. What help would that team or the money you owe be to me now? I need money to restock. I need a hundred thousand dollars."

"Much obliged, Mr. Bell, for your kindness. I won't forget it."

"Hey, Tom. Wait a minute," the cowman called after him. "How did my cows and heifers you got over there come through? Save any of 'em?"

"All but a couple," Tom Ammons answered. "Had them in the corral around the haystack. They buried into it, during the storm. You got some mighty fine young stock over there, calving."

"Well, you'll get your share of 'em."

It was an ironical situation, that the cattle king's holdings should be reduced to a minimum in which the few cattle a settler had saved for him were of valuable consideration.

"About all I got left," Bell repined, "is the damned goats. Have a notion to stock up with goats. Can't kill 'em nor starve 'em out. They can climb to the highest peaks and live on dry shrubs and rubbish.

Yes, a storm could wipe out overnight all a stockman had wrought through the years. He had many disasters to meet, though not many so devastating as this April blizzard which had come in the night without warning in the lamb-and-calving season.

The livestock growers of Wyoming and of all the West had suffered heavy losses, or gone broke, before. But with an indomitable will and plenty of range, they had built again. On their own initiative and their own credit, they had gotten another foothold without aid of government or state, and the livestock industry of the West had gone on and grown, without a New Deal Administration to loan the stockmen money or stock them up again.

This blizzard had wiped out more than cattle and sheep. It had wiped out great barriers between range man and settler of the vast frontier. A force more powerful than the stockmen had taken a hand in the readjustments and a great deal of the curtaining was now done and there was no open range for gigantic outfits to build again!

The plan advocated by development leaders was more growers and smaller herds, summer ranges and winter feed. And shelter. Aside from the economic and commercial, there was the human side of the question. The poor dumb animals should be protected during blizzards and hard winters. Many stockmen were to conform to that system.

Warm sunny days followed and Nature smiled in all her glory upon the land she had so smitten. The snow melted deep into the fertile soil, into the subsoil of fallowed ground, ready for the seed. It would be a good crop year.

Edith Eudora Ammons Kohl

Chapter XXI
THE GREAT DIVINING ROD

In Eastern Wyoming, the bedlam of a year before had changed to steady routine. And the range fence marking America's population center was still moving West.

The sodbreakers planted large fields, knew better how to do it; rye and oats and wheat and potatoes took the place of buffalo and gramma grass over thousands of acres. Mr. Dryer came in one morning in an expansive mood.

"Well, Miss Ammons, I got my 'grain of poverty' sown on that field I plowed last spring and she's up thicker'n hair on a dog's back."

Rye, the grain of poverty, checked the Great Plain in fields of fifty, seventy-five, a hundred acres each.

Mother Van and the Wattses and men who had gotten jobs in the towns for the winter came back with new zeal and money for improvements. Mother Van had "sold" Wyoming to everybody in Peoria that winter. Son Leport was coming again in the fall to do more plowing. In their first year's reports to the government, the colonies stood highest of any like-size region settled under the Mondell (Enlarged Homestead) Act.

New buildings were going up in Van Tassell and so many new people had come in that I was a stranger in my own town, and the trails we had made yesterday had become wide smooth roads hard as macadam. Russell Thorp and other of the "range's dignitaries" often stopped at the printshop as they rode by. They were no longer kings of the open range -- but they would remain kings of character and of courage whether they had a cow or a dollar left. Other ranchers had followed Bell's and Thorp's plan of leasing pasture from the farmers, which brought about a business relationship between the two groups.

The newspaper was in a position to reap some financial rewards from increased advertising and land notices but my work of opening up new territory with a newspaper as the settlers' medium was finished here. From now on, these colonists would have a steady pull, long and hard in places, but straight ahead. The picture they had drawn on the Great Plain lacked only the last touches. But I no longer saw it as a masterpiece on the Creator's canvas. Once I had thought of it as such.

And I had no visions of raw frontiers ahead. I was done. I had been holding on these past few months with a sort of blind grip, sick in body and heart and I had not the resistance nor the valor which had carried me on in the past.

My family was forging ahead. They had bought another horse -- one needed at least three big horses for sod breaking. Old Eagle was a powerful rawboned animal almost as large and strong as a stallion.

The boys took hold in the fields, being up at daybreak wrangling in and harnessing the horses while father did the milking. They had a new breaking plow and were putting in a hundred acres. They and their neighbors exchanged drills and other farm machinery that summer and after the crops were in, Tommy got a job on the Bell ranch, and Mitchell went to work on the paper.

Bell had organized the "Tom Bell Cattle Company" and had borrowed fifty thousand dollars in Denver to restock. He owned two good sized ranches -- the home ranch on the Running Water (Niobrara), and the other up on Lance and Old Woman creeks.

He said, "Give me five years and I'll be back on my feet."

He worked hard, rode the range with his cowboys and became a top-hand for himself; he rented homestead land from the city folk and put up hay for winter feed, or bought their hay. (He was back in less than the five-year time.)

The arrival of a cream separator that my folks ordered was an event in the community. A year ago it would have created no interest in those settlers from the city who had never seen a separator work, but now they gathered around the Ammons milk shed watching the performance.

"My Gosh, look at that," George Coburn said.

Pour in the fresh milk -- and here comes the cream out one spout and the skim milk from another. It was a scientific mystery.

And that reminded me! I must launch the dairy idea before I quit. The regular income would solve the problem of a living for the settlers and the dry-farmers began to buy up cows from the ranchers to "break" to milking.

When the range folk learned the settlers were going into dairying in that section, they were flabbergasted and some of the cowboys outraged.

"Godamighty! There's no cow-milkin' country big enough to hold range-riders," they declared.

They told the story of what happened to a homesteader once, and came into my office with it written out on a soiled, much-handled piece of paper to be printed as a warning.

One time there was a homesteader out on the remote range and now all that was left to tell was a little mound of earth in one corner of the homestead with a wooden slab on which an obituary was crudely printed in big black letters: "He Tried to Milk a Range Cow."

It stood there (I never knew quite where although the cowboys declared they could take me to it) as a warning to other homesteaders that range cattle were not safe when it came to being milked.

In the course of time, the famous Arthur Brisbane picked up a Denver newspaper on the train one morning and a black headline, "He tried to milk a range cow," caught his eye. He was amused at the story and interested in the West's development into a dairy country. The article was signed by me.

He picked up his typewriter.

"I am writing you on the train ... just noted your article. Am also writing an editorial based on your own ..."

And thus, this story of the milking homesteader, which the cowpunchers brought one day for me to print, appeared in the New York American and spread through the press over the nation. The winds of destiny had blown far.

But the truth was that it took a long time for me to reduce my own visions of the far-flung frontier, and its colossal issues, down to the production of milk and eggs.

After many weeks, a postcard that had been mailed during the big blizzard, had turned up out of some lost mail sack, from Lone Star Len. It was bent and torn, and the few, penciled words mottled.

He said, "This is to tell you I was not lost in the blizzard that night. If you ever need me, let me know."

He had given me an address care of a ranch in Montana.

I had wondered if he could have ridden too far into the storm the night he left Van Tassell. Yet, frontiersmen like Lone Star made self-preservation the first law, so I had not been worried greatly.

If I needed him. Why did men still think I needed them?

Robert Kent had written, "If there is anything I can do to help you, please let me know."

From staid-high officials down to Lanky who came to turn my press, men seemed to remember my femininity, no matter how business-like I was. But I did not mind, I loved it.

There were many rich fields lying open for my work. But why should I "labor in the vineyards?" When I thought of all my sister and many others had gone through, I no longer wanted any part in the westward movement.

Leaving Angel to run the newspaper, with extra help on press days, I packed my grip and went to Hot Springs, South Dakota in the Black Hills to recuperate. Perhaps all I needed was a change of surroundings and rest.

Here the Indians had brought their sick across the plain on travois[17] to dip them in the Healing Waters and the Sioux had valued this region above all others because of these medicinal springs.

But I dipped and I dipped, taking the mineral baths and treatment without being restored. These waters could not rebuild the nerve-force in a day nor cure a tired mind and a sick soul.

I was lost on the desert and I needed divining rods to show me where to find the waters of life. But, as on the treeless plane one could find no twig nor reed to locate water, I did not know where to find a divining rod. With more physical reserve perhaps I could have come back, found my way, I deliberated.

Then one day, I met an old, Sioux warrior pussy-footing around Hot Springs and we got to talking, he in Sioux and broken English, and me in broken Sioux. He told me of the wonderful curative powers these springs had possessed for the Indian people.

The reason the healing waters had not cured me, he said, was that no Medicine Man with pow-wow to the Great Spirit had immersed me.

Here was an uncivilized being, of a so-called savage race, with faith that healing lay largely in invocation to the Divine -- that in the Good Spirit lay the power to banish the evil spirit of sickness. And yet here was I, no longer having faith in the mercy of the Great Spirit.

---

[17] A transport sled used by Plains Indians

Angel was going to be married. Her sweetheart who had been ill for a long time was better and was coming onto his claim. He needed her with him and there was where she should be, I assured her. The newspaper was too much for her anyway. So I sold the goodwill and subscription list of The Progress to a Lusk newspaper at a sacrifice for quick sale and shut my door on the dead plant.

For weeks I stayed on in Hot Springs. I know of nothing so hard to crawl from under as a breakdown but perhaps that is because I never had any other physical handicaps to overcome. It is like being submerged under some great weight, or under water, fighting for life.

One evening when a crowd of tourists and health seekers were milling around the Evans hotel, I saw a man coming across the long veranda toward me. I gazed at him as at a ghost from another world. There was a quiet dignity about him that marked him as a man of prestige, with an air of solidity in keeping his splendid physique. He came straight to me, the usually stern face breaking into a pleasant smile.

"Why, Halbert Donovan!" I cried.

In my surprise, I had unthoughtedly called him Halbert. My first reaction after the greeting was one of embarrassment and of pity for myself, as I remembered the happy coquettish girl with the world before her whom Halbert Donovan first had known.

It was his company that had made loans to tide the Brule settlers over in Dakota. We talked of it briefly and he told me those farmers had met their obligations and he assured me this investment was one of the most gratifying he ever made. He knew now how it felt, he said, to have some part in the conversion of wasteland to use.

"And I don't blame you for feeling as you did about your work," he had added.

This investment broker knew the effect of western development on the nation as no one else whom I came in contact. He was emphatic about the expansion of business.

"It has put money into circulation and stimulated trade beyond all concept. And once, you remember, I ridiculed your ideas about settling the West as crazy."

215

"I remember. You denounced it as preposterous but it was you who was seeing too far to look at the barren planes -- a gold mine here in the hills and oil in Wyoming."

"But my opinions did not bear much weight with you," he went on. "You said you wanted to become a voice for the homesteaders -- or at least make a small footprint on the sod."

"And," I interposed, "you laughed and called me a Utopian dreamer and advised me to go back East and recite my poetry."

"Well, Utopia, I want to tell you how wrong I was. I thought it would help you to know how much the settlement of the West had done to boom things. In fact, we are in an era of the greatest expansion the country ever has known."

"Yes," I said, "it takes a lot of material, of everything, to build an empire from scratch."

For a moment, I became the sodbreakers' champion again!

"The fact that big businessmen and financiers have flourished from the achievements of the poor settlers has no interest for me. After they have taken the chances against cold and starvation, made the soil produce, and opened up great domains -- then the big moneyed people come in to reap rewards. Profits! Dividends!"

The last vestige of red blood rushed to my face and Halbert Donovan interrupted me to say, "I'm glad to see that old spark of spirit."

But I went on: "The capitalists are ready enough to make loans on western land and to get their hands on great tracts of it, after a region has been improved. I am glad of a general expansion, glad for the masses, but not for the fortune makers."

The stern, composed, man-of-affairs seemed lost in thought as I had seen him once before when we had gone into the discussion of this matter.

"But you, my friend," I added, "you took the risk of helping the homesteaders at a time when they most needed financial help."

I looked at him intently.

"Do you know, I almost forgot you belong to that financial world where money is a god."

And he said that sometimes he wished he didn't belong to it. Halbert Donovan would be a week in the Hills where he, too, was taking a rest, having come to the Black Hills because of his mining interests in that section.

Strange what broad understanding there had been between this man and myself whose work and whose lives were as far apart as the two poles. Yet, perhaps that was the reason for it. Halbert Donovan was in his forties, and I, in my twenties and visionary. I had cared nothing about his position or success. That, in itself, had won his interest.

I saw him several times during his stay and our mutual interests had developed as we knew each other better. Adroitly, he tried to find if there was some way in which he could help me.

"In making loans on the Brule, I offered one to you but you refused it. What about now -- on your land - strictly business?"

I shook my head. "It's got a mortgage on it."

Next day I was operated on. The doctors, probing around for some organic disturbance that might be affecting my condition (as though there were not reason enough for a slender reed like me to be bent) had at last found a lesser disorder and decided to operate. Nothing serious, they assured me.

Edith Eudora Ammons Kohl

Chapter XXII
THE CLEAN FROM THE UNCLEAN

It was evening the day after the operation as the vespers from the chapel floated through the dimly-lighted hospital. I opened my eyes to see someone in the shadowy light standing beside my bed.

"Hal," I whispered, and in that weak, frightened moment, I groped for his hand.

"I -- thought you had gone."

"I am leaving tonight," he said. "I have kept in touch with Dr. Walker. He -- thinks you are coming out of the operation -- as well as -- could be expected."

My hand lay in both of his, so warm and steady.

"Utopia!" His voice came crisp, commanding. "Don't give up! Once I ridiculed your purpose, your faith, but you've got to hold onto them now, do you hear?"

Was he trying to put them back into me with his own will?

"Yes, I know. I'll try -- I said obediently.

"And remember this - " the man spoke deeply trying to penetrate my subconsciousness. "If you should leave off here, your life has been justified, has it not?"

Who knew? Not me.

He stopped and pressed his lips lightly to my forehead and as I looked up into his serious face, he managed a smile, patting my hand and walked out, the dignified man-of-affairs, again.

Drifting into fitful dreams and incoherent murmurings I re-lived that first meeting with Halbert Donovan. I was skipping across a grassy prairie -- wildflowers in my hair, under my feet.

A stranger's deep voice asking, "What are you, a prairie nymph?"... "No just a homesteader," and the stranger laughing back ... "And what have you found out here at the end of the world?" And I had said, "O, life so big -- and so beautiful. So fresh and free -- the west winds ... listen to those birds!"

And then, in my unconscious wanderings I was floating in the sky and the stranger calling after me, "It's just a dream, my dear girl. These plains are hard. They'll crush you ..."

Halbert Donovan's voice then faded into that of the nurse, the fairyland into the dismal, dreary hospital walls at gray dawn.

"Here, take a sip of this." The girl in white held a spoon to my parched lips and worked quietly over me.

"There, there, you're all right."

The operation failed to turn the trick. Though it was not a serious one, I had been almost too weak for a comeback.

But there was one consolation about that operation. The doctor had taken out the appendix while they were about it. Not that I ever had been conscious of an appendix but one couldn't tell a thing those days about appendix. Which marks this epic as one of the modern era -- after the covered wagon had gone out and the appendix come in.

My father and Mother Van had come and gone and I was left alone again. I had gone into recluse those past few weeks. When I am down on my luck, I run to lair like a hunted animal until at some future time I again bob up before the world with a new foothold.

I had Mr. West sell my Brule homestead. I got in the neighborhood of three thousand dollars for it (a few years later I could have sold it for double the amount). I paid off the mortgage, took one on it, and had some money left to defray expenses. My nest egg was gone but at least and at last, I owned a mortgage on something. Ida Mary and I were always mortgaged to the hilt in our operations. This was probably my last emergency anyhow, I reckoned, and there would be sufficient funds for it. Oh, dear! This financial manipulation was taking more effort than settling a frontier, I complained.

Mr. West wrote me about the deal and said, "We'll get everything settled Saturday, then you will know how poor you are."

And he added a bit of news that he thought would be encouraging, "On my trip to Van Tassell and Lusk, Mr. Dryer showed me his rye and oats with thirteen inch heads. Your father's rye is fine and he has potatoes that will run sixty bushels to the acre. Theilbar has rutabagas big as a full moon. They are all tickled to death about the country."

Even here, I was completely surrounded by the land movement. Townsmen and patients either lived, or had lived on a homestead. Doctors and nurses had claims -- even the rugged Black Hills country was well taken up with landseekers who were spreading to the Bad Lands. Nowhere in the West could one escape the atmosphere.

One day when I was feeling low, a woman walked into my room. "Hello, dearie." She said in a coarse voice. "You remember me?" She sat down, without waiting for an invitation.

I stared at her in surprise. Yes, I remembered. How could one forget? She was the dowdy, frowsy-haired Madam who had talked to me on the train into Lusk last fall. Here was the same, floppy, picture-hat, a little floppier, its long plume worn thin. The same indescribable garments looked shabbier and in the closer observation, I saw the old velvet dress was deep purple.

But her face was brown and minus the heavy make-up. Her hands were red and rough; and she was thinner. She had been taking mineral baths for rheumatism and had seen me at a spring one day some weeks ago and had been all this time tracing me. Well, at last, here she was, she sighed.

After she had gone to all that trouble to see me, I would not send her away.

"So you came to Deadwood?" I queried, a wee bit curious to know the fate she had met in the Clean-up-Deadwood reform which had been in progress.

Yes, she had started her Deadwood House she told me and was doing right well in spite of all the competition (it was a real town) when the law began to make trouble. Not so much the law -- in fact, some of the officers had tried to protect her -- as a few righteous fathers and that big newspaper, damn them, making over Deadwood. Just ruining the town. Swept her House right out.

"But I had to tell you this," she went on. "I said to those smart alecks, 'Just run your highbrow town! But you are not going to run me out of the country!' Time I got through fighting the white feathers (angels) I didn't have money enough left to start up in some new place. Know what I did? Remembered what you had told me about land and took up a claim. Now, would you believe it?"

"No! A claim. You really did?"

"Yes I did. Got away out in the Hills up north of the Springs where the Deadwood prospectors (I never knew whether she meant

221

persecutors or prosecutors) couldn't find me. Been living there all summer. Was plumb wore out and I did enjoy the rest, and seeing the sun come up. Imagine seeing the sun come up! Surprising what abundance there is out here -- fruit and everything ..."

"A few of the girls and I formed a kind of colony, like you had talked about. I figured the Magdalenes had as much right to this soil as the saints."

She was going out to her claim and would be back in a few days.

"Now you want to perk up," she admonished.

When she did not come back, I found myself wondering about this woman of ill-fame whose trail had re-crossed my own so unexpectedly. Just to look at that hat with its fallen feather amused me, and the strange character was a diversion.

It was a lonely Sunday in the quiet convalescent home when she came again. She had on her tawdry jewelry this time -- the long earrings and the heavy bracelets -- and she carried a large bunch of goldenrod. It was really pretty with its bright yellow blossoms. She put the flowers in the water pitcher, flopped into the rocker and took off the hat without being asked. She had brought a jar of chicken soup -- yes, she had a dozen chickens, she boasted.

The friz and the dye were almost gone from her hair which was combed back from her face, there was a new light in her eyes and she did not look so hard. Suddenly, I was telling this so-called moral leper about my troubles -- my sickness and Ida Mary's untimely end.

"Well, dearie," she said, "we gotta take life as it comes and make the best of it. I wish to God sometimes I'd a died in my youth. There's worse things than dyin' young."

She was seeing those girls of hers. Some of them, she said, had been driven to a life of prostitution through hard luck. Others were "just strumpets" -- hard and mean and brazen. But they all met practically the same fate: old before their time, destitute, isolated as lepers.

"Now you -- you got a lot to live for. And you're clean!"

Of course I knew what she meant -- that I was not a prostitute. But I doubted if that alone would separate the Clean from the Unclean.

"Folks a takin' to you -- why I'd a never took land but for you," she said. "Now I'm through living off o' girls; done fighting the preachers

222

and uplifters. I got a little money in my stocking and they can go to Hell. I've got to spend the rest of my life a making, ah --"

"Restitution," I supplied the word. "Or atonement."

"No-o. Respectability, dearie, that's it. I've always hated these smug respectable people. I see women who bleed men and call themselves virtuous. And selfish married women living like parasites. But they got that nice gold bound marriage certificate, so they can hold their heads high. And men. I've known a lot of 'em that were selfish and mean as the devil -- but honorable."

"But now, living among good respectable folk that treat me right, I gotta get respectability. You know, I been a thinkin'. You could come stay with me a while -- wouldn't cost you a cent. I've doctored up a lot o' rundown girls in my time. In return you could teach me --"

"Respectability," I broke in laughing.

Then a pang shot through me. This creature offering me aid, she with her courage, did something to me. I, a developer, a newspaper woman. My Heavenly day! I had come to the place where I could identify my own work only through this retrospection. I was a stranger to myself!

The Madam putting on the big picture-hat said, "I'll have to buy some clothes -- I got a couple o' calico dresses -- real neat -- and a chambray sun hat and a fascinator[18] to wear around home but when I come to town --"

"Wear them to town," I said. "Women in the homestead country wear plain clothes like that --"

Her claim, she said, was out quite a way from the Springs -- she had to get it fixed up for winter but she would come again.

"I'll bet your sister wouldn't a give up very easy – well, goodbye, dearie. And remember, I'm one of your landgrabbers now."

I shook hands with the "moral outcast." A forlorn woman on the downhill of life trying to make an evil life over. But she had done more for me than I for her.

That evening, I picked up an old Homestead pamphlet that had quoted a bit of Ida Ammons' philosophy to the settlers: "When we have

---

[18] A 19th century knitted or crocheted hood or scarf tied under the chin

learned to scorn trifles, lift our aims and do what we are afraid to do, we have fought our greatest battle and are not far from success."

I felt a reaction about Ida Mary's death and in the night came sweet and peaceful memories. Despite the hardships and struggles, she had known the joy of doing, and the devotion of a plain, simple people. And once she had said in speaking of a wealthy girlfriend who spent her life in leisure and luxury, "I wouldn't trade places with Martha."

Then she had laughed, "Sounds like 'sour grapes', I presume."

Ida Mary had gone in the Great Fulfillment with love, youth, and the glory of motherhood, hers. Was not that the pinnacle of earthly happiness for any woman? She had been spared being the dead shell which many became, as I was becoming. And if, in the intricate workings of life, I had been responsible in a way for my sister's sacrifices, then should not I justify her work by carrying it on?

During those days when life had been at low ebb, my thoughts were often of Halbert Donovan. They had brought a warm glow and a sustaining comfort. He came from a solid world. Then he had written me and the communal of interests and of understanding were as some infinite thing, pulling me back to life. In the long, lone hours, I re-read his letters as devout sisters counted their beads. Something strong and calming in them.

But the fall was almost gone. My money was dwindling and over and over I counted it as a precious thing against time and the winter, and the hard reality now blotted out all else. As the cowboys would say, I was "plumb down to grass roots." I must go on somewhere, somehow! And I must find the trail again.

I saw the struggle of others for health and watched the old soldiers from the Soldiers' Home incapacitated, crippled, in the useless destruction of war. What Ida Mary and I -- and countless others -- had sacrificed was for construction, building instead of tearing down, as these men had been called upon to do in the name of patriotism.

Did it matter whether the Frontier was developed? Just cut off the country west of the Missouri and the United States would have the answer in twenty-four hours. Her resources and strength would be cut in two. A back trek would stagnate America. We had to stay!

What was this mighty push to the land, I asked myself again. It must be some universal force that moved these masses for no individual call to the land could create this migration. It was like a natural gravitation to earth.

A quarter-million people had registered that fall for homesteads in the great Couer d'Alene (Idaho) Opening and vast reservations in Montana and Washington were being thrown open, with people by the tens of thousands surging in for claims like armies of invasion.

And with them were coming other hordes to open up commerce and industry in those fields. They were possessing America's Last Frontier. Other nations looked on astounded at this phenomenon in territorial development.

The homestead project (the development of farm units) was becoming the most fundamental of all the movements because in it homes were being carved for the generations to come.

Making the Frontier into an agricultural empire was no longer a dream. Every state had produced food for its people that year.

The noted Senator Frances E. Warren, writing me about it from Washington, had said, trying to urge me on, "It truly is a great Vineyard and the laborers few."

I went to the top of a hill where I could get a scopic view of this new world, the West, that reached endlessly onto the Eternal. And it was Omnipotent.

"O, Lord, give me strength to do."

I was not aspiring to any heights of accomplishment. All I wanted was to walk with the people, the grass and the sod under my feet, the pungent scent of sage instead of drugs and the feel of prairie wind and sun on my cheek. But, God, please let me die with my boots on ---.

I had prayed once more. God? Why, we had to have an all-enveloping Deity to lead us on. What else would tie these multitudes together, this new empire, the world? We had to hold fast to something bigger than ourselves or fall. All of us thrown into these vast spaces were, and must be, a part of a Supreme Plan.

Back home, I went to the telephone in the deserted hall and called a Hot Springs newspaper. Did they perchance know of a printer who could run a weekly newspaper. Where? O -- I didn't know where, not yet. What kind of a paper? The man's voice at the other end of the wire asked. A frontier weekly, I explained.

"Well, I'm a printer working here -- I might be interested in taking the job myself," he concluded. "Where are you?"

"I'm in a sanitarium," I informed him, giving the address. "Come on over. When? Now!"

"I'll be there as soon as I get off duty -- five o'clock. That do?"

"Yes, that will do," I replied and hung up.

I scrambled through the piles of letters and messages forwarded from Van Tassell. Among them a number from development leaders and Immigration Bureaus of various regions asking me to come. Officials of the Department of Interior and Western Congressmen (mainly my sponsors) had written me saying there never had been such a need of supporters in the homestead movement. Friendly letters from Senator Warren and from Congressman Mondell expressed interest in my recovery and in my getting back to the fields.

Among these fields was a region in Montana. Someone from that district had written me about starting a newspaper there.

Young, black-haired Arthur Kenyon came that evening. And the next week, he packed the plant at Van Tassell and took it on ahead of me to Montana. And there in the great Judith Basin which became famous overnight for its wheat, I set up my printing "shebang" and started another newspaper. The fourth newspaper, the fourth expedition into new empires.

It would be a few weeks before I was able to go and I bent every effort to that purpose. I could rest now and sleep and eat.

As I packed to leave, Dr. Walker, the noted surgeon said, "This has cost you a lot. Here, take this. It was a check for a hundred dollars. Pay me back when and if you get ready."

I sent word to Halbert Donovan.

"I am on my way. I do not know how far I'll get. But -- I've found a trail," and signed it, "Utopia."

Winter had come and with it a certain amount of new energy. And so one bright effervescent day, I started out for Montana.

I had closed another chapter of my trail breaking career, leaving it written on the sage and the sod.

To be continued …

OTHER BOOKS BY EDITH EUDORA AMMONS KOHL

Land of the Burnt Thigh

This true story is an absolute must read by all American History buffs. It is about the lives of two young women, Edith Eudora Ammons and her sister, Ida Marion Ammons, and the trials and tribulations they endured on the flat, open prairie of the Rosebud Indian Reservation in South Dakota in the early 1900's. They had no idea of what they were getting into and had no one to guide them. The hardships they endured were mind-boggling. They were trail blazers and true pioneers and they lived their lives with an intensity which always characterized conquerors of the American frontier.

Denver's Historic Mansions

This is a fascinating story of how Denver's early builders shaped their personal modes of living. Many of the great old homes of Denver still stand with all the dignity and substance that were built into them; some have gone forever ... their locations shadowed by skyscrapers.

Denver's First Christmas

This is the story of Denver's first Christmas in 1858 when people with new dreams and new visions were following another Star across another plain to the birth of a new Empire.

ADDENDUM A

Copy of Front Page Article
Written by Edith Eudora Ammons Kohl in 1935

ADDENDUM

The following is an article written by Edith Eudora Ammons Kohl in 1935

FRONTIER TRAILS
By the Noted Newspaper Writer and Trail Breaker
Edith Eudora Kohl
(Copyright 1935, Edith Eudora Kohl)

HOW-KOLA

We had just landed on the homestead, Sister Marian and I, when one day we set out to explore a little further; Marian had wandered off our trail picking wild berries and I was stooped down trying to fan a campfire into life when I heard a strange, snarling sound behind me.

I jumped up to face a big old Indian towering over immobile me. I had never seen an Indian running loose and a lion out of its cage would have looked tame to me beside this savage-looking creature with hard face, long black braids, and strange attire.

I gave one loud scream, and then stood paralyzed with fear. We had not dreamed that we were settling that close to Indians and I presumed when the westerners talked of Indian agencies and allotments, etc. that they were walled off, and the Indians guarded like inmates of asylums or prisons. And here was one loose. We were in an Indian camp.

He kept making signs and muttering. Then seeing my fear, he took me by the shoulder, his leathery features broke into a weird grin as he said, "How-Kola, How-Kola," and sat down on the ground Indian fashion, legs crossed in front of him, and reached for a sandwich.

How-Kola, the greeting of the Sioux. How -- I greet you. Kola -- friend. It meant deliverance to me that day, and with it was cemented a strange friendship through which Ida Marian and I became mediators between a great settlement of whites and that tribe upon whose reservation they later settled.

I like that word with its broad significance, in bringing about through my stories a deeper understanding and appreciation of our western development, and of the people who broke the trails.

"New York City Too Dog-Gone Fur From Everywhere"

"What's the matter with New York City?" I asked Lasso, an honest-to-goodness cowboy who had been roped into going east to show the tenderfoot New Yorkers how men on the cattle range used their influence over a wild steer.

"It's too dog-gone fur from everywhere," he answered seriously. "And them there canons with the high stone walls a stickin' up don't lead nowhere that I could find."

I looked over the great panorama of prairie which stretched before me and smiled sadly at this cowboy's crazy ideas. I had come from a place where chasms of streets were walled with mountains of buildings and so far as I could see, these western trails began nowhere and ended nowhere -- unless it was in an Indian camp.

ADDENDUM B

Complete Copy of the Article
Written by Edith Eudora Ammons Kohl in 1935

"HOW-KOLA"

We had just landed on the homestead, Sister Marian and I, when one day we set out to explore a little further; Marian had wandered off our trail picking wild berries and I was stooped down trying to fan a campfire into life when I heard a strange, snarling sound behind me.

I jumped up to face a big, old Indian towering over immobile me. I had never seen an Indian running loose and a lion out of its cage would have looked tame to me beside this savage-looking creature with hard face, long black braids, and strange attire.

I gave one loud scream, and then stood paralyzed with fear. We had not dreamed that we were settling that close to Indians and I presumed when the westerners talked of Indian agencies and allotments, etc. that they were walled off, and the Indians guarded like inmates of asylums or prisons. And here was one loose. We were in an Indian camp.

He kept making signs and muttering.

Then seeing my fear, he took me by the shoulder, his leathery features broke into a weird grin as he said, "How-Kola, How-Kola," and sat down on the ground Indian fashion, legs crossed in front of him, and reached for a sandwich.

How-Kola, the greeting of the Sioux. How -- I greet you. Kola -- friend. It meant deliverance to me that day, and with it was cemented a strange friendship through which Ida Marian and I became mediators between a great settlement of whites and that tribe upon whose reservation they later settled.

I like that word with its broad significance, in bringing about through my stories a deeper understanding and appreciation of our western development, and of the people who broke the trails.

"New York City Too Dog-Gone Fur From Everywhere"

"What's the matter with New York City?" I asked Lasso, an honest-to-goodness cowboy who had been roped into going east to show the tenderfoot New Yorkers how men on the cattle range used their influence over a wild steer.

"It's too dog-gone fur from everywhere," he answered seriously. "And them there canons with the high stone walls a stickin' up don't lead nowhere that I could find."

I looked over the great panorama of prairie which stretched before me and smiled sadly at this cowboy's crazy ideas. I had come from a place where chasms of streets were walled with mountains of buildings and so far as I could see, these western trails began nowhere and ended nowhere -- unless it was in an Indian camp.

A month had passed since we met old Joe Two Hawk on the trail that day on the border of the Indian camp and yet, the only way Ida Marian and I could find ourselves out on the God-forsaken homestead she had filed on was "three miles from the buffalo waller" -- a sort of scooped-out water hole where once upon a time the wild buffalo had wallowed in cool, tall grass. And unless we used the sun and stars as a guide, we were as likely as not to go in the wrong direction to find that.

But Lasso was an authority in that man's country. Couldn't he lasso anything on hoofs -- four hoofs or two? And the "skirt" homesteaders and school teachers comin' out from the East had better watch their step. "Even some o' them high-headed, high steppin' New York gals" it was reported, "woulda stood plumb still had Lasso throwed his rope in their direction."

That was in western South Dakota. One day, some five years later, when Lasso, nonchalant and breezy as ever, blew into my newspaper shop on a sheep range in Montana where I was publishing … let's see … that must have been "The Bleat."

I said, "Lasso, I think you are right about this frontier west. It may be too 'dog-gone fur' from the veneer of life but it's awfully close to the fundamentals. And the trails do lead somewhere."

That passed over Lasso's head. He grinned at me about as tolerantly as I had at him once upon a time.

"Yeah," he answered dryly, "they've led you from Indians to sheep. And the grass here ain't half as thick."

"Neither are the rattlesnakes," I interrupted in argument of my forging ahead.

For two years, I had lived where the rattlesnakes ran the country. One would think they had been given first squatters' rights and no intention of vacating. I sometimes thought all the rattlers in the world had settled on that one reservation. Most of them had. And Rattlesnake Bill, famous for his research in that line would testify to the veracity of the statement if he were here today. Rattlesnake Bill could tell some creepy snake stories; but after that two years' experience I do not need Bill to furnish me any stories on the subject. I vie with him, or any other as a connoisseur in the fine art.

Ida Marian, coming in one hot day, sank helplessly into a stool in the combination print shop and land office and said, "Sis, what are we going to do about the rattlesnakes?"

Deliberately I whittled off the end of a match, gouged it down in between the type on the form to keep it from falling out. Lifted the form up carefully, put it down and wedged in another piece of match.

"Just let 'em rattle." I answered with the finality of defeat.

We had downed a good many obstacles but this one we had merely dodged; and it took some side-stepping, I'm here to relate. The rattle of snakes became accompaniment to the song of the meadow larks. And then -- but that snake tale is a story within itself. I mention this as one of the impedimenta with which the settlers were confronted in the conquering of the primitive.

"Thar's Riches in That Thar Soil"

"Thar's gold in them thar hills," men said long ago. "Thar's feed on them thar ranges," they said a little later. And then, "Thar's riches in that soil," and along came the droves of homesteaders. They all came to practically untrammeled areas as remote as the very first one in this far-reaching frontier West, a vast part of which was once known as the Great American Desert. And the trails that "began nowhere and ended nowhere" led to the building of one of the richest empires in the world by one of the greatest armies that ever marched to conquer.

232

The truly greatest army, I think, became hungry and ragged and foot-sore and without leadership or direction, they fought, regiment after regiment, the longest and hardest war ever waged for territory. They fought voluntarily and valiantly against the most powerful of all enemies -- the indomitable force of nature. They made their fight unseen, unheard, unheralded by men.

Their families lived in crude makeshifts of shelter -- these "shanties on the claim," crooned about synthetic cowboys, that would disgrace any respectable back lot; and in which no flock of up-to-date chickens would stoop to roost. They suffered from cold where snow blew in through cracks almost as wide as the open spaces. (One of the great mysteries of the homestead world is where the lumber industry ever found all the knotholes it sold the settlers.) They suffered from the searing sun and winds which burnt up their crops and moral courage; and some were parched for water.

Their war munitions in the conquest -- human energy, money if they had any, livestock, were confiscated by the cruel hand of the desert and destiny. The people were wholly unequipped for the job.

"It seems to me," Ida Marion would say, "that it would be a good investment for the nation if our government would help the settlers develop this land." And surely it would have been. It would have come into production and power so many years faster and earlier.

Once I appealed to a large investment broker passing through. "Investment in the development of these new lands is the unparalleled opportunity of big capital," I declared. But he smiled indulgently and called me a Utopian dreamer, a poet. Dreamers, Poets, Huh.

But there was no government or financial agencies to grubstake these armies, or equip, or recruit them. All the government did in those days to get the frontier developed was to give the homesteader a plot in the endless vacant space for a song, IF, by the mercy of providence, he could hold out long enough to prove it up without starving to death; and if he could raise money for required improvements of a shack, a few acres plowed and fenced, with a little crop put in, etc. And if he lived on it the allotted time. That was the foremost letter of the law that he live and eat and sleep upon it.

233

These remote no-man's lands have been enriched with blood from the bleeding hearts and feet of the men, women, and children, who trod them, the toll of progress. But they not only developed a country, they developed men and women. Or rather, while they developed the frontier it developed a people of sterling worth.

And when they laid their sacrifices on the altar of the people for a greater America, a new dominion, the West, there was no blowing of trumpets nor cheering of crowds to hail their feat.

Their victory was signaled by another field of sod turned over, or a lean-to to the shack.

The Last of the Five Thousand

Many there were who fell by the way with only now and then a little wild flower to mark their graves. And there are no tall monuments erected on the border of the frontier to remind the nation they gave their lives to its development -- these heroes who suffered untold privation; who perhaps lay ill and died far away from aid, or perished in blizzards or prairie fires; or just naturally succumbed to the struggle leaving their families to starve, or worse.

Strange, when today we pin laurels on just about anybody, and talk so much about "high standards of living," (when we are already so soft we squash from too much of everything.)

A stripling of a youth sat one night in his bunkhouse on an isolated ranch drawing a picture on a rough scrap of paper. It was the answer to a letter received that day from his uncle in St. Louis who owned the ranch. He finished the drawing and mailed it.

That sketch became world famous. It was Charlie Russell's "The Last of the 5,000," master-piece of the noted cowboy artist.

The picture of a lone starving critter after a blizzard, humped up from the cold, nothing but skin and bones and blocked by snowdrifts with a hungry wolf waiting for the carcass, told the story of what happened to his uncle's large herds of cattle during the terrific blizzard which had swept the plains. It depicts the battle of the cattlemen and sheepmen against the frontier, for supremacy.

A little group of men from St. Louis, who had just filed on land in Wyoming, stood examining a handful of the soil as an old-time cowman came riding over the ridge. A picturesque figure, Tom Bell always made as he rode, and a familiar one over the vast Wyoming ranges. Short, stout, and blocky, he wore white fur chaps and a twenty-gallon hat as white as the chaps, with fancy boots and spurs that glistened in the sun. And he always had a pack of hounds with him. Long, lean, and tall, they trotted alongside the pony, or raced ahead, leaping the barbwire fences of the homesteaders, ignoring these barriers to the open range.

"What do you think of it?" he asked, referring to the soil.

"Well, seems like it's pretty rich."

"It should be," Tom Bell answered calmly. "It has been well-fertilized over these parts."

"Fertilized?" they asked.

"Yes, fertilized by the bones of my cattle and Jackie Mills' sheep that have perished in the blizzards. I found 300 head of my cattle piled up in that fence corner," he said pointing to an old range fence nearby, "when the snow drifts melted one spring. Had been driven by the storm and when they reached the fence they couldn't get any farther."

Herd after herd perished on the plains year after year and there was no government aid, no federal agency to furnish loans for feed or reimburse these pioneers. Yet somehow, they built a sheep and cattle kingdom and became kings of the industry.

Government Ran Lotteries with Land as Stakes

I do not belong to the covered wagon, Pike's Peak-or-Bust era with which the world so mistakenly imagines that the glamour and the romance of the frontier died -- when as a truth they were just an embryo.

None of the immigrants I knew were going to Pike's Peak which was a purposeless destination; and most of them were already busted. I belonged to that last and biggest army which shouted "Thar's riches in this here sod," and tore up the range with their plows.

I had just become well enough set to find the old buffalo waller, three miles away without getting lost, when the sparsely-settled West woke up one morning in the biggest and swiftest stampede of immigration that ever hit any country in the world -- the government lotteries with land as the stakes. One virgin tract after another, millions of acres, with not a track except those made by the wild life inhabiting them, were "throwed open" to settlement through drawings to which thousands upon thousands flocked like grasshoppers in the Kansas grasshopper raid.

"Shucks, it's as simple as fallin' off a log," stage-driver Sam would say to the crowds of excited, confused landseekers. "Just take enough grub to last a couple of days and a bottle or two o' strong whisky and get in line at the land office. The gov'ment will number yuh, put the numbers in a box, shake 'em up and draw 'em out. Lucky numbers win. Like gamblin' on a roulette wheel -- lucky numbers too skeerce for all the suckers that play 'em -- allus rather take my chance on poker."

The players in these drawings had one chance in fifty, sometimes in a hundred, to win. But the land office and the railroads did a "land-office business."

Lucky numbers went wild with the excitement. Surging crowds pushed and jolted and fell down over one another on the border of far-flung, empty space. They had no idea where they were going or what lay before them in the great adventure of this lifetime, for which most of them were wholly unfitted.

The frontier was not ready for this onslaught. Food, shelter and fuel, were a problem. There was no water supply until they went down into the ground after it, and drilled wells which took time and money. And in some of these boundless areas -- "You'll have to drill clear to H -- after it, and then you won't get water," an old-timer once said.

It was like unloading a world army on desert islands. It caused bedlam, chaos. Natives who had been through the thrill and excitement and adventure of the gold-rush, Indian war days, stood dumbfounded at this spectacular invasion.

The Melting Pot

Lone Star Len rode in from the open range one day. "I'm movin' on," he said. "It's too lonesome with all this millin' around. Too bad to ruin a pretty country like this with pesky homesteadin' herds."

"Ruining it? Making it, you mean." He gave no answer.

"Where are you going?" I inquired.

"I don't know," he replied mournfully. "Some place where it won't be so hemmed in with people."

Lone Star was a strange, lone character, belonging wholly to the silences of the plains. And through the falling dusk he rode on West. But I was to meet him again in one of the many strange coincidences of these frontiers.

Coyote Cal thrived on the upheaval. "Never seed as many skirts in my life. Musta been two trainloads shipped in …" purt near" as human as broncs, when you get to know 'em, too."

Coyote's life had run to broncos.

"You don't get much to eat or wear out here," old white-haired Ma Wagor said next day after the big prairie fire that almost had annihilated us with its red tongue. "But you got a lot o' livin' what with blizzards and prairie fires and young folks fallin' in love and cattle rustlers and Indians -- well, it's almost as exciting as a three-ring circus we had back in Blue Springs once … I told Pa last night that I had always hankered after some excitement before I died.

Pa, nearly eighty didn't hanker after excitement but he figured that eighty-acre homestead would raise corn. The old-timers shook their heads and said, "Too bad. The sun has baked his mind."

But raise corn it did -- and Cain, too, for that dear, brave old couple who became parents to the whole settlement.

Young girls there were, whose tiny shacks sat alone, with the weird cry of the coyotes at night, the only sound. Out of sight and sound and reach of human habitation in case of illness or other emergency, they stuck with an undaunted courage and settled up no small part of the broad frontier.

How they did it is beyond human imagination. But the Great White Father must know -- and remember.

Written Upon the Sagebrush and the Sod
Broad region upon region was settled thus over the West through these spectacular openings; and the momentum of this overnight settlement brought flocks of immigrants into other sections -- an epic of development unparalleled in history.

I traveled with these trail-breakers. Most of the way I trailed a little printing press behind me. Sometimes Ida Marian and I bent the tall grass and pitched our "newspaper shebang" -- as Lone Star Len scornfully called it -- in the middle of a No-Man's land ahead of the settlers. Until – well -- Marian, that brave little torch-bearer was one of those who fell by the way with only a little wild flower now and then to mark the graves and no monuments to mark them as heroes. And then I went on alone.

We were not adventurers. A strange destiny or some other unseen force seemed to lead us into these fields in which we plodded next to the lowly early until our job of aiding the settlers through our little newspaper on each frontier was finished.

I have encountered many people and things along the way -- drama and romance and tragedy and progress, where pathos was oft times filled with humor, and humor became pathetic.

And as I come with these stories which have been written indelibly upon the sagebrush and the sod, I say "How-Kola" as a message from those who wrote them there.

AND NOW … MAY YOU ENJOY SODBREAKERS!

Edith Eudora Ammons Kohl

ADDENDUM C

"JUST A CABIN IN THE PINES"
Poem Written by Edith Eudora Ammons Kohl

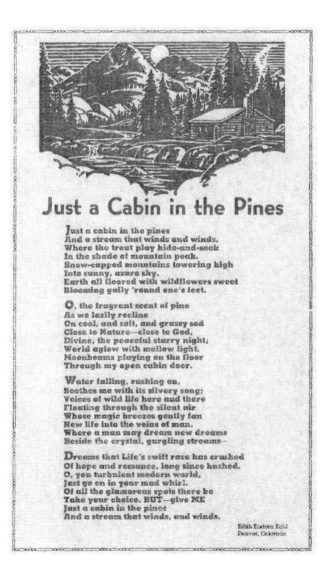

Just a Cabin in the Pines

Just a cabin in the pines
And a stream that winds and winds,
Where the trout play hide-and-seek
In the shade of mountain peak.
Snow-capped mountains towering high
Into sunny, azure sky.
Earth all floored with wildflowers sweet
Blooming gaily 'round one's feet.

O, the fragrant scent of pine
As we lazily recline
On cool, and soft, and grassy sod
Close to Nature—close to God.
Divine, the peaceful starry night;
World aglow with mellow light.
Moonbeams playing on the floor
Through my open cabin door.

Water falling, rushing on,
Soothes me with its silvery song;
Voices of wild life here and there
Floating through the silent air
Whose magic breezes gently fan
New life into the veins of man.
Where a man may dream new dreams
Beside the crystal, gurgling streams—

Dreams that Life's swift race has crushed
Of hope and romance, long since hushed.
O, you turbulent modern world,
Just go on in your mad whirl.
Of all the glamorous spots there be
Take your choice. BUT—give ME
Just a cabin in the pines
And a stream that winds, and winds.

Edith Eudora Kohl
Denver, Colorado

239

Edith Eudora Ammons Kohl

INDEX